HOW TO FIND YOUR LIFE'S DIVINE PURPOSE

Brain software for a new civilization

By the same author:

Ashtanga Yoga: Practice and Philosophy

Ashtanga Yoga: The Intermediate Series

Pranayama: The Breath of Yoga

Yoga Meditation: Through Mantra, Chakras and Kundalini to Spiritual Freedom

Samadhi: The Great Freedom

HOW TO FIND YOUR LIFE'S DIVINE PURPOSE

Brain software for a new civilization

Gregor Maehle

Kaivalya Publications

Published by Kaivalya Publications
PO Box 181
Crabbes Creek NSW 2483
Australia

© Gregor Maehle 2020
This book is copyright. Apart from any fair dealing for the purposes of private study, research, criticism or review, as permitted under the Copyright Act, no part may be reproduced by any process without written permission of the author.
First published 2020

A catalogue record for this book is available from the National Library of Australia

Creator: Maehle, Gregor, author
Title: How to Find Your Life's Divine Purpose/ Gregor Maehle.

ISBN:
Paperback   978-0-6488932-1-9
EPUB   978-0-6488932-2-6

Dedication

To all those who have been to the other side, came back, and reported what they saw.

Acknowledgements

To the ancient seers of all cultures who inspired this work and to each living being that crossed my path. For all of you who became my teachers, without whom this work could not have crystallized.

Contents

Dedication v

Acknowledgements vii

Introduction 1

Chapter 1: What is that "divine purpose"? 9

Chapter 2: Life's divine purpose in different cultures 59

Chapter 3: Practice of finding one's life's divine purpose 115

Chapter 4: Psychology of finding one's divine purpose 131

Chapter 5: Implementing your life's divine purpose 191

Chapter 6: Process of implementing your Life's
           Divine Purpose.. 237

Chapter 7: Results of finding one's life's divine purpose 273

Epilogue: Humanity's collective divine purpose 285

Bibliography 287

Index 291

Author Information 295

Introduction

For most modern people who follow some form of spirituality, their material and professional life, on one hand, and their spiritual pursuits, on the other, are disconnected and, often even, are in conflict with one another. Imagine, for a moment, a life in which the two are not only aligned but actually enhance each other.

But is it really possible to bring our spiritual goals and work life into greater alignment? Before I talk about techniques and methods to bring this about, let me firstly point out that, implied in this very question, there is already a separation between material and spiritual life, between matter and body, on one hand, and mind, spirit, soul and consciousness on the other. This separation is indicative of Western philosophy and society, which has always defined matter and mind as a duality, as two different things or planes that do not come together. Via Hellenistic philosophy, this philosophy of separation has entered Christian thought and, from there, has formed the philosophical bedrock of Western Science, which informs our belief systems today. Eastern religions and indigenous earth-based spirituality do not follow this template. In these traditions, whatever you do and wherever you are in life is more often seen as a worthy expression of spirit and consciousness.

This contrast is beautifully expressed in Hermann Hesse's novel Siddhartha, where the main character, Siddhartha, is unfulfilled wherever he goes and in whatever he does. He starts out as the son of a Brahmin whose main occupation is to chant the Vedas. What some modern Western yoga students would have seen as an ideal starting point to a spiritual quest, for Siddhartha remains unfulfilling, and he leaves his Brahmin father to become an ascetic, practicing austerities in the desert and the jungle. After some years, he finds this pursuit lacking as well. He moves back into the city to become a wealthy merchant, enabling him to have a sensual relationship with a famous courtesan. Although their relationship culminates in a child, Siddhartha is ultimately frustrated and cannot find himself in either of these varied environments and activities.

As he again sets out on his spiritual quest into an unknown future, he crosses the very same river that he crossed between each of his previous stages of life (avid observers may notice that the four phases of his life roughly resemble the four Hindu stages of life, although in a modified order). During each river-crossing, Siddhartha is ferried by the same old ferryman, Vasudeva. During the first crossing, he barely notices the humble old man, but on subsequent crossings, he begins to interrogate and challenge him. Vasudeva, with his contentment, simplicity and lack of drive, is a complete antithesis to Siddhartha's drivenness and desirousness. When asked whether he had no desire to go anywhere, seek or learn anything, Vasudeva replies that all that could be learned, could also be learned right here at this spot simply by listening to this river.

On the final crossing, upon entering the ferry, Siddhartha needs to only briefly glance at the old man to see that something has changed in his demeanour. Although he has never gone anywhere, not done anything outstanding, but only taken his ferry across the river day-in day-out, Vasudeva, Siddhartha has found, has arrived. And Siddhartha, although he has studied the holy books, chanted the hymns, mastered the most ridiculous practices, has mortified his body, attained fabulous wealth,

INTRODUCTION

found his soul mate, enjoyed tantric sex and fathered a child, he, Siddhartha, has not. He is still a stranger within himself and to himself, and a stranger to human society.

Siddhartha then asks Vasudeva to accept him as his student, but we need not concern ourselves with that. The important point is that Vasudeva became a master of life simply by listening to what was present right where he was. The river here is a beautiful metaphor for the river of life, the river of experience, which is always flowing right there were we are. Nothing else is required but to listen to it. You need not go anywhere, you need not do anything, and you need not become somebody else. Life is right there where you are!

Whatever activity you perform right now, however lowly and insignificant it may seem (a ferryman was considered very low), you still perform an important contribution for spirit and society. As a student, I met several Indian spiritual teachers who first served as soldiers, bankers or accountants and, seemingly on the side, followed their spiritual pursuits. Once retired from duties, they then became full-time spiritual teachers. At no point was there a disconnect, a break from their previous life. They never thought that, previously, they had done something unspiritual. Their former professions, once the time was right, seamlessly changed into their new pursuits without there ever being a rupture.

Today, of course, we don't want to stay where we are. The media and education system instil in us discontent and the desire to become more, to become something bigger, to become rock stars, master chefs, real estate tycoons, or derivative traders. But while sowing such desires into all of us may drive Gross Domestic Product, would a society solely consisting of these and similar "sexy" professions actually work?

HOW TO FIND YOUR LIFE'S DIVINE PURPOSE

In the Bhagavad Gita (III.35), there is an important statement where Krishna says, "One's own dharma, even if not glamorous, is more important than dharma not conducive to one's growth." We must then ask ourselves: how do we know whether we are already performing our own duty, whether we are already on the right path? Some people may rightly answer in the affirmative, although it seems that, compared to ancient society, fewer and fewer people seem to be content with where they are, with what they are doing. And more and more people seem to be estranged and discontent with their place in society.

This book deals with how to find out whether you are living your life or somebody else's and whether you are living a life of divine purpose. Like Vasudeva, we need to become better at listening. Listening here is, of course, meant metaphorically. It is metaphorical for cultivating the visceral experience that there is one common intelligence expressing itself through you (ferryman), through the whole world of manifestation (the river) and all beings (those that you ferry across). In ancient societies, this common intelligence that simultaneously expresses itself through everything was called by many names, including God, the Divine, the Dao, the Brahman or Great Spirit. But we don't need to give it a name. Often, in fact, by naming it, more is taken away than gained. Once we give it a name, a label, we also dupe ourselves into the belief that we have understood a phenomenon that is ultimately beyond understanding. More important than understanding it is that we "feel" that it works through us.

Let's suppose now we are not currently in Vasudeva's situation. Our life seems to be working well enough, but there is this nagging voice of discontent, and it almost feels that we are living somebody else's life, not our own. We just cannot "feel" the spirit breathing through us. How, then, can we change this

INTRODUCTION

and come to a point where we truly live our own life?

The most powerful way of opening yourself up to the greater life is to take time daily to state sincerely to the Divine/spirit that you wish to be of service and that you are available as a conduit through which It can work and express Itself. In an unconscious way, this is already taking place. In an unconscious way, we and all living things are nothing but avenues through which spirit lives, moves, acts and experiences itself. But when this unconscious process becomes conscious, it becomes the most incredible thing possible to a human. It is at this point that the seemingly impossible can become possible to us.

For those of you who have difficulties with the concept of a spirit that works, moves and lives in, through and as everything, here is another way of looking at it. In order to be truly alive, in order to live the greater life, we need to bring our conscious, subconscious and super-conscious minds into alignment. Most individuals are completely driven by their subconscious programming. By emulating our parents and, later, our peers, we accepted a more or less robotic programming that makes decisions largely automatically. We come to a point where our thoughts, emotions and even our lives seem to happen to us, rather than being self-authorized, self-actualized.

The next step, then, is to use our conscious minds to re-program our subconscious minds. We do this by taking active responsibility for our thoughts and emotions, and by continually implementing this strategy, our subconscious will eventually accept our chosen thought patterns rather than those that we have been programmed with during childhood. The problem with continuing your robotic programming received during childhood is that life-paths based on it often involve disconnected, egoic phantasies of wanting to become wealthier, more loved, more recognized or more powerful than others. To evolve from here, it is imperative to let the conscious mind receive its inspiration and vision from the super-conscious mind. Like the subconscious, so is the super-conscious mind largely outside of the field of our conscious perception. The super-conscious mind is that part of our mind that connects us to this super-intelligence that expresses itself simultaneously as infinite consciousness, the material cosmos and all beings. Your super-conscious mind is the wellspring of your highest potential, your higher sense-of-self and your noble-most aspirations.

Ultimately, we need to ask ourselves what does the spirit/the Divine want to become as us? When talking to super-conscious mind we need to ask, "How can I serve and as what?" This is, of course, not a one-off act but an ongoing process. Once we have made it a regular habit to ask, the next step is to hone our ability to listen. It is only through our inability to listen from the bottoms of our hearts that we do not hear the messages of the Divine. Practicing listening to the Divine/spirit is the key. The message is at first faint, as the voices of the ego and the subconscious will be louder. But with practice, we hear the voice clearer and clearer.

When you have become used to hearing the messages and acting upon them, you will notice an absence of inner dialogue. There is no nagging voice saying you are in the wrong place, doing the wrong thing, living somebody else's dream or life. It is this state that is known as svadharma (own duty), and Krishna called it "acting for Me rather than acting for reward". This book is about to take you through this journey step-by-step.

The 1st chapter of this book will explain what divine purpose is, and for that purpose, we need to have a fresh look at what

INTRODUCTION

the Divine is. This chapter is influenced by my own mystical experiences but also a lifelong study of philosophy and the world religions into which I will synthesize as diverse subjects as information technology, quantum – and astrophysics, evolutionary biology and neurology.

The 2nd chapter will show that the method shown in this book is not some high-fangled, new age crack-pottery but, in fact, based on sacred tradition. For this purpose, I will quote the relevant passages from the Yoga Sutra, the Bhagavad Gita and the Bible. I will then show that psychologists like Carl Jung, Victor Frankl and Abraham Maslow have also worked on this subject.

In the 3rd chapter, then, the actual core method will be shown. If you are in a hurry, you can jump ahead to this chapter, but I do believe the understanding of the earlier chapters is necessary so that the method can be practised with trust and conviction.

Chapters 4 through 6 will consecutively lead you deeper into the technique, featuring a combination of explanations of concepts and layers of practical steps. In the 7th chapter, you will find a list of parameters that enable us to determine whether we have succeeded in the method and transformed our lives. The book then completes with an epilogue that describes the transformative effect this work can have on the whole of our society. Enjoy!

Chapter 1.
WHAT IS THAT "DIVINE PURPOSE"?

Do you remember when you were about 13-14 years old, and you knew that your life was going to be amazing? When you knew that you were called to make a contribution to the life of others and to life on the planet? When you knew that your life had a higher meaning and you were to follow a higher calling rather than just simply surviving, maximizing your self-interest and passing on your genes?

Intuitively, you knew that there was some form of higher intelligence that expressed itself through you, through the whole material world, and through all living things. You knew, even if only deep down and in a vague form, that this living intelligence was also expressing itself through you. That it was communicating through you to all of its other aspects embodied through all other beings, through everybody else. But what happened then? Why did this great promised life, this becoming yourself through what you do, never eventuate? Like in many other people, the idealist within you may have turned cynical and became a realist.

However, this so-called reality is not one enshrined in nature. It is one dictated by our society, which is very skilled at breaking the life-spirit of our children for the purpose of turning them into industrial wage slaves. Our economy, which worships the god of GDP-growth, has no use for self-realized young people who follow their own higher calling. What it has use for are millions of individuals trained in a handful of industrial, corporate professions, which in many cases offer little apart from mindless drudgery and estrangement. No wonder that many people working in these jobs become depressed, reach to drugs, or become aggressive, being a danger to themselves and others.

The reason why our society is so good at forcing young people to stop listening to their inner callings is because it is organized to deliver every year a greater share of human wealth and prosperity into fewer and fewer hands. Our society and economy are organized to accelerate inequality although both profess to do just the opposite. And to do so, they must first break our spirits. We must first be convinced that we cannot achieve what we came for. That we are not good enough to deserve a purposeful life. And to achieve that, society must first convince us that we do have no purpose. That our life is, in fact, nothing but a purposeless accident.

Before I go on to speak about life's purpose, let's have a quick look at what living a purposeless life has done to us as a collective. Being told that our life is a purposeless accident, that we are nothing but selfish-gene-powered flesh robots, the only thing left to us is consumption, pleasure and gratification. What influence on the biosphere would seven billion individuals have who are constantly competing for higher levels of consumption, pleasure and gratification? We would expect to see clear-felled forests to make space for feedlots for livestock, a poisoned atmosphere, oceans filled with plastic instead of marine life, eroded, acidified and salinized topsoils, plummeting wildlife stocks, more and more extinct species of plants and animals, increase of chronic and mental diseases amongst humans, etc. And this is, in fact, what we do see.

If all of that takes place when we do live a purposeless, meaningless life, what would happen if we followed the call to purpose and meaning? I will answer this question briefly because it is an important one, but it will be answered in much more detail in the course of this book. If we would follow the call to purpose and meaning, we would place ourselves in the service of life. Not only into the service of those around us but all humanity and the larger community of life, including plants, animals, microbes and the entire biosphere. We would act as if life itself, biodiversity, the fact that life expresses itself in more and more diverse forms, is God. With that in mind, let's inquire into what it is that calls us to service and that wants to express itself through us.

WHAT IS THE "DIVINE" ANYWAY (AND WHAT IS IT NOT)?

Let me first answer what it is not: it is not an anthropomorphic god, i.e. a god having human characteristics that wills everything for you into existence. This anthropomorphic god is nothing but an extrapolation, that is, a projection into the sky of our need for an all-powerful father, who governs and controls everything, who judges, punishes and possibly ultimately saves and redeems us if we have been found good enough. In other words, this so-called god that we believed in is not God at all because the true Divine does not have an ego from which to judge you, punish you and redeem you. The Divine is infinite and pure love and judging and punishing requires an ego from which to do these things. What has an ego cannot be infinite, eternal and pure love; therefore, this alleged judger and punisher cannot be the Divine.

To identify the Divine with a giant, irate, bearded, white male who may throw at us locusts, plagues, floods, lightning, etc. is a theological error. It is a superstitious belief from a time in which we were living in tribal chiefdoms that were ruled by exactly such males. Often, they claimed that their power came from a god in heaven that was exactly like them, "as it is in heaven so be it on earth". That is how these chiefs and warlords legitimized their power over us by claiming a divine mandate, that they were acting "in the name of the Lord".

HOW DID THIS PROCESS TAKE PLACE?

A big part of the process which we are here undertaking is the reawakening of our spirituality. But at the same time, it is obvious that a significant section (but not all) of what is today called religion is simply power politics and manipulation. That's why Karl Marx said, "Religion is opium for the people". There is of a lot of truth in that statement, but at the same time, we need to acknowledge that there is also a lot of truth hidden in all sacred traditions.

So, we need to first look into how religion came about and how it became a tool of manipulation. With the work we are about to undertake, it is important that you understand what you can trust and what is not trustworthy. How humanity was manipulated for millennia and were the nuggets of truth are hidden.

All religions are going back to the experiences of mystics, either an individual (such as Buddha, Jesus, Muhammad), or groups of mystics (the Hebrew prophets, Vedic rishis, indigenous shamans).

CHAPTER 1.

A mystic is a person who searches for or has transpersonal, mystical experiences in which the nature of reality is revealed. Because these transpersonal experiences require an expanded sense-of-self and a temporary suspension of ego, it is rather unlikely that a mystic will declare themselves as exclusive (for example, as the only begotten son of God or the only Buddha of this world age). These claims are made later, usually after the founding mystic of a tradition is dead. If the followers of a particular mystic declare that the experience of this mystic is the only valid mystical experience (and possibly that this mystic was the only one entitled to it), then we have the birth of a religion.

The difference between mysticism and spirituality on one hand and religion on the other is that religion takes the experience of a particular mystic and declares it as the only valid one, as the standard. However, you and I and everybody else are entitled to mystical experiences. They are the most powerful, satisfying, expansive, transformational and ecstatic experiences humans can have. To deny them to most or all of humans and limit them to one individual or an elite group is nothing but another form of supremacism.

Summarizing, the timeline of the development of religions starts with mystics who have mystical experiences. A particular mystic may be very good at communicating their experiences via language to the surrounding community. If that is the case, after the death of this mystic, a group of scholars, theologians, high priests, etc. will develop around this mystic's teaching to interpret and explain it. In this context you need to understand the next development.

For the next step, I will pick out the name of the Mesopotamian warlord Gilgamesh. He probably wasn't the only person to set this process in motion, but his is a name we know, and his name is linked to all of the processes here described. Prior to Gilgamesh's era, humans in most places were living in hunter/gatherer bands or nomadic pastoralist tribes. There was little in form of political organization. Bands included only a few dozen individuals and in tribes, a few hundred. Wherever a male leader ascended to power, they could only lead a few people and therefore not cause too much damage with their ambitions. Gilgamesh, however, changed all of that.

Mesopotamia, in which this drama of our civilization arose, is also called the fertile crescent. Mesopotamia was one of the most fertile places on Earth, and it could easily be cultivated. In this area, horticulture was first developed. Humans became semi-sedentary and spent longer periods in one place to grow gardens. Gilgamesh, a successful warlord, was very apt in man-to-man combat and vanquished all of the tribal leaders around him. This enabled him to combine the conquered tribes into one of the first kingdoms. For this to be sustainable, he needed to develop a stratified power structure. Prior to Gilgamesh, humans either hunted or tended to their herds or gardens. In such a setting, when it came to tribal war, everybody dropped the shovel, the digging stick or whatever they used and picked up a spear, club or bow and arrows instead.

Gilgamesh, however, had something different in mind. He created the world's first standing army, warriors who had nothing to do but to fight and to train for war. Obviously, his warriors became much better at war than tribal amateurs who were shepherds, hunter/gatherers or gardeners in the rest of their time. But the difference did not end here. Tribal people, even if they are good at fighting, needed to interrupt war to go back to food production. So tribal wars were always intermittent. Gilgamesh's army, however, was a permanently standing army that could engage in permanent warfare and did not need breaks to go back to food production. He quickly overran all neighbouring chiefdoms and seized a large empire. But here, he struck a new problem. Nomadic pastoralists and hunter/gatherers may interrupt their warfare to procure meat for food. But you cannot run a vast army on meat as it rots much too quickly. Mesopotamia is a hot country and fridges, etc. were a technology of the future. Meat could only be kept for a few days.

Gilgamesh understood that he needed an enormous supply of grains such as wheat, barley, millet, etc., which all can be stored for lengthy periods and can be transported by armies during their campaigns. Gilgamesh therefore had the ancient rainforests of Mesopotamia cleared and turned the land into grain production for his military conquering machine. His military expansions were now largely fuelled by grains and agriculture. As a by-product, he used the timbers harvested for constructing military fortifications in case his many enemies would strike back at him.

The conquered tribes had to provide slave labour or toiled as highly taxed peasants on the fields of the new empire to provide food for Gilgamesh's army. Imagine the life of a person who had, until recently, lived freely as a nomad, hunter/gatherer or gardener. Living such a free life, it is left to your own organisational skills in which order you perform activities and for how long. Now, suddenly, you were under the rule of a vast stratified power structure where you were told to spend your entire life in meaningless drudgery to perform the same actions over and over again because the structure relies on you doing so. Needless to say, the conquered tribes had a habit of periodically rising up against Gilgamesh's rule, he who had turned their free life into meaningless, numb drudgery.

But now, Gilgamesh had his most ingenious idea. He collected a group of tribal priests and charged them with creating a myth according to which there is a giant, bearded, irate patriarch living in heaven. A man very much like Gilgamesh himself but of cosmic heft and with infinite power at his disposal. This heavenly king would sentence you to eternal damnation if you rose up against his rule. Anything you did in terms of disobeying the heavenly king was sin, and it would attach to you forever. Of course, that was not the end of the story, but the important part of it was that the heavenly king had a representative here on Earth, a human man, somewhat smaller in stature than the heavenly king, but he was to rule here on Earth on behalf of the heavenly king (for example, in Russia, the tsar was called the "little father" who had his authority from the Great Father in heaven). He was given divine authority. From that moment onward, a rebel or revolutionary was not only acting against the worldly order. He or she was also acting against the heavenly order and for doing so was branded as sinful and eternally damned.

The tribal druids, priests and shamans that Gilgamesh contracted initially showed little interest in this new philosophy. But they changed their minds when Gilgamesh promised them that they would never have to work the fields again. They would never again have to touch a shovel or spear, they would live in luxurious mansions and wear expensive silk garments and ornaments. They were to become the high priests and founders of a new creation, sky religion. Sky religion is so called because a male human with obvious human characteristics is projected into the sky. The term puts it into juxtaposition to earth-based spirituality, the religion of indigenous people.

CHAPTER 1.

Earth-based spirituality is about the here and now, whereas sky religion talks about a place or state, often called heaven, nirvana or enlightenment, which is not presently available to us and usually is far removed from our current situation. The priests and high priest were to become one of the most important strata of Gilgamesh's power pyramid. They were to give him the spiritual justification for what he undertook.

In order to succeed with our work, you need to understand that sky religion was created not from any form of mystical experience, but it was the re-organizing and reframing of mystical experiences for military and economic purposes. That's all there is to it. So, whenever you notice that in your thought you link terms such as God or the Divine with concepts like sin, punishment, damnation, etc., remember that this link has been made in your mind to manipulate you and your ancestors so that they would not rebel against those in power.

This, of course, does not to mean that all spirituality is bogus. In the hallmark of our ancient, original form of spirituality, earth-based spirituality, each person has their own valid connection to mother Earth, mother nature. It is from nature directly that each person learns what their purpose is and what they are here to do. Sky religion broke this link that all of us had with the sacredness in nature. And sky religion had to do so because only with this link broken could we be mass-herded into the meaningless drudgery of the agricultural/industrial production process.

WHAT IS THE DIVINE, THEN, IF IT IS NOT A PHARAOH- OR EMPEROR-LIKE HUMAN MALE IN THE SKY?

In the following paragraphs, I will outline the sum total of my mystical experiences, i.e. what I believe the ultimate reality to be. There is, of course, nothing original about it. All these experiences have been had by mystics down the ages; they are hardwired into our nervous systems, and we are designed to have them. The descriptions that mystics make of their experiences differ only in regard to semiotics, that is, the differing definitions that they give depend on the symbols they use, the cultural metaphors embedded in their backgrounds and in how far the descriptions handed down to us have been altered by the powerbrokers of those cultures with the objective to turn their teachings into a tool of manipulation.

A description of a mystical experience can never be completely accurate, and most importantly, the experience itself can never be identical with the description. This is so because when you do have a mystical experience, by definition, both your ego (the software that connects your body to your mind and limits you in time and space) and your mind (your word processor) need to be suspended (to be explained in great detail later). Once you return from your mystical experience, your ego and mind will reboot because otherwise you would be incapable of functioning and also you would be incapable of integrating your mystical experience into your life. It is therefore completely normal and healthy after a mystical experience to think, "What was that?" and "What does that mean for who I am to be and for what I need to do?"

But even when making all of these necessary efforts in describing mystical states, we need to remind ourselves that the state is not the description. That's another area where religion errs. Religions have sacred books that they believe to be the state. They are not. They are important books; they have their own beauty, and we can learn a lot from them, but they can never replace our own mystical insights, experiences and transformations.

Often, people then backflip and ask if we cannot describe the state accurately why describe it at all? Why think about it at all? That's, again, an error, an extreme. You need to describe the state so that you can work with it and communicate about it with others. The most important aspect of a mystical experience is not the experience itself but the extent to which your surface-self (your day-to-day persona) is transformed by it. That can happen only if you attempt to understand, analyse, interpret and integrate a mystical experience.

In indigenous religion, the interpretation of an initiate's vision is so important that all the senior shamans/medicine people of a tribe may have to go on a vision quest together if they fail to agree on the interpretation of that initiate's vision (again more on that later).

It's similar to using any word. We all know that the word "plane" is not the same as a plane. But we use the word nevertheless, and so it is with every other word. Now, the word plane is enough for me as a tourist but if I am an engineer working on a passenger jet plane I would not be satisfied with the word "plane". I would want to use a thousand-page engineering manual. But even with a manual of this size, I would still know that the manual and the plane are two different things, right? As Alfred Korzybski said, "The map is not the territory".

This, however, is exactly what happened with religion. We accepted the map as the territory and the engineering manual as the plane. Nothing can take the place of your own ecstatic realization of the Divine, similarly, as no engineering manual, however sophisticated it may be, can actually take off and fly passengers to their destinations.

With this in mind, I'm offering now the sum total of my mystical experiences. It's just a map or an engineering manual. There is nothing holy, definitive or binding about the description itself. It is helpful, however, to identify and navigate to your destination and to keep your plane serviced.

THE GOD TRANSCENDENT

There are three aspects to the Divine. We could say the three aspects make a trinity. This has, of course, already been described in Christianity, so there is nothing new to it. Understanding the three aspects is an integral part to living your life's divine purpose and forms the bedrock on which the whole method rests.

The three aspects of the Divine are called the transcendental aspect (or God transcendent), the immanent aspect (or God immanent), and the divine child aspect (or God as life). Let's look at the God transcendent first because it's the part that is most known and best described in sacred traditions and religion. Transcendental means beyond, i.e., that part of the Divine that is beyond sensory perception and beyond direct experience. The best psychological term we have to describe this part of the Divine is consciousness, but the term is here used to denote what is conscious rather than that what we are conscious of. Be careful here, because in modern psychology, the term consciousness is often used with the meaning of that what we are conscious of, that is, the content of the mind. But that is not the meaning in which the term is used within spiritual systems. Here the term denotes the entity within you that is conscious, that is aware.

If you meditate for a long time, you notice that this entity is completely separate from body and mind because body and mind are changing and changeable; consciousness itself, however, does not change. I experienced consciousness in meditation for the first time over 50 years ago, and when I experience it today, it feels fresh, exactly like 50 years ago. My body, in the meantime, has aged beyond doubt, and my mind has become smarter and more educated (at least, that's what I'd like to believe). Both body and mind feel completely different than my consciousness. This is because consciousness is beyond time or, more precisely, time is a phenomenon that occurs within consciousness, whereas body and mind are phenomena that occur within time.

We could say that consciousness is the container that contains the world and all beings. That is a Buddhist terminology, and it similarly refers to the God transcendent as Krishna's saying in the Bhagavad Gita, "I am the self in the heart of all beings" or "Who see me in all beings and all beings in me, truly sees". Although paradoxical, these words are very accurate. In deep meditation, you see at once that consciousness appears within you ("who sees me in all beings"), yet at the same time, everything seems to be inside consciousness ("and all beings in me"). The mind cannot grasp both these views simultaneously, it can only jump back and forth between them. Consciousness can be both simultaneously. It can do that because it does not modify sensory data, i.e., it does not try to understand itself – it is itself. That means that in order to abide in consciousness, in order to have a mystical experience, you need to temporarily suspend the mind. All practices of all sacred traditions on Earth are methods to, one way or another, temporarily suspend the mind, so that a mystical state can take place.

In the Old Testament of the Bible, we find the beautiful sentence, "Be still and know that I Am God". Also, this sentence refers to the transcendental aspect of the Divine, consciousness. It cannot be seen when the mind is active. Thoughts cover consciousness like clouds cover the blue of the sky on a rainy day. That's why the biblical Yahweh charges us to "be still", lest we can behold Him.

Patanjali, the author of the Yoga Sutra, says the same in Sutra I.2- I.3, "Yoga is the stilling of the mind. Then (when the mind is still) consciousness abides in itself". Note the similarities of the descriptions. Interesting also that the biblical phrase states, "Know that I Am God". It is an accurate wording as, strictly speaking, the transcendental aspect of the Divine is beyond perception and experience. This is reverberated halfway around the world in the writings of the Indian philosopher Shankaracharya who says in his Brahma Sutra Commentary that the consciousness (Brahman) cannot be perceived and experienced but only known.

A similar focus on the God transcendent we also find in ancient China. In the Tao Te King, sage Lao-tzu says, "What can be said about the Dao (consciousness) is not the Dao". Notice again that consciousness is beyond perception and description. Lao-tzu also states that the transcendental is beyond being described through language. The same concept of the God transcendent is illustrated in the Indian prayer to the Nagaraj, the serpent of infinity. Here, consciousness is identified with a one-thousand headed serpent, with all one-thousand heads emerging from the same trunk. The trunk itself is silent; it does not have a mouth to speak with. The trunk represents the Brahman, infinite consciousness. The one-thousand heads growing out of the same trunk all speak in different languages representing differing systems of philosophy, science and religion. But the ultimate truth is only in the trunk, which itself does not have a language, as absolute truth is beyond words. While each head may teach a system that is internally consistent and cannot be refuted when being allowed to start from its own premises, the heads are conflicting each other. Each head may offer a viable interpretation of the truth but never truth itself, which cannot be spoken.

This can be understood by resorting to the work of the important French postmodernist Jacques Derrida. Derrida stated that meaning only derives out of context. The language a person uses and the meaning they give to the words making up that language will never be congruent with the language of the next person and certainly not if the next person has as different cultural background. We all have made different experiences in life which form our context. Although dictionaries give us a vague general meaning of words, these meanings are tinged with our individual experiences. You will never find two people that will use terms like God, love, trust, truth, freedom, etc. with exactly the same meaning. We all take the deeper meaning of these words from the tapestry of our experiences and not from the dictionary. All words or symbols are ultimately conceptualizations and not deep truth. Therefore, a teaching consisting of words and symbols ultimately can only be an interpretation or representation of the truth but not truth itself.

This is one of the reasons why indigenous religions engaged in relatively little speculation about the God transcendent. In the language of the Lakota Native Americans, the transcendental is called Wakan Tanka, great mystery. The anthropologist Richard Walker wrote that the old Lakota seers talked little about the Wakan Tanka. Because nothing concrete could be said about it, it was left to individual experience. As we will see later, indigenous teachings are more interested in the remaining two aspects of the Divine.

Because everything we so far have heard about the transcendental is rather non-concrete, most traditions tend to anthropomorphize it (i.e., give it human characteristics), which can be helpful up to a certain extent. For example, the God transcendent in the Old Testament is called Yahweh, in the New Testament, the Father, and in India, most often either Shiva or Vishnu. Both Yahweh and Shiva were thought to reside inactive on mountaintops looking at the world from afar. This is, of course, to be understood as metaphorical. In India, for example, the mountain on which Shiva sits is called Meru. But Meru is also the term used for the human spine. The mystical meaning of the name Shiva is consciousness. According to yoga, consciousness is experienced when the life force is transported up the spine and held in the crown chakra at the top of the spine (Meru). From that vantage point, consciousness does not look like a blue-skinned, dreadlocked male, brandishing a trident while sitting on a tiger skin (such as the Lord Shiva). But that can be a helpful metaphor.

The setback of anthropomorphising is that most people today, when asked what religion teaches, seriously believe that God is a bearded male sitting on a mountaintop. That was meant to be metaphorical, and to take it literally is bizarre. Unfortunately, mystics themselves sometimes became confused. So did the 16th century German mystic Jakob Böhme state that because man has two legs, God also must have two legs, and because man has a liver, God must also have a liver. The mistake here is that the statement, "Man is created in the image and likeness of the Divine" has here been switched around to mean God is created in the image and likeness of the human. That is the tragedy

CHAPTER 1.

and misunderstanding embedded in modern spirituality and religion. We have projected and extrapolated a giant version of ourselves into the sky. No wonder that we have lost sight of what the transcendental actually is.

THE GOD IMMANENT OR IMMANENT ASPECT OF THE DIVINE

Immanent means here-with-us; something that we can perceive, experience and touch. Unfortunately, religion was so obsessed with the transcendental aspect of the Divine that the immanent aspect has often been forgotten. As the transcendental aspect of the Divine in ancient days was anthropomorphised into a male god, the Father, so the immanent aspect used to be depicted as female, the Mother. Have you ever wondered how the Christian trinity of Father and son was completed not by the mother but by the Holy Ghost/Holy Spirit? The Mother was really ghosted, removed from our perception of spirituality in the wake of Gilgamesh and his succeeding warlord culture turning religion into a tool for their own empowerment and the manipulation of the masses.

For a father to have a son, there needs to be a mother, right? But in Christian theology, following a patriarchal paradigm, the father has been made all-powerful, and the mother completely disempowered. Mary, the mother of Jesus, is so reduced in stature that she does not even get to meet the father of Jesus. Nor can he meet her in person, as she is not his equal anymore. As he would sully himself in the process, an immaculate conception was conjured up.

In earth-based spirituality, on the other hand, the God immanent is anthropomorphized into the Mother. This even continued into some of the religions. For example, in Shaivism (a subdivision of Hinduism), the immanent aspect of the Divine is identified with Shakti, the divine feminine.

Now, what really is the God immanent, and how can we understand it? There is an interesting passage in Shankara's Brahma Sutra Commentary that says, "Consciousness [the God transcendent], similar to a mirror, is of the quality of reflectiveness. If there was nothing to be reflected, consciousness could not bring about its quality of reflectiveness". What does that mean? Try to imagine a giant mirror floating in empty space. Nothing could ever be reflected in the mirror, as nothing else existed. That means the mirror could not reflect anything. But since the mirror is not a mirror outside of it being reflective, the mirror then would not be a mirror. That's really important to understand, and the same is true for consciousness. Consciousness (the seat of awareness) is only consciousness if there is a world to be conscious of.

What that means for us practically is that the transcendental aspect of the Divine, consciousness, is forever conscious of the immanent aspect. The immanent aspect is the cosmos, the world of matter and energy, the entire universe. Since, by now, the existence of parallel universes in astrophysics is considered highly likely, in modern astrophysical language we would say the sum total of all parallel universes, or the multiverse, rather than a single universe.

To use a poetic and devotional expression, all that you see, feel and perceive is God. The entire cosmos is nothing but a crystallization of the Divine. There is no place, no time, no particle, no energy, no radiation, no wave pattern that is not God. The entire material world is the crystallized body of the Divine. That's why the scripture says, "In Him we move, live and have our being". You cannot live, move and have your being in anything else because there is nothing else.

For spiritual seekers, this must come as a great surprise. We have been looking for the Divine everywhere without finding Her, but we are acting akin to fish looking for the ocean. For a fish, there is nothing but the ocean, and for us, there is nothing but God. Wherever you stand, you stand on God. Whatever you look at is God. You breathe nothing but God, and you think nothing but God. That's why in the Gita, Lord Krishna says, "All actions are performed by my prakrti only a fool believes to be the doer". The prakrti (procreativity) is a Hindu term for the divine creative force or energy. It is similar to the Hebrew term Shekinah, God's energy. Both terms are nothing but shorthand for the God immanent.

In the above Gita phrase, Krishna says, "You are not breathing yourself but I breathe you through the divine creative force. It is not you beating your heart but the God immanent is beating it through you. Can you order your arm to raise? No, it is me who thinks the thought, sends impulses through your neurons, and powers your arms. Can you transform food into energy via your metabolism? No, it is me as the God immanent who does so. Can you write your DNA, create proteins, power cells via mitochondria, harvest sunlight via photosynthesis and turn it into proteins?" No, all of these miraculous processes the God immanent performs through us without we having to do anything. That's why Krishna says, "Only a fool believes to be the doer". Our foolishness consists of having appointed ourselves to being the doers whereas truly, these actions are simply expressing themselves through us without our conscious input.

This leads me to the probably most important concept related to the God immanent, cosmic intelligence. When you look at the above paragraph, there is no denying that the cosmos itself is intelligent, since it could produce something as miraculous as life, and particularly complex life. We have often looked at matter as dumb, dead and inert, but the entire material cosmos is nothing but an intelligent incubator of intelligent life, designed to realize itself as an embodiment of that intelligence and to co-create with cosmic superintelligence.

Life is not something that occurred accidentally. The odds for something like that to happen have been calculated and are so extremely unlikely that we can rule out accident. For example, there are over 50 natural, physical constants that need to be exactly as they are for life to occur (discussed in great detail later). Atoms need to hold together and form complex atoms and molecules. Stars need to hold together and create heat and energy. Stars need to eventually explode into supernovae in which extreme pressure sensations take place that weld atoms together to form complex, heavy atoms, like carbon, for life to eventually occur. Look at the golden jewellery you wear. Gold atoms could only come about by matter going through four consecutive lives and deaths of a star (we are talking about a period of many billions of years) for such superheavy atoms being welded together in four subsequent supernova explosions to bring about gold atoms.

Look at the large hadron collider, an international collaboration in Switzerland, the largest, most ingenious, and most expensive machine humanity has conceived and built. The Hadron collider is about 24 kilometres in diameter, has cost trillions of dollars and took 30 years to build. We expended all of that time and energy so that we could accelerate elementary particles, crash them into each other to see what happens. A couple of years back, for a few nanoseconds, these experiments revealed the Higgs-Boson, the so-called God particle. Do you see the irony? We believe ourselves to be so smart, but three million years of existence of the genus Homo, trillions of dollars later and thousands of physicists working on this project, we still cannot outsmart dumb and dead matter?

The reason why we find it hard to outsmart it is because the same intelligence that has crystallized as matter and the cosmos has crystallized as us. There is no difference between intelligence, spirit and God immanent on one hand and matter on the other. Matter is crystallized intelligence and spirit. Matter is the crystallized body of God. Matter is God. Matter, whether presented in form waves or particles or energy is the God immanent.

Notice how different this view is from today's mainstream religions. Religion disempowered the Divine Feminine, the Shakti/Shekinah/Gaia and placed a merely male God into a faraway, unattainable realm, either heaven, Shangri-La or even further away into Nirvana/ nothingness/ emptiness. Disconnected from any spiritual meaning, religion could then declare matter/the world/femininity as an obstacle, something to overcome, something that could corrupt the male seeker. Religion became a sole male domain, from priest, cardinals, the pope all the way up to God all being men, and they are all supposed to stay away from women so as to not become contaminated by them. That's because women, supposedly, are representing lowly matter, which is unspiritual. That's why Yahweh, according to scripture, did not have conventional intercourse with Mary to conceive Jesus, and that's why in most religions today, women still can't ascend to high spiritual offices.

We need to get over this brainwash that has been going on for at least five thousand years. Neither matter nor women present any spiritual obstacle whatsoever. On the contrary, matter and women *are* crystallized and embodied spirit.

Notice also that although there is this supposed conflict between religion and science, both actually agree in the fact that matter is spiritless and meaningless and therefore can be exploited and manipulated to one's heart's content. Notice that for the first 300 years of Western scientific development, all the founders of Science were firstly men and secondly Christians. Men like Rene Descartes and Isaac Newton simply followed the biblical injunction to "make the earth thy dominion". The term dominion comes from the Latin dominus and means Lord/master, but it is actually the name of the Roman slaveholder caste. Now, it becomes clear why humanity could completely disregard the spiritual value and beauty of nature, wilderness, rivers, mountains, forests and oceans. Our religions first devalued the divinity of these entities. Only then by means of science did we manage to coerce, manipulate and destroy them so that now in the 21st millennia we are looking into the yawning abyss of environmental holocaust, ecocide and our own extinction.

Rene Descartes, for example, traced the beginning of his scientific career to an experience he had as a young man. An angel reportedly appeared to him and said, "Control of nature is obtained by number and measure". Descartes then went on to lay a big part of the foundations of today's mathematics, geometry and physics. Our obsession with measuring and controlling is, unfortunately, caused by a misunderstanding that sees us as separate from nature rather than an integral part of it. The results of this view now becomes apparent. Centuries

CHAPTER 1.

after Descartes, this belief of separateness has led us to the point where we are destroying nature at an ever-accelerating pace and are sawing off the very branch we are sitting on.

The compound of religion and Science have provided us with an evolutionary cul-de-sac that leads nowhere (we need to differentiate here between the scientific method and the philosophy of science, which is materialistic reductionism and objectivism, but more on that later). By realizing the divinity of the material cosmos, we come to understand that humans were meant to be nothing else but guardians of this garden of Eden and not its looters, ransackers, pillagers and plunderers. But unfortunately, that is what we have predominantly done throughout the last 10,000 years. There is, however, a human culture that has existed for more than 100,000 years that managed to live in harmony with nature, and that is the indigenous culture. When you analyse indigenous religion, you understand that indigenous people have always looked at the whole of the world and nature, including all life as divine. It is, after all, possible then!

THE THIRD ASPECT OF GOD, GOD AS LIFE

We now have two closely interlinked divine aspects; firstly, the infinite consciousness (the God transcendent) and secondly, the entire material cosmos (the God immanent), a crystallization of divine intelligence, reflecting itself in infinite consciousness. But these two aspects are not enough to make the Divine whole. In order to understand this, I need you to participate in a thought exercise. Imagine for a moment you were infinite consciousness, the God transcendent, cosmic consciousness, if you so wish. Being this cosmic consciousness, you are now conscious and aware of the sum total of the God immanent, the entire material universe (or to be more precise, the sum total of all parallel universes, but this thought can make the exercise somewhat mind-boggling).

Rest in this sensation for a moment until you understand that the transcendental can only be aware of the immanent in a general form as in "I am aware of the whole cosmos" but you cannot zoom in and be aware of, let's say, a particular person on Planet Earth reading Gregor's book and reflecting on its content. This is really important to understand. In many ways, this is the key to finding your life's divine purpose. Because you are (for the purpose of our thought exercise) cosmic consciousness, you can only be aware of the material world in a general form seeing the whole of the cosmos, but you cannot be aware of its particulars. You cannot be aware of a particular situation in time and space, for example, now on planet Earth in a particular place and time.

And there is an important reason for this that has been overlooked. As cosmic consciousness, you cannot focus on a particular situation in time and space because you do not have an ego. If you did have an ego, you could not be the God transcendent, the Cosmic. Ego is a piece of software that limits consciousness in time and space. You can only be one or the other, either cosmic consciousness or consciousness identifying itself with a particular body/mind in a particular spatial and temporal setting.

A brief interjection here: as humans, we can temporarily suspend the ego and for a limited time abide in cosmic consciousness. During that time, we are unable to identify with our current body and mind, we are beyond time and space. During that time, we are also unable to direct body and mind and attend to our survival. During a peak experience of cosmic consciousness, eating, walking, speaking, thinking, etc. is impossible. However, once the peak experience is over, the mind and ego will quickly reboot. Otherwise, we could not come back from this state. This means that the normal day-to-day egoic body/mind state and the mystical state can take place sequentially but never simultaneously. They literally exclude each other, one is egoic and the other is para-egoic (beyond ego).

Because the God transcendent, the infinite consciousness, the Unified Field does not have an ego, it cannot experience itself as a particular being within the God immanent other than through us. In other words, an individual such as you or I is nothing but the God transcendent individuating through us within the God immanent. It is exactly for this reason that theology began to talk about the Divine child or the son of God. Shame only that theologians misunderstood Jesus to be the only begotten son of God. This is a theological error. God does not have an ego from which to bestow son-hip on Jesus and withhold it from the rest of us. We all are collectively the Son begotten of the only God or better to say, we all are the Divine Child, the third aspect of God. Jesus actually knew that when saying, "and have I not said, ye all are Gods ye all are children of the most high". Important also to understand that the sonship does not only accrue to humans, but it accrues to all living beings, including animals, plants and microbes (we still tend to think in terms of speciesism, i.e., discriminating on the basis of species). To invoke now the holy trinity, infinite consciousness is the father, the material universe is the mother, and all life is the divine child. Rather than saying we are all children of God, it is scientifically more accurate to say that all life, humans, animals, plants and microbes, (i.e., the entire biosphere) are jointly and collectively the divine child.

You can observe that at play everywhere in nature. For example, the physical parameters here on Earth allow for life to exist. But most of them are not produced by the bare rock of planet Earth. Instead, they have been created and are maintained by the biosphere. For life to continue to exist on this planet, we are relying on a process called homeostasis of the bio parameters. Homeostasis means that the bio parameters, such as temperature, chemical make-up of the atmosphere, salinity, ph and temperature of the oceans, precipitation, seasons, soil consistency, etc., oscillate and fluctuate only within a very narrow band.

That the bio parameters stay within that band is not due to the geological formation of the planet but due to the sum total of Earth's organisms. So is the atmosphere on Earth created predominantly by plants and animals. In the beginning, there were plants only. They created so much oxygen that the air become oxygen-hyper-enriched. A single lightning strike set the whole world alight. After that, animals came about. Animals take up the oxygen, turn it into carbon dioxide and feed it back into the system. Then plants metabolize the CO2 and turn it back into oxygen. Note that for plants, oxygen is a useless by-product, and so is CO2 for animals. But together, they metabolize each other's metabolic wastes and use them as food to thrive.

This principle occurs everywhere on Earth. Let's look at ocean salinity. Ocean salinity has been more or less constant, operating in a very narrow band for 2 billion years. In periods when ocean levels drop or when giant continental salt deposits crack open through tectonic movements and subsequently get washed into the oceans, salinity will rise. All oceangoing organisms will sense that and, as directed by a common intelligence, they will filter out salt via their kidneys and deposit it in their bones. As they die, their bones sink towards the bottom of the ocean and get sequestrated away through sediment. This process goes on until salinity is returned to the average level. If Earth heats up and ice shields are melting, water levels rise and salinity in the oceans decreases. Maritime organisms will then exude salt into the oceans until salt levels are back to normal. This way, maritime organisms have maintained ocean salinity as if directed by one common intelligence. And not only "as if" but as directed by such an intelligence.

It is important that we humans understand that the entirety of life constitutes the divine child, directed as it is by the cosmic intelligence of the Divine Mother. Have a look now how this plays itself out as biodiversity. If the sum total of all organisms will excrete a by-product that is toxic to all existing organisms, a new organism will appear that is able to metabolise the new by-product. It will then return the metabolized substance into the biosphere in a form that can be consumed by the existing organisms. In this way, as time goes on, more and more organisms get introduced, and the biosphere becomes more and more complex, i.e., biodiversity increases. The more biodiversity, i.e., the more different organisms there are, the more stable the joint superorganism will be. That is, the more it will be able to weather crises. Hence, as humans, we should not think that we don't need the delta smelt or the monarch butterfly (two of many endangered species) just because we can't put a monetary value on them. Their purpose is in supporting an extremely complex superorganism, Gaia, which in turn supports us.

Next, let's consider methane. One of the greatest concerns climate scientists have is that the rising temperatures on Earth will lead to a release of giant amounts of methane, which is many times more toxic than carbon-dioxide. Methane is locked into the frozen tundra but also into ocean floors. Recently, these areas have begun thawing, and methane is starting to be released into the atmosphere. The process is well out of humanity's hand, and no present technology would be capable of harvesting and sequestrating away such enormous quantities of methane. The only question is: will methane-consuming microbes multiply fast enough to metabolize the methane and return it into the biosphere in form of harmless compounds? Theoretically, this is possible, but it is made less likely through our war on microbes. Microbes are our friends; they are on the same team. We need to support them. Without microbes, we are stuffed.

To take this subject further, consider that the more specialized an organism is, the narrower a band of homeostasis it requires. The more specialized an organism is, the more sensitive it is to fluctuations exceeding that band. The most specialized organism on Earth are we, humans. Hence, it is in our interest to support the stability of the current biodiversity as we need it more than any other organism on Earth.

There are organisms such as archaea (a basic single-cell lifeform) that can live millions of years without oxygen, deep down in the Earth under massive tectonic pressure, in extreme heat and under extreme toxicity. For example, in the Mariana trench (the world's deepest oceanic trench between Japan in the north and Papua New Guinea in the south) are located undersea volcanoes that exude toxic, sulphuric burps. On the spouts of these volcanoes, archaea have been found flourishing not only in the presence of this toxic cocktail but also under atmospheric pressure 1000 times higher than what we are used to. Imagine how a human would fare under those circumstances?

Archaea have also been found when drilling through the sediment under Lake Titicaca in the Andes, the world's highest navigable lake. The lake is situated at an altitude of 3500-metres above sea level, and it is 280 metres deep. The sediment deep under the lake has not been in contact with oxygen in hundreds of millions of years. It also is exposed to one of the highest tectonic pressures on Earth (which is still raising the Andes skywards). In this sediment, archaea have been found happily flourishing. They are being squeezed a bit, but they are good sports and don't mind a bit of foul play. Again, imagine humans under these sorts of circumstances. What I want to show here is that we are an incredibly fragile species, yet for the last 400 years, we have been throwing our weight around on this planet as if we are the crown of creation, which we so obviously aren't. There are much, much tougher guys on this planet, and most of them are microbes.

It is we who are supported by all of the other organisms on Earth. It is we who are standing on their shoulders, but at this point, we are not returning the favours. We are making 100 species of plants and animals extinct every day. 100 species less every day who were working on keeping the biosphere safe and stable so that complex organisms like us can thrive. Again, we can see that the indigenous people who looked at themselves as the guardians and keepers of the garden were on the right track. But we modern people always seem to know better because we supposedly know progress. At least that's what we are duping ourselves into.

God as life does not mean God as an individual or God as humanity. It means the sum total of all lifeforms, the complete community of life. The purpose of each life form is to create more life, nurture life in all forms and to create more life forms. To place oneself into the service of that means to foster biodiversity and the blossoming and flourishing of all lifeforms.

THE MONTE CARLO GENERATOR

Let's now look at the dichotomy between the cosmic and the individual. The Divine, both transcendent and immanent, can be personal to us, but It cannot be an individual. Consider the difference closely. It needs to be well understood. To be an individual means to have an ego by which your consciousness can identify with a particular body and mind specific in space and time rather than another body/mind in a different space/time. The Divine cannot do that. It is everything, everywhere and at all times. If It had the ability to reduce Itself to a particular moment and location, It would need an ego for this purpose, and that would impede Its capability of being everything, everywhere and all the time. In other words, you can only have it one way or another.

Teachings that promote that the entirety of God could be embodied as an avatar or as the only begotten son of God are committing theological errors born out of anthropomorphic thinking. Anthropomorphic thinking here means that we are creating a god in the image of humanity rather than seeing the human being created in the image and likeness of the Divine. It is important to think these points through and come to a complete understanding.

Once we have understood these realizations, we are then ready to comprehend that, since the Divine cannot Itself become an individual, It must individuate through us (It is this principle that forms the bedrock of this book and all ancient Earth-based spirituality). And this is exactly what the Divine has been doing for the last few billions of years of spiritual and natural evolution of life on Earth.

Now, we are ready for the next important step in our reasoning. For the Divine to individuate through us, through all life forms, a new piece of evolutionary software was necessary, the ego. Spiritual people often completely misunderstand the term ego. The person who made the term famous was the psychologist Sigmund Freud. Freud, who wrote in German, used the term "ich", which in English means "I". Obviously, the term "I" does not have any of the heavy connotations that the term ego has. When Freud's texts were translated into English, the term "ego" was borrowed from Latin to make it sound more scientific. However, today, when we hear ego, we immediately think about an egotist with a huge ego. Freud did not have these connotations. He believed that somebody functioning properly must have a healthy sense-of-I, and if the I/ego was injured in a child, this would become the source of many forms of pathological tendencies later on. Interestingly the term sense-of-I is one of the possible translations for the Sanskrit terms asmita and ahamkara, important concepts used in yoga. The other possible translations for these terms would be I-am-ness or ego. It becomes more fascinating when we realize that the term asmita was actually used in the ancient Yoga Sutra with two separate meanings. The term appears first with the somewhat pathological meaning of "egotism" listed amongst the forms of suffering (the so-called kleshas) and secondly with the meaning of pure ego or I-am-ness listed amongst the samadhis (stages of ecstasy and revelation).

The difference between both is simply this: when I'm coming from pure I-am-ness, I'm thinking "I am". When I'm coming from egotism, I am thinking instead, "I am great. I am better than this person. I am this or that" as in "I am a wicked person, and I deserve punishment. I don't deserve what I have or, on the contrary, I am entitled to anything the world can offer, and others aren't". Notice that when pathological ego (egotism) enters, it generally comes with ambitiousness, comparison, self-loathing and competition. On the other hand, the revelatory aspect of ego comes with realizing that our individuality is nothing but the Divine individuating through us and as us (because It itself cannot be an individual but must do so through us).

This is something that Jesus also knew and expressed. Unfortunately, he is quoted in the King James Bible as having said, "Unless you know that I am He, you shall die in your sins". But this is actually a corruption of the original. The King James, although of beautiful poetic language, abounds in corrupt translations reflecting the theological biases of their translator and the predominant view of the time. Better to look into the New International Bible, a text that is constantly updated by hundreds of Hebrew and Greek scholars. Here, we find the saying as "Unless you know the I-AM you shall die in your sins".

Translated into modern language and our context, this means nothing but, "Unless you recognize your ego/I-am-ness as a piece of software that enables you to become a conduit for the Divine to individuate through you, you shall die in your sins." If you want to compress the meaning of this book into one sentence, it would be this saying of Jesus.

A note here on the term sin: "sin" in the original Hebrew is a term that was first used in archery and it means "missing one's mark". In the original, there are no connotations of eternal sullying that the term carries now. The use of the term "sin" simply implied that we should stop making mistakes (i.e., missing our mark). If we kept making mistakes, though, their consequences would finally catch up with us. If we add this understanding to Jesus's statement, the final updated version would then be "Unless you recognize your ego/I-am-ness as a piece of software that enables you to become a conduit for the Divine to individuate through you, you will keep missing the mark (and ultimately die in that state)." That's, of course, something that we want to avoid, and the rest of this book is dedicated to how we can achieve that.

However, before we go to the practical part, I will have to take you through a few more foundational concepts. You may ask, what is the difference between somebody being a so-called avatar (a personification, i.e., God becoming human) and a being opening itself up as a conduit for Divine purpose? The difference is simply that: We are all Divine (ye all are gods, ye all are children of the most High) to exactly the same extent because the Divine does not have an ego to withhold Itself from us. The Divine can only express Itself in Its entirety through the totality of all beings. That means it would be correct to say that all beings collectively are the avatar of God.

To understand this a bit more, I would like you to look at the Monte Carlo generator. A Monte Carlo generator is a computer program that was first used to find out how many possible permutations or number combination occur when you play roulette. Let's say you spin the wheel, and you get an 18. You spin it again, and you get a 25. Spin it again, and you get a 3 and so on. A Monte Carlo generator can tell you how often you have to spin the wheel until all numbers have occurred. It is also capable of telling us of the likelihood of a certain number combination to appear. And it can also tell us if we spin the wheel 100 times, how many different paths or permutations of number combination can occur. It is this last information that I would like you to understand. Each being is a possible permutation, computation and path that the Divine can become as an individual. The Divine is not a particular individual, but the Divine is all of these paths, permutations, computations collectively in their totality and in the aggregate.

You have to understand that you cannot actually stop the Divine from computing Itself through you. You do have a choice, though, whether you do this unconsciously or consciously. If you do it consciously, it leads to living-in-the-zone and to consciously co-creating your life with the Divine. If you remain unconscious about it, then it may feel as if your life is being enacted on you, somehow as if you are a robot without having free will.

Understanding this will also lead to a completely different way of looking at conflicts. You will understand that another person/being will react differently than you in the same situation, as they represent a different path/computation of the Divine. The Divine enacts something different through the other person, since being-you is already enacted through you. There is no point in doing it twice. This also explains the sacredness of all life because each being is absolutely unique whether we notice that or fail to do so.

QUANTUM PHYSICS

There is another way of understanding the relationship between the Divine and the individual that we need to discuss, and this is through science. The mainstream view today is that science and religion are in conflict and you can accept either one or the other. I have already shown that this is a misconception since

CHAPTER 1.

religion has invented science. To give you another example, you may be familiar with Occam's Razor. Occam's Razor is one of the most important principles of science today. It states that if various explanations of a phenomenon are available, and one is simpler or requires fewer components, then the simpler one should be preferred (in other words, one shouldn't construct unnecessary complex models to explain something). So, who exactly is Occam, the founder of this principle? He actually was a 14th century Benedictine monk. Until rather recently, most scientists came either out of the spiritual profession or had a spiritual worldview.

Today, science and religion have splintered, and it is exactly this illogical split of spirit and matter, or more precisely, the idea that matter is not spiritual, that has brought us to the abyss of ecocide, environmental holocaust, and our possible extinction. All of our destructive actions are informed by this erroneous and illusory split. We cannot escape this catastrophe unless this split is healed.

One way (but not the only way) in which this may play out is that science must inform our theology. That means as a theologian, and even if for no other reason, I should at least study scientific progress and new-found knowledge so that it can inform the way in which I understand the Divine. In turn, science itself must be placed into the service of a wholistic worldview and not in one in which humans try to make themselves master of the universe, only to self-destruct in the process. Humanity is here to serve creation and not be its master. Creation itself is the master and luckily so, otherwise we would be long done and dusted.

The possibly most important scientific breakthrough that must inform our view of the Divine is quantum physics, or quantum mechanics, as it is also called. In order to not alienate or bore anybody with too much nitty-gritty detail, I will keep this discussion as short and basic as possible.

Quantum mechanics arose from the double-slit experiment, in which light was sent through an aperture and, depending on whether an observer was present or not, light either displayed wave or particle characteristics. Some experiments proved light to be a wave and refuted the hypothesis that light consisted of particles. Other experiments proved light to be a particle and refuted the theory according to which it is wave-like. Ultimately, it was found that, under certain circumstances, light possessed wave characteristics, and under other circumstances, it had particle characteristics.

It was found that the determining circumstance whether or not light was a wave or a particle was the presence of an observer, a witnessing individual consciousness. If no witness (i.e., observing scientist) was present, light behaved like a wave, i.e., one could make only statements about the probability of light reaching a particular area. As soon as a witness appeared, the wave function collapsed (scientific lingo for the fact that we can now make precise statements where the light hits), and the wave turned into a particle. These experiments have been repeated over and over again with more and more sophisticated set-ups. Upcoming experiments will, for example, focus on whether the same applies when non-human observers will be used, such as animals.

Practically speaking, this means that a room is only then a room consisting of fixed walls, furniture, etc. as long as a witness is able to perceive it. As soon as the last witnessing consciousness has turned away from the room, the room dematerializes into wave-functions, and from now on, we can only make assumptions about the probability of the room being there in a particular form. The room will definitely remain in the particle state if we can still see it via CCTV and probably even if a louse is still contained in it, but that's not proven yet. A louse probably wouldn't prevent the entire room from entering the wave state, but if a bedbug was in the mattress, the mattress may remain in the particle state, but the rest of the room may enter the wave-function as it is not perceived by the bedbug. Most of this can be easily proven with small particles like photons, but experiments have gone on to show that it applies to electrons, too. It most-probably applies to large objects as well, but seeing that billions of witnessing consciousnesses observe planet Earth, it is unlikely that experiments will catch the Earth turning into a wave-function anytime soon. One scenario in which this could occur would be if we blinked all at the same time. The Monte Carlo generator could tell us how long it is likely to take for all of us to blink at the same time.

This confirms the importance of the third aspect of the Divine, the Divine as life. Remember that the God transcendent (cosmic consciousness) is aware of the God immanent (the material cosmos) only in a general, universal way. That means that prior to individual life, the entire God immanent, the universe, existed only as a wave-function. The wave-function shows the probability for something to be there in material, particle or fixed form.

The third aspect of the Divine, life, had to appear for the material cosmos to enter into the particle state. The third aspect of the Divine, life, did so through the introduction of the software called ego/I. Only if consciousness is filtered through sense-of-I/ego and now becomes "I am aware that I am this body and mind in this particular space/time", does it have the power to make the wave-function collapse and the material cosmos enter the particle state. That means that the material world appears before your eyes only because the transcendental aspect of the Divine has limited Itself in time and space via ego to become you. It did so that it could experience Itself in form of the God immanent, the cosmos, through billions of eyes, ears, tactile organs, etc. These sense organs are ours, i.e., of the children of the Divine. I know it's baffling, but that's what it is. Think it through. If you understand this, you are likely to succeed with the method described in this book.

Cosmic consciousness (the Brahman, the Dao, Nirvana etc.) cannot by itself collapse the wave-function, because it cannot observe anything particular. But what it can do is make the entire cosmos appear as the God immanent, which is the sum-total of all wave functions.

Only once consciousness is limited in space and time via ego (what we would call an individual or the observer or witnessing consciousness) can this observer now provoke a particular object in space/time to turn from a wave into a particle. If you want to learn more about this subject, please read Biocentrism and Beyond Biocentrism by Robert Lanza and Bob Berman. Another great subject to study if you want to take this further is Archibald Wheeler's Participatory universe.

ASTROPHYSICS

Another part of physics that needs to be consulted by any budding theologian is astrophysics. You don't need to understand all the nitty-gritty details of this, but read over it to get a sense of wonder. The cosmos is an amazing thing, and cosmic intelligence has organized the physical parameters of this universe in mysterious ways. For example, the density of matter in the universe is exactly what it needs to be to prevent a reverse Big Bang, a collapsing of the universe. Another mystery involves the so-called cosmological constant. Particle physics predicted this constant to be over 100 times larger than it has been found to be, but if the cosmological constant were only several orders of magnitude larger than what it actually is, the known universe would have expanded so quickly that no celestial bodies like stars or planets could have ever occurred and hence, no life.

Then there is a set of constants called the dimensionless physical constants. They were found to be fine-tuned to allow the appearance of matter as we know it and with it, life. Had the so-called weak interaction of these constants been slightly stronger, all hydrogen would have converted into helium. This would have meant that the fuel source for stars such as our sun would have been eliminated, and photosynthesis, which forms the basis of life, would not have been possible. Additionally, with hydrogen converting to helium, no water would be available, and water is one of the most important ingredients to life. The same scenario would play out if the so-called strong interaction, another part of the dimensionless physical constants, would be slightly larger. It is important to understand that while we take water, light, stars, etc. for granted, the likelihood of all of these parameters to be aligned in the right way is incredibly small. It appears that the entire cosmos is a super-intelligent incubator of life. It is inconceivable that all of this could have happened randomly.

Another area that is mysteriously fine-tuned are the forces that form atoms. Slight changes in the so-called weak and strong force that act within atomic nuclei would have meant that these nuclei would have flown apart, and matter as we know it could not have formed. There are also numerical relations between the age of the universe, the mass of the proton and the gravitational constant. Would they have been slightly out, no life could have ever appeared.

Another surprising fact is that in the early days of the universe, only simple atoms such as hydrogen, helium, etc existed. Heavy and complex atoms such as carbon (we are carbon-based lifeforms) were only welded together in solar explosions, so-called supernovae. Supernovae are really labs in which components of future planets and lifeforms are manufactured, welded together by mind-boggling gravitational forces. Many large atoms in our bodies have gone through two, three or even four supernovae (stellar explosions), meaning it took a multi-billion-year complex process to manufacture atoms like carbon or gold. The process by which these increasingly heavy atoms are brought about is called nucleosynthesis, and it takes billions of years. Stars have to be created, and when they finally explode (akin to the death of a star), such an enormous pressure is created that nuclei combine. Then the process starts again. A new star is born, lives billions of years, explodes and forms even heavier nuclei by fusing the existing ones together. This means that our universe first had to reach a certain age and maturity that it could even bring forth life. A young universe does not have the capacity to bring forth small planets like ours. The strange friendliness of our universe towards life has given rise to theories such as the one according to which this universe is a simulation created by a super-intelligent lifeform (see James N. Gardner – *Biocosm and The Intelligent Universe*). I do agree with the author of this theory that the life-friendly universe we know is too unlikely to have come about randomly. However, I think that the universe itself is intelligent. It does not require a foreign agent to order it, but matter itself is crystallized intelligence and the immanent Divine.

EVOLUTIONARY BIOLOGY

It was no one else but Nobel prize winner and co-discoverer of the DNA double-helix, Professor Francis Crick, who suggested DNA was so complex that it could never have developed by random mutation and natural selection during planet Earth's short existence. In other words, to create DNA from scratch by random mutation would take much longer than the short 4 billion years that life exists on our planet. If you look at DNA and compute how long it would take to develop randomly, you arrive at trillions of years, not billions. Charles Darwin had the luxury of developing the belief that life was created by random mutation and natural selection because DNA and its complexity was not yet discovered. Crick saw no other way but to suggest that an earlier galactic civilization had seeded DNA here on this planet. This theory is known as directed panspermia.

A lot of people will consider this theory outlandish, but that is only because we take DNA for granted. The attitude is, "It's here, so let's not think too hard how it developed". But that head-in-the-sand method does not work for those seriously inquiring. The random mutation and natural selection hypothesis is out, as it takes too long. This leaves us with an omnipotent, Yahweh-like anthropomorphic god creating DNA according to his liking or possibly directed panspermia. Personally, I am no fan of directed panspermia, but I think it's important that Crick pointed out that DNA can't have developed here according to Darwin's ideas. However, panspermia only postpones the problem. How did DNA develop somewhere else by random mutation? The average life-span of a star is also only 15-billion years, and by then it would have nuked any DNA-incubating small planets in its vicinity into oblivion. I'm suggesting instead that the material cosmos (God immanent) itself works like a super-intelligent supercomputer that reproduces itself as life. To liken the cosmos to a supercomputer is, of course, metaphorical. A computer itself is not sentient, but the sentience is conferred by infinite consciousness (the God transcendent). Consciousness here has the role of a catalyst. A catalyst itself is not transformed in a chemical reaction, but the reaction can only take place in the presence of a catalyst. Life, then, is the interface of the Mother (material cosmos) and the Father (infinite consciousness). We all are the divine child. Again, the anthropomorphic terms father, mother and child are metaphorical, but they give us a way to reconcile mystical experiences with scientific theory.

BIO-SYMBIOSIS AND MULTICELLULAR LIFE

Another area in which we find mysterious life-creating and life-advancing forces of creation at work is the coming about of multicellular life. Until about 750 million years ago, there were only single-celled organisms. Many of them were so-called archaea, which I have already described in some detail under *The third aspect of the Divine*. Another form of single-cell organisms that appeared are bacteria. They invented photosynthesis, that is, the ability to turn sunlight into energy and protein. Then came the great miracle. An archaeon and a bacterium fused in a bio-symbiotic act and became one. The new being included the tough outer hull of the archaeon, and the bacterium became the mitochondria of the new creature. They had a lot of energy available, could move around, procreate, and all complex life today is a descendant of this new creature. What are the chances of that happening randomly?

Furthermore, if you read the accounts of scientists describing this event, they insist that the encounter between the two microbes took place "violently". They say that the archaeon swallowed the bacterium, but for whatever reason, the bacterium survived and become part of the archaeon. That's too much science fiction to me. A bit like Ridley Scott's *Alien* with a twist, i.e., instead of killing you when entering, the alien fuses with you and bio-symbiotically you both create a new advanced organism.

But how do they actually know that a particular act that took place 750 million years ago did so by means of violence? Because in the language and belief system of the scientists, there is no other way it could have taken place. That means the term "violence" only reflects the perceptual biases of the scientists looking at the phenomenon. And that is because we humans have convinced ourselves that violence is a viable way of sorting out our differences, and so we are projecting that on single-cell organism fusing to form a new advanced lifeform.

Another example of this tendency was the recent (16 October 2017) merging of two giant neutron stars (as measured by LIGO and Virgo interferometers) that gave us the first chance to measure a gravitational wave (predicted by Albert Einstein in 1916) in real time. Again, the scientists in charge of the observation insisted that the merging of the two stars took place "violently". Even stars can't go about their business unscathed without us humans projecting our negative emotions on them, hence anthropomorphizing them.

BRAIN DEVELOPMENT

Another mystery of evolutionary biology involves our brain development. Not that long ago, we presumably sat on trees, munching on bananas. Then the African jungles dried out and were replaced with savannah. Looking for a new food source, our ancestors climbed down from the last remaining trees and within 100.000 years, our brains grew to a size that ultimately enabled us to write symphonies, build computers and space ships, and conceive the Vedas, the Iliad, Hamlet, Guernica and quantum mechanics. Science has no explanation for how this could happen in such a short time. Again, random mutation and natural selection would take tens of millions of years if not longer.

And why would a brain grow that huge anyway? Most of what we have created from the Ramayana to Beethoven's Ninth Symphony and on to Claude Monet's Les Nymphéas is stunning and beautiful but confers no evolutionary advantage whatsoever (to the contrary, it often makes surviving harder). For what evolutionary purpose does an ape create stunning beauty?

There are various theories that try to explain this massive brain growth and increase in cognitive power. One theory says that due to starvation we turned cannibals, and the eating of one another's brains provided us with such a quantity of growth hormones that our brains expanded to double the size. Another theory suggests that because we had to throw spears to hit running prey, our brains grew large quickly so to better hit the target. Again, a much smaller brain would have actually been better if the design brief was that simple. For many of us today, this huge brain with its many distracting considerations is

CHAPTER 1.

actually an obstacle when it comes to procuring food. Although from our current point in history, we take it for granted to have created the Sanskrit language, the Gizeh pyramids and the Acropolis, from a mere survival of the fittest point of view, they have actually distracted us. The question still stands, why do we have such a huge brain that enables us to create all these amazing things?

Then there is, of course, Terrence McKenna's stoned-ape-theory. McKenna theorized that when looking for food in the African savannah, we came across magic mushrooms, and their psychedelic content enlarged our brains in a short time. This idea would be appealing to users of psychedelics, but it still makes our evolution accidental. According to this theory, had those jungles not dried out, we'd be still sitting up there in the trees happily throwing bananas at each other.

I find all of these theories ultimately unsatisfactory. None of them connects the purposely intelligent quantum realm with the purposefully intelligent astrophysical realm and the purposefully intelligent jump to multicellular life. I propose that matter and the cosmos are crystallized cosmic intelligence, which is animated by infinite consciousness. We are its interface. According to this view, there was no way life could not have evolved towards more and more complexity and intelligence because not only is the cosmos itself intelligent and complex, but it is undergoing a process towards more complexity and intelligence (see Alfred North Whitehead – Process and Reality).

A fallacy that we often fall for is that we just accept that we are here, have DNA and have large brains. But we can't explain how we got here. Random mutation and natural selection cannot explain any of that, as our evolution took place in a much shorter time than random mutation could explain. If the random mutation and natural selection theory cannot explain our development, then we must look elsewhere.

SCIENCE AND MATERIALISTIC REDUCTIONISM

I have previously outlined the importance of science for all modern mystics and theologians to improve the models they use to describe their experiences. I must now also speak about the great limitation and even danger that science poses for our future welfare. For the great environmental destruction that took place over the last 400 years did not just accidentally become possible through science, but it is part of the very fabric of science, the belief that we are separate from nature and have to dominate and control it.

The term science generally refers to any system of knowledge. More specifically, it is applied to gaining knowledge through observation and experiment. As we get more sophisticated, we may add double-blind studies, peer reviews, etc. Karl Popper held that what cannot be falsified cannot be seen as science. Science was always designed to deal with the empirical only, that is, it deals with the physical and not the metaphysical. Scientists like Newton and Descartes were material scientists, but they had designed science in a way that it dealt only with the physical. In the last 80 years, this has gradually changed. Science, which itself is designed to deal only with the empirical, now has gone on to deny the metaphysical because it states that there is no empirical data for it. Do you see the irony in that? If science was to make binding statements for the non-empirical, it needed to have been designed differently right from the outset to include non-empirical ways of ascertaining the truth.

CHAPTER 1.

What science shouldn't do is to arrive at a belief system that makes it impossible for scientists to look at evidence contrary to this belief system. But this is exactly what is happening today. Western science, a great methodology, has married itself to a belief system, materialistic reductionism, that in itself is difficult to prove or refute. Materialistic reductionism is the belief that mind and consciousness are the result of bioelectrical and biochemical processes in the brain. Scientists convinced of its viability usually refuse to look at contrary evidence, and scientists who do may lose funding, may lose their tenure, will not get invited to conventions, and their students are informed that if they stay with their mentors, they might damage their academic careers. It would not be wrong to talk about a new inquisition within science to stamp out everything that conflicts materialist reductionism. For more information on this subject, please refer to Mark Gober's *The End of Upside Down Thinking*.

Max Planck, the father of quantum physics, said, "A new scientific truth does not triumph by convincing its opponents and making them see the light, but rather because its opponents eventually die, and a new generation grows up that is familiar with it." This statement was later simplified to "Science progresses one funeral at a time". The dilemma in which we currently are is that part of the old paradigm of science, the belief that we are an entity separate from its environment (the so-called subject-object split), is exactly what fuels environmental destruction and, hence, our demise via the sixth mass extinction. Because the old paradigm of science is built on this belief, science has difficulty accepting that the brain is not an organ that produces mind but one that filters and reduces cosmic consciousness/mind and that each individual, human or otherwise, is only a localization of cosmic mind. If this understanding could assert itself, we could make quick progress in ensuring a return to natural balance and harmony and, hence, our survival. With the continued holding on to the subject/object split and the belief that the brain creates mind and consciousness, science is continuing our separation from nature and due to that, our attempts to dominate it. As long as science cannot change this course of action, it will continue to work towards our demise. Again, please note that I am not against the methodology of science. It is a method that I am using myself. What I am critical of is the philosophy of science, materialistic reductionism. Unfortunately for many today, they have become inseparably intertwined.

SRI AUROBINDO

Let's look at an earlier attempt to a holistic philosophy. The Indian mystic Sri Aurobindo said in The Synthesis of Yoga that the whole multi-billion-year process of natural evolution of life on Earth (God as life) is nothing but a giant act of yoga of nature (God immanent) to bring all matter to the state of cosmic consciousness (God transcendent). While this statement goes well with the philosophy expressed in this book, it is also peculiar. I am wondering whether matter must really be brought up to cosmic consciousness or whether it is already crystallized cosmic consciousness (this being my position). But the great Indian seer managed to bring in a single sentence the three aspects of the Divine, the trinity, in relation to each other. In all likelihood, humans cannot but look at the God transcendent (consciousness) as the origin and ultimate destiny of everything that exists. It certainly does act like a catalyst upon the God immanent (nature, the material cosmos) so that it, like a giant incubator, brings about life. Life, which is the interface of the transcendent and immanent, connected together by ego, firstly makes the immanent crystallize from the wave state into the particle state. In this way, it moves the God immanent from the general to the particular, or from a potential or probability to the manifest or concrete.

On one hand, infinite consciousness, for the first time, can become aware of the universe in particular details. The immanent then, on the other hand, does not just exist as a potential anymore, a probability, but the observing consciousness encapsulated in life forms forces it to abandon its indeterminacy (Heisenberg's principle) and transform itself from waves into so-called solid matter and what we call reality.

Life, then, evolves until it itself becomes aware of the influence it has on waves and particles. It becomes aware that it itself is the interface of the transcendent (the father) and the immanent (the mother) as the divine child. Up to this point, life unconsciously co-created reality with the Father and the Mother. We must use the term co-created here because the transcendent and immanent cannot by themselves alone create specific reality in space/time. They can do so only through us and by becoming us.

From the moment that life has realized this, the process of conscious co-creation goes underway. About this moment, the Bhagavata Purana stated poetically, "When the devotee recognizes Me I cannot but rush to the place and embrace the devotee". To recognize that a cosmic intelligence and consciousness embraces you and enacts themselves through you as a conduit is the most liberating, enabling, expansive, healing and satisfying experiences available to the human being. It is this process of conscious co-creation that this book is dedicated to.

SUMMARY AND CONCLUSION

In this chapter, you have learned what cosmic consciousness is, that is has a transcendental aspect, but that it is also in you. Consciousness all by itself can do nothing. But simply by being conscious and aware of the immanent, the material cosmos, it brings about its quality of awareness. The immanent exists as an infinite multitude of vibratory patterns, waves. These waves crystallize into the particle state (matter) only once the third aspect of the Divine appears, God as life. Life is the interface of the immanent (through its body and mind) and the transcendent (through its consciousness/awareness). Life is the divine child, and both the transcendent and the immanent create reality through it and as it. The purpose of life is to become conscious of this process and to offer itself as a conscious conduit so that this process can be accelerated. For life forms to receive their divine purpose and meaning, it is essential that they understand that the transcendent and the immanent are capable of delivering such instructions, that is, that they can teach us. Religions and mystical schools have often limited how this instruction can come about and what the relationship of the individual to the cosmic has to look like. This led to the development of distinct yogic paths such as the path of devotion (bhakti), of knowledge (jnana), of intellect (buddhi), of action (karma), of mind (raja) or of the body (hatha yoga). However, these yogas are indeed one, and their difference is only in suitability for different types of practitioners. One of keen understanding and progress practises them all simultaneously.

Chapter 2.
LIFE'S DIVINE PURPOSE IN DIFFERENT CULTURES

In this chapter, we will trace the importance to finding one's life divine purpose to different cultures. This is to give the reader the confidence that the subject has not been made up by the present author but in fact dealt with by many reputed sources, and it has been a mainstay of human civilization dating back to its dawn. Our current materialistic reductionist culture is actually one of the few which has neglected this subject. The belief that life is a purposeless accident is actually leading to untold suffering in many individuals. Unfortunately, by its very definition of being materialistic reductionist, our modern civilization has excluded the cure for many mental disorders from its healing repertoire. Modern psychology, in many instances, consists of little more than patching up suffering individuals with pharmaceutical chemicals so that they can continue to compete in a meaningless rat race. This is not to say that these medications may not be necessary in some cases until a more holistic solution has been found, involving, amongst other things, lifestyle choices.

FINDING ONE'S LIFE'S DIVINE PURPOSE IN INDIGENOUS CULTURES

Clearer than many other sources, the stance of indigenous cultures towards finding one's life's divine purpose is described in Richard Walker's *Lakota Belief and Ritual*. Walker was a medical doctor who was assigned to the Pine Ridge Reservation in South Dakota, USA after the massacre at Wounded Knee, 1895. Walker served as a medical doctor to the Oglala Lakota for 18 years, during which he became more and more interested in their spirituality.

Ultimately, he asked them whether they would consider initiating him into their religion. At the time, there were only six of the old medicine men alive. They initially declined, telling him that white people were too unspiritual to understand their beliefs. Walker insisted, and eventually, the old medicine men undertook a vision quest to ask their gods whether they could initiate a white man. Luckily for us, the gods came back with a positive reply but maintained that Walker had to go first through the long gruelling training of a shaman. Ultimately, he completed the entire training and became a Lakota holy man. During that process, the Smithsonian institute got wind of his initiation and trained him as an anthropologist. His book *Lakota Belief and Ritual* (1905) is a fascinating insight into indigenous religion.

The defining element of the Lakota religion and most indigenous forms of spirituality is the vision quest, usually undertaken at the onset of puberty. The ways and methods by which indigenous people bring about visions differ, but their purpose is the same. When Walker asked the old medicine men about the vision quest's purpose, they replied that it is to bring each individual in contact with the *Wakan Tanka* (great mystery, great spirit). Through this contact, each individual experiences what their natural gifts are and what they are here for. By following the vision and fulfilling the role seen in the vision, individuals earn self-respect, a livelihood and the respect of the community around them. The Lakota considered the vision quest to be so important that they would go to all lengths for all members of the tribe to obtain a vision informing them of their life's purpose. If an individual failed to obtain a vision, their old mentor had to go on a vision quest with them. If this failed, too, it could mean that the entire council of old shamans had to go on a vision quest together to break the deadlock.

When asked why it was considered so important that all members of the tribe had a vision showing them the direction of their future life, the old shamans answered that people who never had a vision of their life's purpose usually became angry and a danger to themselves and the community around them.

Do you see the drama of our valueless culture in that sentence? Apart from outcompeting others in career, sports, education, consumption, etc., our culture doesn't show our young people any values (it should be argued that competitiveness is a destroyer of values not a value itself).

Because our culture has lost all initiatory rituals, our young people grow up angry and confused and without self-respect. In order to gain self-respect, they display dangerous, reckless behaviour, drug use, sexual excesses and mental disorders (as I did, too, when I was young). At this point, we recognize that these young people are a "danger to themselves" but we fail to recognize that it is our valueless and non-initiatory society who forces our young people to self-initiate through drugs, crime, sex, violence and danger.

But even more concerning are the ones who are "a danger to the community around them". We consider an individual accomplished if they have a strong competitive drive. We are celebrating billionaires, athletes and politicians who have only one objective and that is to ruthlessly rise to the top of the pile. Electorates vote into power politicians that do not care at all for the disadvantaged but who display an unbridled will to power and greed for no other reason than their own self-aggrandisement.

The connecting theme between those who "are a danger to themselves" and those who "are a danger to the community around them" is that both groups come from an attitude of wanting to get, to take and to receive. The Lakota and other indigenous cultures show us that a satisfactory life is not defined by what you receive, take, and get but by that what you are able to give, that is, by the contribution you are capable of making to the lives of others.

It is a great mystery of our life that what makes us really feel good about ourselves is to be able to make a valid contribution to the lives of others. This is, of course, not what you read in the media and what you learn at school and university. Here, the mantra is to compete, out-compete and get ahead of others. But have you noticed that no amount of success built on out-competing others insulates you from depression and suicide? This is because the philosophy of ambitiousness and competitiveness does not take into consideration that humans are wired to be social animals, and what makes us happy is to facilitate the flourishing, blossoming and growing of others.

And this is exactly what indigenous people experienced during the vision-quest. What indigenous people called the Great Spirit is nothing but the cosmic intelligence that expresses itself as the continuing expansion and growing biodiversity of the biosphere. As previously shown, this intelligence makes all lifeforms act like one life to keep the bio parameters fluctuating only within a narrow range, maintaining the possibility for life. Indigenous people knew that a satisfying and fulfilling life is possible only if individuals can place themselves consciously into the service of this intelligence. If you manage to do this, your life will be fulfilling. You are set to benefit by finding out what your nature gifts are and how to place them into the service of the community around you. And from that, you develop self-esteem from the experience of being a giver.

These founding concepts of indigenous cultures are near universal, found all around the world. The vision-quest of the Lakota is called walk-about among Australian Aborigines, but the purpose is the same. It is to show the young human how they can be a support for their community and a guardian of the nature around them. It shows them that they are not an accidental by-product of a random evolution but an integral part of the web of life and all matter. Aborigines often refer to geological formations, i.e., mountain ranges, etc. as their ancestors, and they usually display an expanded sense-of-self when making statement such as, "I am the land".

For a modern Westerner, this is difficult to understand as we were enculturated with the erroneous concept of a discrete self, estranged in a hostile or at least indifferent world "red in claw and tooth" as Hobbes would have it. But for one who has received a vision, it is clear that the same cosmic intelligence that has formed galaxies, stars and planets has also formed continents, mountain ranges, oceans and finally, has also given life to us. Mountain ranges, oceans, etc. who came before us are therefore correctly seen as our ancestors, because the same cosmic intelligence that has formed us now has formed them before.

An important concept of indigenous spirituality is to be in service of all life. This is in stark contrast to modern ideas such as Adam Smith's "economic man", that is, a person being primarily interested in their economic advantage. Our modern delusion is that we are here to maximize our own self-interest and hopefully pass on our selfish genes to even more maximized egotists than ourselves. After we have followed this so-called philosophy of science for several centuries, we have come to the point of making extinct every day 100 species of plants and animals, and by that continued activity, we are making every day our own extinction more likely.

This is very clear to indigenous people. So learned, for example, the African shaman Malidoma Patrice Some during his initiation from his elders that the white man's way means death (Malidoma Patrice Some – *Of Water And The Spirit*). Because some had adapted to the way of the whites, his elders told him that there was something dead within him that did not like to confront anything having to do with life. A stark warning of the effects of modern culture issued by a people that have lived in harmony with nature for tens of thousands of years. A similar warning about the results of following a life bereft of divine purpose comes from a prophecy of the Cree Native Americans, "When you have shot the last buffalo, felled the last tree, and poisoned the last river, you white people will finally realize that you can't eat money".

DIVINE PURPOSE IN THE YOGA SUTRA

I will continue now by tracing the philosophy underlying this book in some classical spiritual texts such as the Yoga Sutra, the Bhagavad Gita and the Bible. It is essential that you, dear reader, understand that this teaching is not some New-Age bugaboo, conjured up by the present author, but an essential, ancient teaching that is only re-applied to modern society.

The Yoga Sutra is a few centuries older than the Bible and most likely older than the Gita, too. A theme recurring in the Yoga Sutra is that the mind needs to be cultivated like a farmer would cultivate a field. The Sanskrit term for cultivation is bhavana, and it is the most frequently appearing term in the Yoga Sutra. Sutras I.2-4 state, "Yoga is the stilling of the mind. When the mind is still the seer abides in its own true nature. At other times the seer emulates the forms of the thoughts." These three opening stanzas of the Yoga Sutra (stanza 1 merely says, "Now then introduction to yoga"), are akin to the biblical "The Kingdom of Heaven is within", "close your door and enter the closet", and "the secret chamber of the Most High".

There is a space within us, which upon entering, will bring us in contact with the infinite. The Yoga Sutra says that then we will experience (more precisely, abide in) our true nature, which is consciousness. This space is already here in all of us, but most of us have difficulties accessing it due to the long process of enculturation that we underwent. In order to access it, we need to turn inward, shut out sensory distraction and the chatter of the mind. If we don't do that, we are under the tyranny of the mind. Reflecting that the Yoga Sutra in stanza I.4 says "[when the mind is not still] we become one with the thoughts". That's all right as long as your thoughts are noble, but at times when they are conflicted, being one with one's thoughts is a recipe for disaster. Serial killers, mass murderers and other psychopaths, when asked why they did what they did, usually respond that there was a voice in their heads telling them to do what they did. Listening to the voices in one's head and following their advice is probably the most hazardous human pastime. In this book, you will find a method connecting you to the one voice drawing you towards your sacred destiny.

Sutra I.10 says, "Deep sleep is the intention of non-becoming". The message of this stanza supports that of the stanzas above. During 11-17 minutes per night of deep, dreamless sleep, the subconscious becomes completely motionless and merges with the consciousness, which is eternally awakened. Because the mind is completely still during this period and there is no subconscious activity whatsoever, we are essentially in a self-realized, liberated state, were it not for the fact that we are fast asleep and that there is little memory upon awakening (there is some form of memory of that, though, and yogis work on increasing it). We could say that samadhi, the yogic state of ecstasy, revelation and superconsciousness, is nothing but the deep sleep state experienced once fully awake.

The reason why I describe this here is so that you realize that you are much closer to freedom than you think. We all experience this deep sleep state nightly. It is only upon re-entering the dream state and, later, the waking state that the mind boots up again and exits us again from the Garden of Eden. Poetically, the deep sleep state is called "resting in the embrace of the Divine". It is really only your mental activity that stops you from accessing that state or making it conscious. It is natural for you to go to this place daily, the only thing we need to change is to link your conscious, waking state of mind to your superconscious mind. More to that later.

CHAPTER 2.

Sutra I.23 says, "[samadhi can also be achieved] by placing yourself into the service of the Divine (ishvara pranidhana)". The phrase ishvara pranidhana is so important to Patanjali, the author of the Sutra, that he repeats it in four different locations where it serves four different functions. Here, it initiates a series of stanzas that discuss and define the Divine. The stanza does this by suggesting our relationship to cosmic intelligence be one of service. It is not enough to simply have spiritual experiences and not be changed by them. Spiritual experiences are only valuable to the extent that we learn to embody them and live and work for the common good. Placing oneself into the service of the Divine, of course, means that we need to learn how the Divine wants to be served (note: remember to not think of the Divine in anthropomorphic terms).

Practically speaking, in meditation we need to open ourselves to the Divine influx, set our surface personality aside and let the Divine teach us and express Itself through us. Managing to do that will result in spiritual freedom for us. You may say, how can that be, don't we fulfil, then, somebody else's will? The answer to that is that this will is not "somebody's". The Divine is not an individual, it is the cosmic, the universal. Additionally, there is only one will and that is the will of the Divine. The art is to place ourselves into the service of that will. Only then can we be free. There is no freedom from the Divine because the Divine is freedom. There is only freedom from the tyranny of our minds. Additionally, the Divine is not somebody else, but it is your innermost core. As Krishna states in the Bhagavad Gita (10:20), "I am the self in the heart of all beings".

In stanza I.24, the Yoga Sutra says, "The Divine is a distinct consciousness, untouched by forms of suffering, karma, it's results and residue". Here Patanjali defines the Divine. Ultimately the stanza says that a human being, through spiritual practice, can become similar to the Divine in that we can become free, but there will always be the difference that we do carry a karmic residue, meaning we always know that there was once a time when we weren't free. The Divine will never carry such a residue as there never was a time when It wasn't free. Patanjali also uses the term *distinct consciousness*, that is, the Divine is not just the sum total of all consciousness, a view that pantheism holds. Distinct consciousness means that it is more like a cosmic being that is not individual. All beings are in it, but it is more than just an amalgamation of all beings. It is a being that is not limited in any way. A personality, an ego, etc. always means limitation. If you are such-and-such a personality, you cannot be its opposite. The divine is, therefore, an infinite, cosmic being, but it is not a person or individual. The fact that the Divine has to individuate through us has already been explored. Another reason why Patanjali uses the term "distinct" is because the ability to distinguish the voice of the Divine from other voices means that we have a reliable avenue to be instructed by the Divine and to not confuse this voice with other voices.

Sutra I.25 states, "In the Divine is all knowledge". This is a really important stanza for our subject. 1.24 defined the Divine as consciousness. But knowledge is something completely different from consciousness. Consciousness is that which is conscious. Knowledge is part of the contents of consciousness. Whereas stanza 1.24 dealt with the God transcendent, 1.25 deals with God immanent. When Patanjali says that all knowledge is in the Divine, he means to include all scientific laws we have discovered and also those we are yet to discover. The statement includes the order by which elementary particles assemble to atoms and atoms to molecules. It means that the principles by which stars assemble to clusters, clusters and black holes to galaxies, galaxies to universes, etc., are all in the intelligence of the Divine. Laws of harmony that J.S. Bach applied in his fugues, tenets of linguistics expressed by Shakespeare, rules of electric engineering discovered by Nikola Tesla, specific relativity as formulated by A. Einstein are all held in the intelligence of the Divine. They were only downloaded and applied by these geniuses. They have not invented them. Vincent Van Gogh and Salvador Dali showed us new ways of seeing. But they did not invent them. They were merely conduits of divine expression. The Divine is constantly seeking expression. The question is only can we open ourselves to its influx? This stanza here says that the Divine in its form of God immanent is Cosmic Intelligence. This is made clear by the fact that consciousness as such is formless, quality-less, infinite and eternal. Any form of knowledge pertains to form and quality and is, therefore, not part of the God transcendent but the God immanent, which we can poetically call the Divine Mother. Interestingly, most Hindu schools of thought see the entire manifest cosmos, including all matter and all beings, as feminine.

In sutra I.26 we find, "Because the Divine is beyond time it is the teacher of the ancient teachers". This stanza deals with how spiritual knowledge such as yogic knowledge is derived. Yogic knowledge comes in so-called lineages, but however far back they reach, the founding teacher ultimately received their knowledge by tuning into a wavelength of the Divine. The

Divine, because it is outside of space and time (or we should better say space/time is within the Divine), is the wellspring of all spiritual systems whenever and wherever they arose. Importantly for us, this means that wherever we are spatially and temporally, we can always access the Divine. It is as clearly here and now as it was in India or Israel five-, three-, or two-thousand years ago, respectively. Do not be discouraged from accessing the Divine, nor be duped into the belief that it is harder or even impossible now. That thought is scientifically absurd. The Divine is as much here now and as it has been in ancient days and has been so at all times and places throughout history. Of course, psychologically and subjectively, it seems more difficult today, and that is because our society has turned profoundly materialistic. Let's not be distracted by this apparent contradiction.

Sutra I.27 states, "The Divine projects forth the Big Bang". The Sanskrit term pranava means the Big Bang. Pranava is also the name of the sacred syllable OM, which stands for omniscience, omnipresence and omnipotence. But again, OM is just another word for Big Bang. OM means omniscience because all knowledge was right there when the Big Bang initiated. Matter didn't have to make up its mind along the way how exactly to form hydrogen or helium atoms, stars, supernovae, quasars or black holes. All of that takes place according to already established principles. All of this is already known, formed in the primordial vibratory pattern OM. Similarly omnipresence. Prior to the Big Bang, there was no space. Space can only be determined once we have different points of reference that are separate from each other. Prior to the Big Bang, however, all matter and space were compacted

CHAPTER 2.

undifferentiated in a single point, smaller than a pinhead. Hence there was no space. But the primordial vibration OM was already present in that spot. As the Big Bang projected forth space and the universe with it, it took the primordial vibration with it, or better to say it was the primordial vibratory pattern that laid out and projected forth space and the universe. Hence, the primordial wave is wherever space is and therefore omnipresent. There is no space where it is not.

Similarly, it is the primordial vibratory pattern OM that makes everything manifest, i.e., projects forth the entire cosmos by giving birth to an infinite number of daughter vibrations, wave patterns. Hence, it does and produces everything, and there is nothing that is not made by it, and, therefore, it is omnipotent.

A disclaimer here, the primordial vibration OM does not and has not produced consciousness, but consciousness is uncreated and unmade. It is not, therefore, subject to any potency, nor subject to time or knowledge. It is simply eternal, infinite, uncreated, formless and quality-less. Consciousness is the God transcendent; OM is an aspect of the God immanent.

Sutra 1.28 continues this thread through, "The mantra OM should be chanted and its meaning realized/cultivated". Here, for the first time, we find the important Sanskrit term bhavana (cultivation). It implies an agricultural metaphor where soil and crop are not simply seeded and then abandoned but cultivated over a long time. Similar to a farmer producing a crop not in an afternoon but through the work of an entire year, so the realization of the purpose of OM cannot take place in a single sitting. We can become conscious of the grandeur of OM only through a gradual process. The meaning is that behind the visible process of creation there is a super-intelligence, which, although not a giant human or person, nevertheless has certain similarities with us so that it can rightfully be said that the human is made in the image and likeness of the Divine.

The similarities lie in the fact that the Divine is conscious (the God transcendent) and intelligent (the God immanent). However, it is both to such a magnitude that we cannot really comprehend and appreciate it. But we must try. We must try to understand that out of trillions of universes that could have arisen, ours is finely tuned to bring about intelligent life. The likelihood of this fine-tuning to come about at random has been estimated to be 1x10 to the power of -130 (James Gardner – *The Intelligent Universe*), which is as close to zero as we could possibly get.

Again, try to appreciate that if our human evolution really would have come about by random mutation and natural selection, billions of years would have needed to take place, but our human evolution took place in giant leaps in a few 100.000 years. The reason why modern critically thinking people have difficulties connecting the dots is because theologians have not precisely spelled out in what way humans differ from the Divine. And they simply could not do that because they would have to forsake many of their favourite concepts of exclusivity that most religions abound in.

For example, the Divine (God transcendent) is infinite, eternal, quality-less, formless and egoless. Because it is everywhere and at all times equally in everything, there cannot be such things as God's only begotten son, or that one person is an avatar while another person isn't. God, having no ego, can neither choose an individual as their favourite nor a people as their chosen. Infinite consciousness can also not limit itself to produce only

CHAPTER 2.

one awakened one (Buddha) per kalpa (world age). Because all space and all time is equally in the God transcendent, no place, no person can be separated from or closer to the Divine in any way. Since the God transcendent is not separable in compounds (because it is not assembled from compounds) it follows that the Divine is in all beings completely and fully. It follows that we are all the avatar, the son of God, the Awakened and chosen one.

It is important to think these things through logically. Because it is those age-old misconceptions that stop us from becoming conduits for divine consciousness, intelligence, love, beauty and creativity. Or to be again more precise, you are already a conduit for divine consciousness, intelligence, love, beauty and creativity, but you are not conscious of it. The bhavana, i.e., the cultivation mentioned in this sutra, is to cultivate awareness of the fact that the Divine is already creating through you. Because It cannot limit itself to Jesus, Krishna, Buddha, etc., It must do so through all of us. This understanding needs to be cultivated to find one's life's Divine purpose.

Sutra I.32 then states, "For the purpose of counteracting the obstacles one needs to place oneself into the service of the Divine". In sutra 1.30 we find a list of obstacles to yoga which include sickness, mental rigidity, fear, doubt, etc. Sutra I.31 states that these obstacles will surface in three planes, i.e., body, breath and mind. With stanza I.32 starts a list of methods to alleviate the obstacles, the first of which is to place oneself into the service of the Divine. But what does that actually mean? The Bhagavad Gita states in stanza III.35 that better than performing someone else's duty well is to perform our own in a mediocre way. So, to place oneself into the service of the Divine does not mean to accept some general guidelines that serve everybody, but it means to do exactly what the Divine wants to do through you, to become a conduit for divine will. For it is, of course, most important that you allow divine inflow of information through intuition and vision practice. What it does not mean is to follow some spiritual leader who tells you what you should do. Nobody else can hear the frequency on which the Divine speaks to you and through you. You *are* that frequency.

How can service to the Divine alleviate and prevent all these obstacles? Mainly by creating an atmosphere of certainty and removing any internal dialogue about what you should do and what you shouldn't. It creates an atmosphere of congruence, a state in which the various layers of your being are congruent about what needs to be done and are not like a set of horses that all pull in different directions. With your entire being in a state of congruence and alignment, the obstacles can easily be overcome.

In sutra I.33, we read, "Clarity of mind is produced by cultivating benevolence towards the happy, compassion towards the miserable, joy towards the virtuous and forgiveness towards the wicked". The key word here is cultivation, the second time that the term bhavana appears in the Yoga Sutra. The above attitudes do not come suddenly just because we desire them but must be slowly cultivated like a farmer cultivating crop and soil. We have certain ingrained attitudes that are based on seeing others as threats and competition. If they are happy, we react with envy (i.e., we ask why do they deserve this but not me), but if they are miserable, we might react with judgement (we think they have brought it on themselves). If we see a virtuous person, instead of celebrating them, we react with cynicism (such as wondering whether their behaviour is just a PR stunt) whereas if somebody's error of judgment has been revealed, we call for retribution and punishment although we would hope to be let off lightly if caught in the same situation. The stanza asks for a resetting of our attitudes towards others, which currently are still built on competitiveness. By understanding that it is the same Divine working through others that works through us, too, we can gradually let go of permanent conflict and competitiveness with the people around us.

Sutra II.2 reads, "The purpose of introductory yoga is to cultivate samadhi and the reduce the forms of suffering". The stanza explains what is behind so-called introductory yoga (Kriya Yoga) which is a simplified yoga taught to novices. This sutra states that the various forms of suffering cannot be overcome all at once, but one must do so gradually. This comes together with gradually cultivating the mind with the objective of experiencing samadhi (ecstasy of revelation). The significance for us here is that the mind does not tend to tune into our life's divine purpose all at once. It has doubts, gets distracted and finds arguments to return to behaviours based on the concept of the separate self, such as ambitiousness and competitiveness. These will not disappear all at once, but the mind has to gradually be cultivated to adopt a philosophy based on bio-symbiosis and mutual support of all life-forms.

In sutra II.21 we find, "The nature of the seen is only for the purpose of consciousness". The term "the seen" refers the material world, including our bodies. When brought up in a materialistic-reductionist society we may accept toxic beliefs such as that life is an accidental by-product of random colliding forces in an essentially dead universe (which lead us to the attempt of dominating nature and as a result self-destruction). This present stanza gives us a different vision of life. It says that the entire universe exists for life to realize itself as consciousness, which in our language is the God transcendent. That means that on the cosmic scale, the material universe was projected forth so that infinite consciousness could bring forth its quality of reflectiveness. Without that, consciousness would not have been consciousness.

On the individual scale, your body exists so that you can work through your mental limitations that stop you from realizing your true nature of consciousness. On the way towards that outcome, you are traversing a vast journey from single-cell organism to cosmic consciousness, having experiences of a Krishna, Buddha and Jesus on the way. Jesus went as far in saying, "The works I do you shall also do and greater works than these you shall do" (John 14:12). I do not think that Jesus was flippant when he said this, but that he actually could see a future in which humans who continued to pursue their spiritual evolution would achieve what he did and even outdo him. Jesus had a clear vision of our evolutionary future. And the key to that is to understand that this is a spiritual cosmos in which lifeforms have a body so that they can spiritually evolve.

Sutra II.33 states, "When there is bondage due to conflicting thought, cultivation of the opposite is prescribed". This is the fourth time that Patanjali lists the term cultivation (bhavana). The reason why I keep pointing this out is because Patanjali does not believe progress to "spontaneously" take place but that it is a gradual process of fine-tuning. This sutra anticipates that you did have some form of vision/revelation and now gives advice on how to deal with your subconscious mind that contains beliefs contrary to your vision, which manifest as obstacles. Technically speaking, we can describe a vision as the process of downloading information from your superconscious to your conscious mind. Your divine purpose (svadharma) is already there waiting for you, but you are currently not aware of it because your conscious mind (the part of your mind you are conscious of) is not connected to the superconscious mind. The superconscious mind is the part of your mind that you are sharing with cosmic intelligence, the intellect of the Divine. It is called superconscious because it is above our day-to-day awareness. Through yogic techniques and general vision practice (described later), we are downloading information from the superconscious mind into the conscious mind.

However, that's not the end of story. Your whole life long, whatever you felt, said, thought, and did was recorded in your subconscious mind. The subconscious mind is beneath your threshold of awareness, and it is the seat of all your fears, limiting beliefs, hang-ups, etc. The subconscious mind is a recording of your entire past. It is similar to memory, although most of it you can't consciously access. This is a safety mechanism that prevents your conscious mind from being cluttered with anything apart from things that are necessary for day-to-day survival.

The reason why we have a subconscious mind at all is so that not every time when we have to make a choice we have to sit down and consider which one. Embedded in the subconscious mind are millions of behavioural patterns that we can activate quickly for the purpose of survival.

The terms super and sub are used here only metaphorically. These forms of mind do not have locations, but the superconscious mind is so called because it contains your highest aspirations regarding your spiritual evolution. The subconscious mind, on the other hand, contains painful experiences of the past (shame, guilt, etc.) that prevent you from soaring to meet the aspirations of the superconscious mind. They hold you down and in the past. They were essential during our evolutionary past as reptiles, mammals, and primates; however, as humanoids, we are now gradually outliving their usefulness.

When the present sutra says, "when there is bondage due to conflicting thought" it refers to the fact that the negative, self-limiting beliefs held in your subconscious mind (often related to your childhood) tend to be in conflict with the new beliefs downloaded from your superconscious mind. A typical example: At some point in my life, it dawned upon me that I could, in fact, have a role in aiding the spiritual evolution of others. The moment when I consciously accepted this thought for the first time, my subconscious mind violently regurgitated all the negative judgements that I ever heard about myself. Many were not even consciously linked to my person but were ideas of self-hatred and self-loathing, etc., which I had subconsciously picked up from my parents, siblings, teachers, priests, peers, ancestors, and so on. A big part of it was simply ancestral karma, but some of it also related to silly things I had done as a child and then experienced shame, guilt, etc. Stanza II.33 now says that all these things will come up in form of conflicting thoughts. It is to be expected. How do we deal with them, because if we let them again take over our conscious mind, our progress will be impeded?

If they do come up, we simply restate the vision from our superconscious mind without getting agitated. For many of us, this is initially difficult. If you grew up like me in a Western

CHAPTER 2.

dominator-society, you may have learned that in a conflict situation it is helpful to express your position with great force and possibly supported by emotions such as agitation, anger, etc. We learn to coerce and manipulate our opponents by emotionally overpowering them. However, when living in Asia, I learned that in a negotiating situation, the most important thing is to avoid pushing your opponent into a situation where they experience loss of face. It means that, in a tense situation, you never get angry or excited but always ever calmly re-state your original proposition. If you do that, your opponents will realize that what you say is really important to you, and they can then contemplate ways of adjusting their position, meaning they can consider performing an organized retreat from their own position. If, however, you get angry at them or expose them in any way, they will lose face, i.e., backing down will now be experienced as humiliation.

When interacting with our subconscious mind, we need to employ exactly the same method. Stomping our feet, hollering, bickering, manipulating, getting angry, excited, eventually exhausted, all of that does not work. When your subconscious mind sends up feelings, thoughts, sensations that are not congruent with the vision of yourself as downloaded from your superconscious mind, you need to "cultivate the opposite". This means the opposite of what the subconscious mind throws up. For example, your subconscious mind may say that you are unworthy of doing what your superconscious mind suggests. Or it may say you are incapable, or even a genuinely wretched person that does not deserve anything good at all. "Cultivating the opposite" simply means to, over-and-over again, calmly, without getting agitated, re-state the vision that your superconscious mind gave you.

The Sanskrit for cultivating here is, again, our important agricultural term *bhavana*. It implies that reconditioning the mind is a lengthy process that will only show results once a critical mass of new impressions, which are in alignment with our vision received from the superconscious mind, is reached. More about that later. But for now, remember that you need to be in it for the long haul. You won't change your subconscious mind over a weekend.

Sutra II.34 follows on with, "Conflicting thoughts, such as harmful ones, etc., whether done, caused, or approved of [], will result in more pain and ignorance. To realize that is to cultivate the opposite". This is the fifth time that the term bhavana (cultivation) occurs in the Yoga Sutra, and it's linked here to an important concept. We imagine the process of cultivating as an attitude of wilful effort that has sweat drip from one's brow. And there may be that side of it, too. But it cannot be limited to that. An important side of cultivating an attitude is realization and understanding. I will later on describe the active, wilful aspect of cultivating creative thought-patterns in great detail. But here, the Yoga Sutra states that an important aspect of this work takes place via realization. Without realization and understanding, there will be little sustainable progress on our path.

The present stanza points towards understanding the cycle of subconscious imprints/conditioning and new harmful actions based on it. Let's say that I harbour thoughts of self-hatred and self-loathing. That may be a harsh statement, but often, the people who are the loudest out there proclaiming their own greatness and superiority are not the ones who are confident about who they are. To the contrary, they often have a total lack of self-esteem and make this up by bragging, blustering and putting others down. This apparent contempt for others is actually nothing but an externalized inner conflict, an inner insecurity. Because, if in the privacy of my own four walls and the dark of night, I consider myself a low-life, in the marketplace and in the public eye, I will project that on others and put them down.

The sutra here states that it does not matter whether I harbour and develop those ideas myself, approve them in others or cause others to think that way (by means of manipulation). It will be equally harmful to me. The current sutra also states that harm and demerit don't actually start with a violent act or hurtful speech, but it always starts on the thought stage, on the level of thought. A hurtful speech or action will not spontaneously come out of nothing, but it is something that we gradually prepare ourselves for through repeated application of thought into a particular direction. We are gradually talking ourselves into the action, are psyching ourselves up to perform it.

As an example, let's say I verbally abuse somebody. If I check myself honestly, there will have been a gradual build-up over days and weeks until the top popped off and the anger came out. The present sutra calls for making conscious all these processes while they are still in the thought stage. Once we have committed ourselves through hurtful speech and actions, the tendency is much harder to change. The earlier the intervention, the easier the change.

Now, the actual causal chain the Yoga Sutra wants us to understand is the following: conflicting, harmful thoughts lead to harmful actions. Harmful actions lead to a new cycle of painful, self-deprecating thoughts and those to more negative actions. And so, the cycle keeps revolving and often, it actually accelerates. Currently widely discussed in public discourse, for example, are substance abuse and repeat-offending. But these are just the tip of the iceberg. Patterns of relationship breakdown, isolation due to cruel speech, constant conflict in one's work environment or family are based on the very same pattern.

We must first understand the fact that many negative, self-destructive and self-harming behavioural patterns are, in fact, caused by our own negative thought patterns. Once we understand that, there is the chance of dropping or changing the pattern.

Have a look, for example, at holy, righteous anger. How much investment does our culture have with experiencing righteous anger at those wretched, debased people (whoever they currently may be). We often think that we may be entitled to harbour negative thoughts against others and that may well be true. But, ultimately, it is ourselves that we are harming and damaging through these thoughts. And this is because our subconscious mind works like a recorder and can only say yes to whatever we think into it. That's the secret why children until about the age of twelve are so efficient learners. They are in a hypnotic state in which the conscious mind does not block the subconscious mind from absorbing anything they hear. It is only at a later age that we become self-conscious and may reject thoughts and ideas, particularly those about us.

The problem with negativity against others is that the subconscious mind (which makes up the vast majority of our mind) can only think in one mode. If you do experience hatred against another, the subconscious mind can only think "hatred" and will turn that automatically against us, too. The subconscious mind cannot think "hatred" against our enemies and "love" towards ourselves. It can only think either love or hatred, which will then direct simultaneously outwards and inwards. That's why Jesus said, "love thy enemies" and also "do not place an offering on this altar if you harbour ill against a brother in your heart" (Matthew 5:23-25). He understood than any ill will, whether held against foe or friend, will poison the entirety of our heart and therefore any offering as well.

When beginning to follow our life's divine purpose we need to understand how our psyche, currently built on wrong assumptions about competitiveness, coercion, domination, etc. holds us back in our evolutionary development. Understanding is the first step on the journey to letting go and change.

Sutra II.36 then states, "When established in truthfulness, actions and their fruit will correspond to one's word". This stanza says that, to the extent to which we have made our mind congruent and concentrated, will our thoughts and words form reality. There is lots of talk about the law of attraction, that is, that we are attracting things in life based on the types of thoughts that we think. There is truth in that and, of course, even Jesus has stated as much. But the degree to which this happens depends on the level of congruency of our mind and being. The level of congruency, on the other hand, depends on the alignment of our subconscious, conscious and superconscious minds. While we can train a subconscious mind to be congruent with our conscious mind, we can never force the superconscious mind to become congruent with the conscious mind. The conscious mind, in fact, has to download divine purpose from the superconscious mind and, by means of this, become congruent with it, not the other way round. The process will be described in coming chapters.

Most of us will have some experience with the fact that some thoughts are better avoided lest they should turn to reality. The saying, 'Watch what you wish for' gives testimony to that. The reason why most of us have a mediocre return-rate on our thoughts coming true is because our minds are generally not concentrated and congruent enough. And for good reason. Imagine that anything that you would focus your mind on would come to pass. That would be the fastest way to turn one's life into a complete mess.

When the current stanza says, "established in truthfulness" it means to be established in Divine law, that is, to not utter anything that is contrary to Divine law. The term Divine law here is just shorthand for realizing that there is a greater cosmic harmony according to which the many parts of the cosmos work together in harmony. If we want to create reality, that is, "action and fruit to correspond to our word", we must place ourselves into the service of that perfect harmony and beauty. That is the reason why people like Jesus, Krishna, Gandhi, Mozart, Bach, Einstein, Newton, Shakespeare, etc. could do what they did. They could see a higher order in their mind's eye, and whether we call that higher order religious or scientific is here completely irrelevant. Those terminologies are actually interpretations of the framework in which those views of higher order take place and not the actual vision of higher order itself.

Sutra II.45 then says, "Samadhi comes from placing oneself into the service of the Divine". Samadhi is a complex term in yoga, because there are eight different types of samadhi not just one. I have written an entire textbook on it, but here I only want to skim the subject. Samadhi, ideally, is a state of ecstatic, divine revelation, a state in which the nature of the cosmos is revealed

CHAPTER 2.

to us. It is possible to bring about this state through concerted effort and technical discipline, but this is largely accelerated by placing oneself into the service of the Divine. According to one school of thought within yoga (called Bhakti), all technical effort you undertake is nothing but getting better at placing yourself into the service of the Divine. Samadhi is ultimately something to be received rather than willed or created. Placing oneself into the service of the Divine, on the other hand, is nothing but the process of finding your life's divine purpose and following it. It means that your life becomes deeply meaningful, that you are living in the zone and that you are guided by the same cosmic intelligence that expresses itself through all life and all matter. It means that your life will be divinely guided.

In stanza III.33 we learn, "Or from vision, everything". This stanza is from the third chapter of the Yoga Sutra, and it is part of a long sequence of stanzas that state on what you have to meditate/concentrate, to get what type of knowledge or power. At the end of this sequence, Patanjali, the author of the Yoga Sutra, states that any form of knowledge not mentioned so far can be obtained through vision, a statement showing the importance of vision or intuition. The term pratibhad is often translated as intuition, but it also means vividness, coming from the verb root bha, to shine. It refers to something that shines forth in the mind, hence, vision is probably the best translation. The stanza suggests that all important knowledge can be received through a vision. In later chapters of this book, you will find the process outlined in detail.

The reason why we are all designed to attain knowledge through vision is because there is only one universal mind, the intelligence of the Divine. In that ocean of cosmic intelligence, each individual is only a centre of awareness. Our brain does not produce our mind but is actually a filter, a reduction-valve of cosmic intelligence. The less brain activity there is, the less filtering takes place. In deep meditation and during vision, we are shutting down brain activity as much as possible so that the barriers between individual and cosmic mind are de-activated. This is the process of divine vision or divine intuition, and we employ it to find our life's divine purpose.

THE BHAGAVAD GITA

Let's move on now and have a look at the Bhagavad Gita regarding sources for our life's divine purpose. The Gita needs little introduction as it probably is the most influential text on Indian spirituality. It contains elements of three different systems of philosophy, i.e., Samkhya, Yoga and Vedanta. As the core section of the Mahabharata epic, it contains metaphorical layers but also psychological, historical, mythical and mystical elements. The Gita is presented in form of a dialogue between the deity Krishna and the warrior prince Arjuna. On the metaphorical level, Krishna represents our higher self, the atman, whereas Arjuna presents our surface self, the jiva.

In stanza II.67 we read, "the mind following in the wake of the wandering senses, carries away his discrimination as the wind carries away a boat on the waters". Similar to the Yoga Sutra, we find here the idea that the mind needs to be cultivated and not left to its own conclusions. Sensory data tends to confuse the mind by pulling it towards the surface and away from our psyche's divine core, the consciousness. While empirical data needs to be considered to live one's life and to survive, it cannot tell us who we are and what our purpose in life is.

Stanza III. 27 of the Gita says, "All actions are wrought in all cases by the divine creative force. Only a fool believes to be the doer". Our modern society brings us up in the belief that we are the performing agent. But have a look closely at your heartbeat, your breath, your metabolism, your movements, your thoughts. All these actions are not performed by us but by the divine creative force (prakrti). The term *prakrti* is also translated as nature. Nature moves electrons around atomic nuclei, arranges DNA, holds atoms in molecular grids, lets organs function miraculously and holds planets, stars, galaxies and black holes on their trajectories. Shouldn't we put ourselves in the service of that cosmic power? But no, so the Gita. We prefer to make fools of ourselves believing that we are the doers and agents in this life.

In stanza III.30 Krishna states, "Renouncing all actions in Me, with the mind centred in the Self, free from hope, egoism and unclarity, do thou act". One of our greatest mental problems is that we are taking the credit and the blame in life. When things turn our way, we take it to be a sign of our greatness. When things turn against us, we interpret it as a sign of failure. Krishna here suggests doing neither but to offer all actions to the Divine. That means to act to the best of our abilities as a service to the Divine and all beings but not to be concerned about the outcome.

Although we all try to create certainty and safety in our lives, we have to understand that life is entirely unpredictable. Faulty actions may have a great outcome, and even the wisest may encounter failure. It is important not to make one's happiness dependent on the outcomes, which are entirely beyond our control. This is so because we live in a vast world in which many factors contribute to outcomes. Important is to know that our life has a divine purpose and to pursue it whether we appear to fail or to succeed. Truth be said, what appears like failure in the long term can look like a blessing. On the other hand, what initially looks like a great success years later turns out to be our greatest blunder. The key is to stick to the idea of service and to follow our life's divine purpose, which is to serve the Divine and all beings. Whichever way our life then turns, we have done the best we could by focussing on the process rather than the outcome. Whereas the outcomes of our actions and the many situations we are confronted with are beyond our control, what is within our scope is the standard to which we hold ourselves.

The most important stanza in the Gita in regards to our subject is III.35. Here we read, "One's own dharma, even if not glamorous, is more important than dharma not conducive to one's growth. Even dying when performing one's own dharma leads to good, whereas performing dharma foreign to one's maturation will lead to downfall". In this stanza, the concept of svadharma is explored, which is nothing but our life's divine purpose. Dharma means right action, to do the right thing, and there is a collective right action that all should follow. But there is also a course of right action for an individual which is different from that of the next person. The prefix sva means own and svadharma implies the particular duty or course of action appropriate for a particular individual. The stanza also implies that this particular course of action is so important that it is better to fail following it than to succeed in performing the duty of another.

Have you ever asked yourself whether you are living your own life or somebody else's? In the public sphere, certain professions are glorified and others never mentioned. Particularly living a meaningless life of consumption, gratification and sensory stimulus is often projected as the best outcome for one's life. For example, in the last 25 years, the tone of marketing emails in my spam box has changed from, "Why work your whole life when you can retire as an investment millionaire at 40" to "Why not retire as a stock market billionaire at 24". Very few occupations have been as glorified as that of an investor. But can an entire society sustain itself if the bandwidth of occupations is reduced to master chefs, rock stars and hedge fund billionaires, just because they are currently considered glamorous? The Gita quote states that it is your own path which you need to find and excel at. Because even if you do get good at performing another's duty and profession, the nagging question in the dark of night whether you do live somebody else's life will never cease.

The Gita also states that following one's own path leads to psychological growth. This is something we will explore further in the chapter on the results of following one's divine purpose. If you never step onto your own path, you will never reach your destiny but somebody else's. You will always miss out on your own life. Your growth, however, does not end by finding and accepting your own destiny. In truth, that's where it starts.

Finding your path is not a single incidence, but every time you choose to follow your own path, its future outlines become clearer to you. The details of your growth will not become clear until you start walking your path. You cannot grow, develop your own divine potential, your own nature gift, unless you live your own dharma. Only following your own dharma, your life's divine purpose, will lead to psychological and spiritual growth in alignment with your dharma.

The Gita even goes as far as saying death while following one's path is preferred to success on somebody else's path because that will lead to downfall eventually. Relatives often find solace by eulogizing a deceased loved-one as having "died while following their dream" or "died while doing what they loved", even if the activity during which they died may sound absurd to us. What would you prefer, dying doing something you loved or dying doing something you hated? But the Gita, of course, goes much further. It states that the purpose of one's life is not survival but to grow while doing what we have to do, doing what our divine purpose is.

In stanza IV.18, we find, "He who sees inaction in action and action in inaction, he is wise among men; he is a Yogi and performer of all actions". Inaction in action means to realize that it is not us but cosmic intelligence and cosmic consciousness that move us and embody through us. If we step aside and leave our own personal ideas and let the Divine express Itself through us, we can do incredible things, although seemingly being inactive. Because we let a force greater than us do Its works through us. It is the "Father in me and not me that doeth the works" as Jesus said. "Action in inaction" here means that when we let the Divine act through us, we are still active, even at times when we seemingly do nothing. Because when walking on the part of the Divine, cosmic intelligence is still aligning things for us even at times when we are not moving. And that is because it is moving everything in this cosmos. "He is a Yogi and performer of all actions" means that we are capable of much more if we are making ourselves available for the Divine and living our divine purpose. It is then that we can act for the benefit of all and not just for the satisfaction of our personal egotism.

In stanza V.30 Krishna says, "He who sees Me in all beings and all beings in Me, he does not become separated from Me nor do I become separated from him". In the core of all beings is the atman, the pure consciousness. The pure consciousness is the God transcendent as Krishna confirms (Gita X:20), "I am the self in the heart of all beings". But at the same time, the world of phenomena, the space/time with all its universes, galaxies, all matter and physical beings is contained within consciousness. That's why Krishna here adds, "and all beings in me". Suggested here is a fractal-like organisation with the Divine as the consciousness that contains all beings. Yet within the heart of all beings is again the Divine, within which is, again, the whole world with all lifeforms and so forth. He who is capable of maintaining this view is permanently in a reciprocal relationship with the Divine, and that is the view that we want to have when following our life's divine purpose. The Divine is inside of us, yet we are inside of the Divine.

In stanza XVII:3 of the Gita, we then find the following phrase, "whatever a person believes about themselves that verily they become", a phrase that is also found in the Bible (Book of Proverbs 23:7). Here is a powerful warning for us. If we do believe about ourselves that we are a purposeless accident and that we are here to maximize economic self-interest, then that's what we will become and, in fact, that's what we have become.

This stanza explains that one needs to take responsibility for one's beliefs. Belief systems should not be chosen through some form of petty attachment, but we need to take their results into consideration. For many centuries, we believed that life has no meaning and that we are here to make the Earth our dominion and exploit, coerce, dominate, loot, ransack, rape and pillage our sacred Mother Earth. After many centuries spent in such pursuit, we are now being presented with the bill, i.e., the mass extermination of life quite possibly including our own. We should reject the materialistic-reductionist philosophy alone based on what it has turned us into, a genocider of all life.

THE BIBLE

The Bible is definitely one of the most important texts regarding our life's divine purpose. When wanting to understand what the Bible has to teach us about finding one's life's divine purpose, we must first do away with remnants of belief in the literal understanding of the text. So said, for example, the 1st century church father Origen, "When there is a story about God planting two trees in the garden of Eden, then we must not think of God as a human gardener rolling up the sleeves and reaching for the shovel. No, it's meant metaphorically". The metaphorical reading of the Bible was en vogue until the times of the theologian St. Jerome (3rd century). Unfortunately, in the wake of St. Augustine, the literal interpretation garnered more and more followers. More and more, the Father was imagined as a giant bearded male hovering above the clouds, who loves you as long as you accept his sole authority but gets cranky if you don't. Just like a human father in real life.

Of course, this is a view that cannot be held by a rationally thinking person, and it is this literal interpretation that got religion into the cross hairs of science. The air-born, giant, irate, bearded male is an extrapolation and projection of our own limited human psychology and a longing for the super-daddy that we never had. It is also not a pure Christian concept. If you look at Michelangelo's depiction of the Father in the Sistine Chapel and compare it with artwork depicting Zeus, and later, Jupiter, you realize where the image really comes from.

CHAPTER 2.

Ironically, this imagery is actually pagan, whatever connotations one may have with that word.

Having established the importance of understanding the Bible metaphorically, let's first look as Jesus's parable of the prodigal son (Luke 15:11–32). The parable is about a father who has two sons, and the younger of them asks his father to give him his inheritance in advance. The father agrees and divides his property between both sons. Upon receiving his inheritance, the younger son travels to a faraway country and squanders his inheritance through extravagant living. After that, he becomes so destitute that he has to work as a swineherd, eventually realizing that even the swine are better fed than he.

He finally understands that he has to return home and ask his father for forgiveness, hoping that the father will give him some lowly occupation. To his great surprise, the father comes running when he sees him from afar, greets him exuberantly and reinstates him in a place of honour.

Upon hearing this, the elder son is not happy. He berates the father, arguing that the younger son needs to be rejected or punished for his poor choices. But the Father says, "You are ever with me and all I have is yours".

Interpretation: The Father in Jesus's language is representative of the God transcendent, pure consciousness. The Father is what, in other traditions, is called nirguna Brahman, Shiva, the Dao, the formless absolute. The inheritance the Father has given us all is the purusha (term used in the Yoga Sutra for individual consciousness), the atman (term used in the Upanishads for the self, i.e., the consciousness), the part of ourselves that is eternally one with God.

The son wanders out into the world, wrongfully believing that he can squander his inheritance, his consciousness. He seems to lose his identity by identifying with the sense objects, leading a life of largesse and hedonism. He eventually falls into the trap and starts to believe in his separation from the God transcendent (Father). Ultimately, he falls so low that he is beginning to herd swine for a living. The swine are a metaphor for being stuck in the mire of materialistic stupor. After the son has reached the apogee of separation from the Father, he finally returns home, hoping to be hired as a lowly servant. To his surprise, the Father makes no mention of the period of separation but immediately reinstalls him as his beloved son.

This is a really important point to understand. For the Father/God transcendent/infinite consciousness, no separation has ever taken place. The Father can only ever see his (infinite consciousness) union with the son (personal consciousness). This is so because, in consciousness, there is no separation, since consciousness is eternal, infinite, formless and quality-less. The son only *believed* to be separated from the Father through his sensualist life, but the truth is the union of infinite consciousness (Brahman) and individual consciousness (atman), the so-called inheritance, is divinely willed. Therefore, it is not within the scope of the son to squander his inheritance.

This is really important to mull over. We all, in some way, deep down, yearn to return into the embrace of the Divine, but for manifold reasons, we believe that we can't. At the core of this denial is usually a deep-seated feeling of unworthiness, of not being good enough, having made too many mistakes, etc. All of these reasons are swept away by the fact that, in the original covenant, the Divine has created us in Its image and likeness. That means that the consciousness, the deep self within us, is permanently one with the Divine, whether we are aware of this or not. This fact is so willed by the Divine, and because the will of the Divine is infinite and ours is limited, the undoing of our union with the Divine is not within the scope of our exertion. We actually cannot separate ourselves from the Divine, whether we are trying or not.

Furthermore, the Divine can only see us in the original perfection in which It has created us. And that is so because the Divine cannot see anything contrary to Its own nature. Therefore, the Divine cannot see what we believe to be our shortcomings. From the viewpoint of the Divine, these shortcomings exist only in our minds and have no underlying reality.

When the son returns, the Father acts as if nothing has happened. This is of great significance. The God transcendent can see only what is in alignment with Its own nature and what is real. The God transcendent has created us in Its own image. Therefore, our permanent union with the Divine is real and can be seen by the God transcendent. We have created a separate surface-self, based on our own ideas, but from the viewpoint of the God transcendent, this separate surface-self has no reality because it is not in alignment with divine nature.

Because this so-called separation from the Divine is created only by us (who have no effective power outside of our union with the Divine), to the Father, no separation has happened. In Jesus's parable, the father remained one with the prodigal son although the son had to go through all sort of travails. Please think this through because we, today, are all in exactly this situation.

The elder son, being human, is less generous. He argues with the father that the younger son should be judged for his shortcomings, and he points out to the Father that he, the elder son, was never afforded an exuberant welcome-home feast. The elder son, like the younger one, also identifies with the separate surface self, whereas the father represents the supreme self (In this regard, the roles are the same as those Arjuna and Krishna in the Gita). However, by saying "You are ever with me and all I have is yours" the Father reminds the elder son that both the father and the son are consciousness. You are ever with me – in consciousness there is no separation. With the statement, "All I have is yours" the God transcendent affirms that It does *not have an ego from which to withhold* an inheritance, love, grace, mercy, forgiveness or whatever may be required at a particular time.

These realizations are foundational for the context of this book. Because we have undergone a millennia-long process of enculturation, we have brainwashed ourselves into the belief that we are:

   a. Separate from the Divine
   b. Unworthy of mercy, love, forgiveness, etc.
   c. Incapable of receiving instruction from the Divine

It is these realizations that need to be deeply contemplated. We are not separate from the Divine, and the Divine has no ego to withhold love, grace and instruction from us. We have all made mistakes in life, and unfortunately, religious teachings portray the Divine like the elder son in Jesus's parable. Our oneness with the Divine is divinely willed, and no amount of wrong actions performed by us can cancel this original covenant. Love, forgiveness and personal instructions for all of us are eternally pouring forth from the Divine, but it is our ego, not the ego of the Divine (which cannot have one because the Divine is infinite and eternal and ego means limiter in time and space), which gets in the way. So, the process of receiving visions and instructions from the Divine is an inner, psychological process in which we allow ourselves to receive, nothing else. The instructions are pouring forth at all times, but it is we who are currently not listening.

Let us look now into further quotes from the Bible. Psalm 82:6 states, "I say, 'Ye are gods; ye are all children of the Most High." Jesus actually quotes this very stanza in John10:34-36. In John 10:30, Jesus states, "I and the Father are one". For any yogi or mystic this is a very innocent statement, albeit one that can be unhealthy to utter in the marketplace. When Jesus said "I" he did not speak from his mortal frame, his body. He did not say the human body belonging to the man Jesus is God. Instead, he spoke from his eternal self, the atman, the consciousness. The Father in the Bible is what the Upanishads call the Brahman, the infinite consciousness. So, if Jesus says, "The consciousness in me is one with the universal consciousness", he makes a statement that appears in the Upanishads on every second page. His contemporaries, however, understand him to have referred to his mortal frame and personage, and take up stones to kill him for blasphemy. Jesus now defends himself, "I say, 'You are gods; you are all children of the Most High' [Jesus is here quoting the Old Testament verbatim]. If he called them gods to whom the word of God came—and Scripture cannot be broken—why do you call it blasphemy when I say, 'I am the Son of God'? After all, the Father set me apart and sent me into the world."

There is a very powerful message here, so let's analyse it step-by-step. Firstly, Jesus quotes the Old Testament, where it is stated that all beings come directly from the Most High (God transcendent). Because the God transcendent cannot be divided, all beings contain the transcendent in Its entirety and, therefore, are divine, too. Then Jesus continues, "If he called them gods to whom the word of God came." This is exactly the subject this book deals with. "to whom the word of God came", is a somewhat arcane wording for somebody having a divine vision about how the Divine wants to embody through them. But as we know already from our chapter on indigenous cultures, this was something that everybody was entitled to. Not only entitled to, but it is something that is essential for each individual's mental health. It is also essential for the healthy functioning of a society that its individuals are divinely inspired.

There was a time on this planet when all human beings were expected to have a personal relationship with the Great Mystery/Great Spirit. Only through a long history of middlemen (shamans, druids, priests, gurus, brahmins, etc.) did we become more and more disconnected from what used to be the essential factor determining our mental health.

There is nothing more natural than 'the word of the Divine coming to you'. However, we have been disempowered and disconnected from this wellspring of inspiration through the monopoly of a priestly elite so that it now seems normal to us. It may be normal but certainly not natural. Natural is to live a life of divine love and service stemming from divine inspiration and divine vision.

Jesus goes on to say, "Why do you call it blasphemy when I say, 'I am the Son of God'? After all, the Father set me apart and sent me into the world." Setting apart simply means, making into an individual. Technically, that means connecting consciousness to a piece of software called ego so that the consciousness is limited in space and time and identifies itself with a particular body and mind. In that state, you are 'set apart' from the rest of the world by what you believe to be included in you and what seems excluded. Again, when Jesus says 'I am the Son of God', he does not wish to express 'only me and not you". This would be actual blasphemy because it would be implying that the Father/Brahman/God transcendent has an ego from which to withhold sonship to the rest of us. Remember, "Ye all are gods ye all are children of the most high".

"After all, the Father set me apart and sent me into the world." This is the process that I described at the outset, of the God transcendent becoming itself as an infinite number of paths, permutations through which it computes its infinite potential. Because the cosmic (Father) cannot itself become an individual (because that requires ego and identification with a particular body in space-time), the Father must do so through us, i.e., "set us apart and send us into the world". This is a magnificent teaching that Jesus relates here, but unfortunately, it was considered so potent and revolutionary that it probably would have upended most of the world's authorities had it been allowed to run loose. It was defused and emasculated by turning it into a religion. Instead of following Jesus's great example and following his admittedly sometimes very demanding instructions, we were asked to simply believe that he is the only begotten son of God. Only, this very belief is totally contrary to what he actually taught.

In Matthew 6:33, we find, "But seek ye first the kingdom of God, and his righteousness; and all these things shall be added unto you". All these things shall be added means that modern society saddles the horse from the wrong end. We worry first about all these things, i.e., success, career, education, fame, wealth, power, etc., and if there is a bit of time left, we might consider ethics, mental health and spirituality. But Jesus implores us to do it the other way around. First make contact with the Divine, have a vision and divine inspiration and become clear what you are here for, "his righteousness", which the Gita calls *svadharma*. That means to make one's life an act of glorification of the Divine, and the way to do so is to follow the instructions one receives through vision and inspiration.

So far, so good, but where is that kingdom he's talking about? This is what the Pharisees were wondering, too, and when they questioned him, Jesus said, "The kingdom of God is not coming with a visible display. Neither shall they say, lo here! or, lo there! for, behold, the kingdom of God is within you" (Luke 17:20-21). It is already within us, so we just have to shut up our minds and open our hearts and ears and listen. That's all there is to it.

Admittedly, after 10,000 or more years of enculturation and brainwashing, listening with one's heart is not that straightforward, but we need to understand that the Kingdom of God is within us and has never left. The same has been said in the Chandogya Upanishad, "In the centre of the chest is a small triangular shrine and within burns an eternal flame (the consciousness), and within that space miraculously is this entire vast universe with all its planets, oceans, continents, mountain ranges and beings". Again, this saying is reverberated in the Gita where Krishna says, "Who sees me in all beings and all beings in me".

The next passage in Jesus's reply is, "is not coming with a visible display. Neither shall they say, lo here! or, lo there". This means the Kingdom is not found within the outer world, but it is an inner space. We could call it the innermost, i.e., the space within our hearts where we are one with the Divine. Psalm 91:1 says about this place, "Whoever dwells in the shelter of the Most High will rest in the shadow of the Almighty." This means that as long as our life is aligned with a vision of our highest

CHAPTER 2.

potential, we will be safe, we will be taken care of, as we are resting in the shadow of the Almighty (the God transcendent, the infinite consciousness, the Great Spirit).

So, the question now becomes, how to we access this place? About that we learn in Matthew 6:6, "But when you pray, go into your room, close the door and pray to your Father, who is unseen. Then your Father, who sees what is done in secret, will reward you." Of course, we need to have some form of privacy when accessing the Divine, as little distraction as possible. But "going into our room and closing the door" is not just meant spatially. It also has a psychological meaning as in going inside and shutting the sensory gates as much as possible, i.e., closing the eyes, etc. "Pray to your Father, who is unseen", means that we need to address the Divine, i.e., ask for a vision and not look for the answer on the outside but inside, such as an inner voice, an inner feeling.

And we can be sure that we will be answered, for in John 16:23 we find, "Whatever you ask the Father in my name he will give you. Ask and you will receive". To reiterate "asking the Father in my name" does not mean to ask a giant, Zeus-like, bearded male on behalf of a Jewish gentleman who died for our sins 2000 years ago and was the only human recognized as his descendent by said giant, bearded male. When Jesus uses the term son of god, he is referring to his divine self (atman, purusha) whereas when he uses the term son of man, he is referring to the body and the phenomenal self (the self that is bound-up with the phenomena, the lower self). So "asking the Father in my name" means to ask the God transcendent on behalf of one's higher self, the atman/consciousness, which is the son of God.

Now, "Ask and ye shall receive", does not refer to one's material needs and comfort, but it does refer to our life's divine purpose, i.e., what the Divine wants to embody as us. For once we know what it is and start to implement it, "then everything else will be added on" because "we are resting in the shadow of the Almighty".

Summarizing, the above statement explains that for us to receive a vision, inspiration and instruction how the Divine wants to embody as us, we only need to ask. And the asking is only for our sake. Because the Divine does not have an ego from which to withhold instruction, the teaching is actually constantly pouring forth. It is only we who, by asking, are moving ourselves into a position where we can hear what is being said.

The next thing we need to look at is our investment and belief into our unworthiness and into being incapable of fulfilling a higher purpose. "Who, me?" we might say. "Who am I to live a life of Divine purpose? And what can I achieve anyway, I am nothing". To that we find in John 14:12, "Very truly I tell you, whoever believes in me will do the works I have been doing, and they will do even greater things than these, because I am going to the Father." Jesus often made statements uttered in great exultation. When he said "believes in me" he did not mean believe in the human man Jesus, but he was in a transfigured, transformative state in which he had realized himself as the infinite consciousness. He says if you realize that you are infinite consciousness you will become infinite and can do greater things than I. It is important to understand that he is teaching a repeatable method that can be learned. He wants us to follow his example rather than just believe that he was the only begotten son of God. The last statement, "because I am

CHAPTER 2.

going to the Father" is a call for urgency. Jesus realizes that his presence here is to express a path or potential, a computation of the Divine. Once this is done, his and our jobs here are completed, and we become one with infinite consciousness, we are "going to the Father". Hence, Jesus means that we need to realize ourselves as consciousness so that we can embody the Divine and do greater things than he has done, because he won't be around.

The clearest proof that Jesus was teaching a repeatable method that we were meant to emulate is in the parable of the fig tree (Mark 11:12- 24). On the way back from Bethany, Jesus is hungry. He approaches a fig tree but finds it empty of figs and says "May no one ever eat fruit from you again" as the disciples are listening. Jesus curses the tree because the tree refuses to give him fruit. After that, they go to Jerusalem where Jesus drives out the salespeople and money changers from the temple of David. Again, the high priests are plotting to kill Jesus, and he leaves together with the disciples. As they again pass by the fig tree, the disciples notice that it is dead. Simon Peter says, "Look, Rabbi! The fig tree is dead". Meaning, he is asking, "How did you do it?" To this, the Nazarene says, "Truly I say to you, whoever says to this mountain, 'Be taken up and cast into the sea,' and does not doubt in his heart, but believes that what he says is going to happen, it will be *granted* him." Jesus clearly says that the powers he is displaying are not because he is different from us but because he has received a divine mission, and he is following it. Because he has received his mission in the form of a vision and divine realization and not through simply choosing something that his mind fancies, he completely believes what he is saying and has complete trust in it. His mind is congruent. He knows that he is not doing his own bidding, but he is making himself empty so that the Divine can work through him like through a conduit. *It is not me doing the works but the Father in me is doing the works* (John 14:10, also 5:19, 8:28).

Exactly this same teaching is also given in the Yoga Sutra (II.36), i.e., that the mind is transformed until it has reached total congruence. At this point, the mind becomes a tool for realizing a new reality, which is then projected outwards where it will manifest. This is not something to toy with. The method is not to be used for any self-aggrandisement, for procuring riches, or for making one's life more comfortable. But it is to be used for living a life of Divine purpose, for placing ourselves into the service of all life and a power greater than us.

In the next stanza (Mark 11:24), Jesus gets more precise, "Therefore I say to you, all things for which you pray and ask, believe that you have received them, and they will be *granted* you." The meaning here is this: do not want a divine vision, do not want a divine purpose and do not wish for having it. Instead, believe that you already have it. This means the vision cannot be an idea of the future. There cannot be a future when asking for a future. There can only be the present moment. In the moment when you bring your entire mind in alignment and into the present moment, the vision is there. The mind must totally accept the vision as being given there and then (which it truly already is, but our mind is a great postponer and always finds reasons why it is not yet ready, but later…).

Only if the superconscious mind (the part that bestows the vision), conscious mind (the one who receives the vision), and subconscious mind (the one who holds the beliefs about who we are) are in complete alignment in present time, can we receive the vision. As in many other places of the Gospels, Jesus here displays a profound psychological understanding.

And just to make it absolutely clear, "As far as possibilities go, everything is possible for the person who believes." (Mark 9:23). Again, Jesus is here talking about the subconscious mind (this term will be defined in great detail later on). We don't want to resort to believing in situations when knowledge can be obtained. But the subconscious mind does not deal with knowledge but with our beliefs, values and belief systems and how they have been shaped by our past. As long as we doubt, as long as the concentration of our mind is fractured or dispersed, our results will be mixed. Success in our mission will come when the subconscious mind is brought into complete alignment. It needs to be in alignment with our mission and vision received through our superconscious mind.

DIVINE PURPOSE IN THE YOGA VASISHTA

The Yoga Vasishta is a complex and lengthy Indian text having the form of a dialogue of the sage Vasishta and his juvenile student Lord Rama. During the dialogue, Vasishta states that there is no destiny for one of true self-effort. People often display a great desire to find out what their destiny is, and the title and subject of this book could be misconstrued to believe that your destiny was already set, and the only thing you can do is to find out what it is. This needs to be clarified.

Our life can often feel as if there is a fate that we cannot overcome and whatever we do drags us only ever closer back into the same ruts. That it seems to be that way is because our mind is subject to conditioning. Every time we experience anything, a subconscious imprint is laid down in our subconscious. The older we get, the more there is a tendency to refer back to the past and expect the future to be the same. That's why old people tend to say that nothing can surprise them anymore. Because you have been imprinted and conditioned by your past in a certain way, you tend to mentally and emotionally react in the same way when a similar situation again comes around. When this happens often enough, we may think that this is our destiny, and we may say to others, "Well, that's just how I am. Too late to change that now".

However, in the context of this book, this tendency is something that we want to increasingly become free from. When Vasishta says there is no destiny for one of true self-effort, he means that any shackles of the past can be thrown away as long as you really want to and are ready to take the appropriate steps. Destiny or fate in this context is something we want to break free from. But the important question here is where to? There is no point in breaking out from our past if we don't know where to go from there.

It is this moment when visioning comes into the equation. We need to connect to our superconscious mind to receive a vision regarding our highest potential. This is completely different than making up in our mind willy-nilly a future that tickles our fancy. Because chances are that this mind-born idea of our future is ego-based, usually involving what we have instead of who we are.

Starting a new direction by defining what we are wanting to receive instead of getting clear about what we want to give implies ego-involvement. Additionally, the ego will base visions of the future on comparison and competitiveness. It will, for example, imagine ourselves to be great and powerful in the future. Great in comparison to whom? Full of power over who and what? If we follow such impulses instead of going into the future, we may simply repeat the past.

DIVINE PURPOSE IN MODERN PSYCHOLOGY

The psychologist Carl Jung stated that in his whole life of clinical practice he had never seen a return from neurosis without restoring a person's spirituality. He understood that humans are meaning-making and sense-making creatures. Right from the dawn of our existence, we humans were trying to make sense of the cosmos. We are creating the worst condition for mental health if we say to people that life is a purposeless accident. That itself leads to depression in some and a flight into addictive and destructive behaviour in others. Because when you take meaning away from people, often the only way out is empty hedonism and sensory stimulus.

On the other hand, the most healing experience possible to us is one of expanded self. When life started from basic levels, lifeforms regarded only what was beneath their skin as self. This is very obvious in single-cell organisms and all the way up to reptiles. However, already with mammals, the sense-of-self expands. Here, territory and family come into play. Mammals may defend their young, their partner and their territory even if it costs their own life. Beginning with apes and going on to humans, we find a much-increased sense-of-self that will include a whole tribe, including individuals to which we are not related and increasingly material and intellectual property. Humans are often happy to die to defend ideas they hold precious. This is because these ideas have become part of their sense-of-self, their identity.

As our spiritual growth increases (with the activating of the heart chakra) our sense-of-self expands to first take in the entire human community around us, later (with the opening of the throat chakra) the non-human community of life and natural formations such as forests, lakes, rivers, mountains and ocean. Eventually (with the activation of the third-eye chakra), our sense-of-self increases further to embrace cosmic intelligence, which has crystalized as the entire animate and inanimate universe. Our sense-of-self finally reaches its full extent (with opening of the crown chakra) with the inclusion of infinite consciousness in which space-time is contained.

More interesting research was published by psychiatrist Victor Frankl in his book *Man's Search for Meaning*. Frankl, an Austrian of Jewish ancestry, was rounded up by the Nazis when they took over Vienna and was first interned in the concentration camp Theresienstadt and later in the death camp Auschwitz. While at Auschwitz, he started to chronicle what made inmates capable of continuing to function (and later to meaningfully reintegrate themselves into society), when faced with daily abuse, torture, dehumanization and threat of annihilation. He noticed quickly that it was not the seemingly toughest prisoners that survived but it was the ability to continue to find meaning in one's life that increased the chances for survival.

Inmates sometimes found meaning in their religion, in joining the resistance or in reframing their experiences so that they would be able to express and experience love for their loved ones more clearly once their ordeal would be over (this was the case for Frankl himself). In all of these cases, we find a purpose or meaning that is outside of the individual, a greater context, a greater good, or of serving individuals other than oneself. Again, in all of these instances, we find an expanded sense-of-self and the need to devote oneself to something greater than one's own pleasure or sensory apparatus. Frankl found that inmates who

CHAPTER 2.

could not make this step usually quickly fell into despair and found no more reason to pursue their survival because their life had become meaningless.

An important reminder that Frankl gives us is that life is entirely uncertain, and while we do believe that we have control over our life, any moment things may happen that shatter this illusion. The best way to be able to function in adverse situations is to have an understanding of who we are on the deepest level without having to resort to defining ourselves through external factors such as property, success and reputation. We need to know that deep down there is a very particular divine purpose for each of us, albeit one that is not dead-set but evolves before our eyes as we are pursuing it. We must, therefore, engage in a soul-searching or spirit-searching discipline to find out what that purpose is, and the closer we get to it, the more robust our psyche will become, and the easier we can deflect cross balls that life will surely hurl at us.

If we manage to get into more or less complete alignment with our divine purpose, we will experience a loss of internal dialogue, i.e., we will perceive inner silence. The nagging voices that ask whether we do, in fact, live somebody else's life will cease. Because we don't. When we do find our life's divine purpose, we live in a trancelike state called 'being in the zone' in which there is complete congruence amongst the various layers of our psyche, and all its components start pulling into the same direction.

The humanistic psychologist Abraham Maslow in his work focussed on increasing the potential of the healthy human psyche or what he called self-actualization. Maslow gained many of his great insights through mystical states. He said that in order to be ultimately at peace with themselves, a musician must make music, an artist must paint, and a poet must write. We can see from this statement that Maslow believed in a definite mission for each individual, what the Bhagavad Gita calls the *svadharma*. Maslow also understood that without following ones *svadharma*, inner peace is impossible. We may be successful as accountants, hedge fund managers or master chefs, but if our calling is to be a gardener, there will always be this nagging voice that we are living somebody else's life. This voice will never leave us in peace. We often see celebrities who seem to live an enviable life only for it to suddenly come undone. They may live a seemingly great life, but it is not their own. Unless we are living in alignment with our own divine purpose, inner peace is not possible.

Maslow confirmed this when saying that if you plan on being anything less than you are capable of being, you will probably be unhappy for the rest of your life. The reason why this is the case is because your inner voice, the voice of your heart, will constantly remind you that you are living somebody else's life. It may be a great life, esteemed by many, but that is not the point. The point is that there is within you a divine essence, a pathway through which the Divine wants to express Itself as you. You can try to avoid it, to not listen to it. In fact, many people do. But because that voice continues to talk, people will eventually try to drown it out with alcohol, drugs, and/or addiction to sex, power, fame, wealth or any form of sensory stimulus. But, ultimately, there is no escape because, as Maslow said, what a person can be, they must be. Again, here is the understanding that there is a particular potential to which we are called. And once you are called to it, there is no escaping.

Now, you may wonder why is this not more widely taught? Why is this not part of the school curriculum? The reason is because our education system is merely a conveyor belt for industrial wage slavery. Industry and multinational corporations may need in a particular decade so and so many accountants, engineers, mechanics or lawyers. The education system is then tweaked to provide them. The higher calling of a particular individual plays no role here. The focus of the education system is to funnel worker bees into the GDP-increasing world economy, which is designed to make the already obscenely wealthy even more rich. The spiritual desires of an individual worker bee to self-actualize is only in the way.

This is not to say though that it cannot be your life's divine purpose to be an accountant, engineer, mechanic or lawyer. In fact, we can with certainty say that there will be people who have exactly this as their life's divine purpose. There is nothing wrong with these professions, per se, but as with any profession, you need to feel a higher calling for it to fulfil you. However, many standardized professions get spruiked because they are feeding nicely into the needs of the globalized industrial GDP-increasing machine and not because they are the appropriate thing for you to do. People are often talked into learning these standardized professions by instilling fear in them that they would otherwise end up a failure.

Maslow, to the contrary, believed that one's only failure was failing to live up to one's own possibilities. But he did not mean here the race for career and accumulation of wealth. He said that we need to accept the reality of higher human needs, including the impulse to self-actualization and the love of one's highest values. Self-actualization for Maslow was self-fulfilment based on what your highest potential is. Notice the terms highest values and highest potential. Maslow's use of the term self-actualization is very similar to the term life's divine purpose as it is used in this book. Your life's divine purpose is not necessarily what gives you the most financial payback (although it could well be, but that's not the focus). It is also not what gives you the greatest fame or social status (and again, it could be). But the focus is on the fact that you have been given a particular potential, and it is only you who can find out what that is. If you develop that and live in alignment with it, you will attain inner peace and an absence of internal dialogue. The voice that tells you are falling short and are living somebody else's life will then become silent. Finding your life's divine purpose is about expressing your core nature. It is about finding your life's true goals and not what the society and economy around you are trying to dictate to you.

For Maslow, self-fulfilment meant to become actualized in what your highest potential is. Highest potential, in this context, means to become truly what you are and to become everything that you are capable of becoming. That does not mean that there is unconscious ambition to be somebody but rather a desire to develop your highest potential. Maslow believed that the realization of your potential was not something related to your environment but part of your true self. This is a surprising statement for a modern psychologist, but it is in alignment with what the Taittirya Upanishads states in the teaching of the five layers. The second deepest layer, the Vijnanamaya kosha, is indeed part of the true self, and it is where your divine purpose is encrypted. More on that in chapter 4.

CHAPTER 2.

Importantly, as Maslow pointed out, self-actualized people are growth-motivated. That is, they know that they do have an of yet undeveloped potential and want to discover and develop it. The motivation is not extrinsic, that is outward directed towards money, fame, power, but intrinsic, i.e., one knows that there is internal potential that is still untapped, one is curious what that is and endeavours to express oneself fully.

According to Maslow, a self-actualized person is somebody who is fulfilled and is doing everything they are capable of. He stated, "The specific form that these needs will take will of course vary greatly from person to person. In one individual it may take the form of the desire to be an ideal mother, in another it may be expressed athletically, and in still another it may be expressed in painting pictures or in inventions". Significantly, the people that Maslow identified as self-actualizers reported what he called *peak experiences* (which are here called mystical experiences). Peak experiences involved feelings of ecstasy, harmony, strength, goodness, beauty, luminosity, clarity, deep meaning and feeling at one with the universe. It is clear that Maslow found these were not simply successful people but that they experienced a deep feeling of spiritual oneness and divine meaning and purpose.

Summary: From indigenous traditions via the classical religions to modern psychology, we find that there is one underlying truth in regards to the sacredness and meaning of our life. All sacred scriptures describe the Divine or the infinite in different ways, but it is apparent that the seers and prophets experienced the same and then went on to describe it in their own language and cultural metaphors, which differed. What counts is to get in contact with the Divine and to be inspired by It to take on one's higher calling. This higher calling usually involves being of service to others and to make a valid contribution to their life, often even to all life. This way, you become an agent of spiritual evolution, peace and harmony on this planet.

Chapter 3
PRACTICE OF FINDING ONE'S LIFE'S DIVINE PURPOSE

In this chapter is outlined the actual technique by which to find your life's divine purpose. I would like you to simply get started. After you have practised the method, the following chapters, such as the one on the psychology of finding your life's divine purpose, will make much more sense as if approaching them only from a theoretical perspective.

Place: Firstly, you will need to find a quiet place where you can sit down so that nobody disturbs you. For me, personally, outdoors works best. When I lived in suburbia, I would sit early in the morning in our garden. Now, living out in nature, I can just walk out of our house, and there I am. I do believe that the message of our divine purpose is broadcast by an intelligence that could most aptly and simply be called *nature*. For that reason, it is most readily available in nature, and that's what indigenous people taught, too. According to them, the person seeking a vision would go out into nature alone by themselves. However, there are many classical religions whose practitioners have obtained visions, and the emphasis was not necessarily placed on being in nature but instead achieving closeness with the Divine.

The best way of looking at it is that being in nature is a help. However, we still want to be able to do the practice when a nature-setting is not available. The practice is too important to neglect it, especially when living in a city. A compromise could be that sometimes you can go out into nature for a few days and then focus on vision-practice and after that to use your time in the city to work out the finer details of your vision.

If you live in the city, it may not be feasible to go out early in the morning, especially not if you live in an area deemed unsafe. In this case, find a room where you can close a door so that you are not disturbed. If such a room is not available, then you may have to get up before everybody else does. If you feel closed-off in your vision practice, try different places. Locations seem to have a spiritual power of their own. In some, it is very easy to obtain a vision, while in others, more effort is required. Many spiritual traditions of humanity accept the idea of sacred sites, and in my own practice, I did find that locations do have a spirit of their own.

Time: The ideal time is early in the morning. In India, the time before sunrise is called brahmi muhurta, the divine time. Traditional Indians believe that during that time we are closer to God. Certainly, early in the morning, the mind is quietest, and the longer the day goes on, the busier the mind becomes. If early morning is not possible for you, try other times, but during the day, the mind tends to be the most agitated (rajasic) and in the evening heavy and dull (tamasic). It is in the early morning that the mind is inclined to the sacred (sattvic).

The easiest way to fall into a meditative trance is to be out in nature before sunrise and to then perform your vision-practice as or even before the sun rises. In the Vedas, there are hymns to the dawn, but from the descriptions of the seers, we understand that they were not just talking about a nice sunrise but that the dawning of the light in the world was accompanied by the dawning of inner light. Most potent this practice will be if you actually start it right before the crack of dawn, that is, during the last remaining starlight. This is easy in the tropics and in moderate latitudes in winter, but too early during summer for regular practice.

Sensory deprivation: Once you have decided on time and place for your vision practice, the next step is sensory deprivation; that is, close your eyes if there are distracting things around you. If you are out in nature, you can keep your eyes open. I suggest that you put your handheld device on flight mode and, of course, have no distracting music, radio or television on.

Stating your intent: We begin the formal practice by addressing the Divine with our intent that we want to be of service and want to be a conduit, a canal for the embodiment of divine intention. Ideally, you do that in your own words using your own terminology. However, to get started, you can use the words suggested below. If you have a divine image, you can visualize it as you make your statement. Or, if you do have a sacred object or holy book, you can place it in front of you. If you have an altar at home, you can do the practice in front of the altar. If you practice an established religion, simply use all of its symbols and integrate them into this practice.

If you do not have a religion and especially if you are a very critical, possibly atheistic person, then don't try to override this by superimposing anthropomorphic imagery onto your atheistic believes. That won't work. Atheists often have a supressed fear that they should give religion a final crack. That's not what we are doing here. If you are a critical person that does not want to believe, then don't. There's nothing wrong with you, and I'm not trying to convert you. Try instead to get used to the fact that you are directly addressing cosmic intelligence and infinite consciousness, rather than a deity. Ultimately, that's what you are doing even if you are practising a religion. It was the Chinese sage Lao-tzu, who said in the Tao Te king, "The Dao that can be described and put in words is not the real Dao".

After you have stated to cosmic intelligence and infinite consciousness that you want to be of service and want to become a conduit that it can manifest itself through, take a moment and feel your sincerity and resolve, backing this statement up. Try to feel a deep feeling of love and appreciation for cosmic intelligence and infinite consciousness. Then comes asking.

Asking: Once you do feel your own sincerity, formulate a question along the following lines:
- How can I serve You?
- As what and as who can I serve You?
- As what do You (the Divine) want to embody as me?
- How do You want to become Yourself through me?
- Who do I need to be and who do I need to become to serve?
- How do You want to embody Yourself through me?

Repeat these questions until it is clear in your mind what you are asking for. You can replace the above questions with phrases from your own language and vocabulary that seem more appropriate.

CHAPTER 3

Listening: The next step now is to listen for the answer. And when I say listening, I mean that metaphorically. It is not that the answer will shout from heaven in the allegorical thundering voice. I mean listening with your heart. It is only through our ability to listen from the bottom of our hearts that we can hear the messages of the Divine. Practicing listening to the Divine is the key. The message is, at first, faint, since the voices of the ego and the subconscious will be louder. But with practice, we hear the voice clearer and clearer.

What to do when I can't hear anything? A big part of the remainder of this book deals with this question. Let me give a quick answer now before we return to the technique. For many people, simply understanding the underlying psychology cuts through the Gordian knot of spiritual dryness, and they become ready to receive. Religion has indoctrinated us with the belief in an egoic deity that randomly accepts some requests and rejects others, simply to underline its unlimited power. This is a theological error that is based on an extrapolation of the common human psyche onto the Divine. Instead of a human created in the image and likeness of the Divine (i.e., a human fulfilling its divine purpose), we have created a false image of a Divine after our own image and likeness. Please do understand that the true Divine cannot withhold Its message from you, because the Divine has no ego to withhold from.

The Divine is infinite consciousness and cosmic intelligence. Both are everywhere and simultaneously at all times. Ego means limiter in space and time. An individual can be in a particular point at a particular time because it has an ego. The Divine cannot. Being egoless means it can be limitless consciousness, intelligence, freedom, love and beauty. But with this comes automatically that It does not have the capacity to withhold Itself

119

from you. It can only individuate through us but not alone by Itself. That is, in order to individuate, It must do so through us. That's why you and I are here. For many practitioners, to think through the above accurate theology and reasoning removes the barriers and we can start to listen.

Please understand that the information of what the Divine wants to become through you is being transmitted all the time whether you are listening or not. It is not that the Divine is waiting until you become ready. The message of the Divine for you is transmitted independent from time because the Divine is outside of time or, better to say, time is inside of the Divine. The Divine has no concept of you having to become ready to listen. And that is because the Divine can only perceive you as its own child in eternal perfection. And that is good.

Contemplate the above several times and then try to listen again. The transmission of the Divine to you is eternal and existed before time and space were introduced. When time and space became introduced via ignition of the Big Bang, the transmission was carried everywhere and became hearable at all times. If you do find it hard to listen, it is usually because your own mind cannot open itself to the message or, alternatively, it is the ego that shuts the message out. This makes sense in both cases because the message is outside of the mind's and ego's limited self-image pertaining to you. We will go into much detail later on about what can be done in these cases.

'Hearing' the message: The term hearing is used here with the same meaning as 'seeing' or receiving a vision. Because we are physical beings, our cognitive apparatus developed in context with our senses. We are using sensory terms metaphorically for computing data. It is not important whether your brain tells you that you heard, saw or felt a message or vision. The brain will simply use terminology that fits into your belief system, so that you can understand and relate to what is being transmitted.

Usually, a vision becomes more powerful if more senses are involved, and ideally, we aim at getting all senses involved. Consider, for example, Moses encountering the burning bush. Moses saw the fire (a metaphor for higher intelligence, in yoga called agni). He also heard a voice come out of the fire. We can assume that he also felt the fire, too, because we are told that its quality was cool. The more senses involved, the more powerful. Different people may be attached to saying that they saw, heard or felt a message, but this is generally related to whether you are more inclined to visual, audio or kinaesthetic representation. A combination of all three is great, but it does not have to be that way.

Taking notes: Sit in the vision and wait for it to crystallize and condense in some form of verbal description. Once you have that, write it down.

A few points here regarding writing down the vision. Let the vision simply flow through you without judging whether what you see, hear or feel is right or appropriate. Simply receive and then write down. In the beginning, it's important for the creative progress to get flowing and for you to get writing, rather than activating your critical function. Otherwise, nothing might ever come through. So, simply write down whatever comes to mind and leave the editing, curating and spell-checking for later.

Contemplating the vision: From now on, every day, contemplate your vision. In the beginning, it may be helpful to do so twice per day in the morning and the evening. Good times are shortly after waking up and shortly before you go to bed. Simply read through your written description of the vision and feel how it is to embody it. Do so in the present, in real time, rather than imagining it as a future state. Contemplating the vision means to envision yourself embodying the vision in present time, now, rather than in the future. There may be various levels of resistance that you have to overcome in this process. Typically, they are related to your belief that you are currently not good enough to see yourself as embodying the vision in the present. However, for your superconscious mind to start removing the obstacles, you have to envision yourself embodying the vision in the present tense.

Editing the description of the vision: Now we come to an important new step and that is to check your vision for egoic content. Remember, you do this never while the actual visioning is taking place but always later. Look out for any egoic contents, including ways of describing yourself as what you have and what you receive. Remember Jesus's "seek ye first the kingdom of God and all these things will be added on". Try to change what you *have* and what you are *willing to receive* into terms of what you *are* and what you are *willing to give*.

Also look out for any comparison and competitiveness in your vision of self. Remember that the Divine does not have an ego and is all encompassing, omnipotent, omniscient and omnipotent. So, any concepts of property, exclusion, comparison or competition might be entertaining, but by definition, they cannot come from your divine self. Ideas such as being great or greater, or intelligent or powerful must be exchanged with concepts of biosymbiosis or service, and if that's not possible, simply deleted. Why? Ask yourself, 'Intelligent compared to whom', 'Having power over what or whom'? Comparison, ambitiousness and competitiveness always involve raising yourself above somebody and something that you exclude from your sense-of-self. That means, by definition, such statements were made during a time of experiencing a contracted sense of self, i.e., ego.

I remember when I first noticed egoic content in my vision that I was quite embarrassed. As if I had gotten caught. However, that's not the point. It's natural and important to have an ego. You couldn't actually function without one. The ego is a piece of software that binds body and mind together (try functioning through a schizophrenic episode and you'll be yearning for a healthy ego). The ego also enables you to embody in a particular space/time and via that for the egoless Divine to individuate through you and billions of other individuals simultaneously.

However, the ego has not place when receiving a divine vision. It will limit your highest potential to what you think you are capable of in that particular space/time. And the very point of visioning is to go beyond that, to get a glimpse of who you could be, if you could let go of the limitations imposed by your ego here/now.

Once you have identified egoic content, simply rewrite it to fit an egoless, serving-the-good-of-all-type perspective. In most cases, that works. If it doesn't, the simply delete the entire passage. Once you have gone through these steps several times, your mind will start to auto-delete egoic passages, and they won't come through anymore during vision practice. But, again, it is important to not right away filter by egoic content because it could stop you from having any information come

123

through at all. In the beginning, it is more important to be non-judgemental towards oneself.

Filtering: You may ask yourself now, 'How do we know that it's the right voice'? In the beginning, you can't worry too much about this question. Simply listen. It may, in fact, be the case that early voices are mainly reflective of ego, and that would not be surprising. Remember how much our society has trained us to compete. Have a look at a much-celebrated idea of the Olympic Games. For two weeks, apparently, the young people of the world come together to celebrate. At least, so goes the advertising rave of the Games, but that's not what's really happening. We are coming together to thwart each other, and the hardest and most competitive thwarter gets rewarded. Then comes the medal table sorted by nationality. An artificial border is erected between 'us' and 'other'. The Olympic Games are one of the most powerful tools to create national ego, and for this reason dictatorships, totalitarian regimes and communist countries are the ones that invest the most in coming up tops on the medal table. So, don't be surprised if comparison and topping others in the beginning is mixed into your life's divine purpose. We will have a bit of work to do to unlearn history.

The voice of your higher, divine self is the voice of silence. It will talk without any bluster, fanfare and aggrandisement. It will also come without any internal dialogue about whether you are good enough, or not quite good enough, or should try harder to reach your goals, or whether you are never quite as good as somebody else or possibly even the greatest all the time.

The voice of the higher, divine self is simple, and it is the voice of your heart. There is certainty, restfulness, self-love and love for all others. In fact, it will not differentiate between you and others. That's why it always thinks in terms of service. The higher self gets reward from serving others because it knows that we all share the same self. There is only one. There is only one consciousness, which we all share.

Reimprint and update practice: From here on, daily read and re-imprint your vision. That means that you feel it as if embodying it in real-time. The more closely and authentically you can feel it with all of your senses, the faster you will get there in your life. You can also perform an update practice as often as you like. That means that you go through all of the steps above again and again to get more clarity of your vision. It is normal that you can't see the complete vision at first. But gradually, you are honing your ability to see, hear and feel.

There is nothing wrong with daily asking for the vision or more details to the same vision and then writing it down. You will gradually end up with more and more precision and texture, particularly in regards to how you have to change in order to embody the vision. In the first month or year of your practice, the vision may constantly evolve, but later on, it may do so only gradually. Why does your vision evolve and change at all?

Evolving vision: What you can see, hear and feel in the beginning is not the Divine's view of you in its totality. It is only the part that you can handle. The psychology here is similar to a severe trauma, only we are looking at a positive state. If you have been subject to a severe trauma, the experience itself may be sequestered away in your subconscious, since constant remembrance or even a singular remembrance may be too destructive for your surface-personality. You generally will only remember as much as you can handle.

A similar mechanism is at work here. The Divine can only see you in your divine perfection, since the Divine can only reason from an already established premise, i.e., the perfection of the Divine. In the new testament, the Father says to Jesus, "You are My beloved son; in you I am well pleased" (Mark 1:11, Matthew 3:17). Remember also that Jesus repeated the dictum of the Old Testament, "Ye all are gods, ye all are children of the Most High" (John 10:34, Psalm 82:6). In other words, God's statement to Jesus was addressed to all of us as we are all children of the Divine. The Divine can only see all of us in our divine perfection, since the Divine is not capable of perceiving anything contrary to Its own nature. That means that the Divine can only see that part of you that is identical to Its own essence, your Buddha-nature, your Christhood, the Krishna within you.

Think for a moment what would happen if you could see this view right now in its entirety? You would experience the same that happened to Arjuna when Lord Krishna in the 11th chapter of the Bhagavad Gita gave him the celestial eye (XI.08ff). Arjuna was so overwhelmed that he asked Krishna to take away the state for which he had hankered for so long. Ultimately, if you could really see your atman, your divine self, in all its glory, you would not be able to function normally anymore, because to experience your atman means that, temporarily, your ego is suspended. That is why the Divine, who is constantly in this state, cannot limit Itself to a body in space and time (a so-called avatar) but can only do so by filtering Itself via our ego through us. That is what we are. A divine core (atman, purusha) funnelled via an ego into a body embedded in a particular space/time.

Therefore, initially, when starting your vision practice, you will only be able to see as much as you can currently integrate, because otherwise your subconscious would totally balk at the task. It would also balk at the non-congruence between what it, the subconscious, believes you to be, and what the Divine believes you to be. The Divine believes you to be its perfect child, perfect in love, beauty, freedom, harmony, intelligence and consciousness, but that is too much for your subconscious mind to accept now. Through vision practice, you can gradually come around to this view and bit by bit accept who you already are.

Integration: At first, you will see only a part of the vision. That part that you are capable of understanding and therefore integrating. You then go through a process of integration, and once that is complete, you can then see, hear and feel the next step of the vision to whatever extent necessary. The more you embody initial steps of the vision, the further down the road you will be able to see. Late stages of vision at this early point are still too outrageous for you to see. Every time you have embodied a new aspect, undertake a new course of the vision-technique. Of course, there are no black and white guidelines what exactly is requited to 'embody a new aspect'. As a rule of thumb, if no new material has come through for a while, it is important to focus on embodiment and integration of the existing material.

Method of embodiment: It is absolutely essential that you do not get stuck with "How do I embody the vision? What do I have to do?" You have to do nothing, just be. Just be yourself in the vision and just feel yourself being present as cosmic intelligence enters you, comes through you and expresses itself through you.

Have you ever asked yourself how to beat your heart, how to breathe, how to digest and metabolize your food, how to heal a cut in your skin? No, all of these things and many more are all happening because the Divine, a superconscious, super-intelligent cosmic being expresses and computes Itself simultaneously through you, all other beings, and all matter. This is what is meant when Lord Krishna says in the Bhagavad Gita, "All things are done by my prakriti (divine creative force). Only a fool believes to be the doer."

Understand that your integration, your embodiment of the vision, is not done by you. It is done by cosmic intelligence itself. The only thing you need to do is to get out of the way, to stop impeding the process. We could say you need to let go and surrender into the process. Trying to do it is actually an obstacle.

Let me give you an example: when I received my vision, the first part was to experience all sorts of beautiful and expansive mystical states for which I was thirsty. But the second part was that I had to pass it on and communicate it to everybody who was asking for it. That was the deal, and little did I know that it meant for me to travel around the world and teach constantly changing audiences. As a recluse-level introvert, that was completely out of my comfort zone and certainly not something that I desired. Had I known that bit, I would have refused right away. When it came to embodying, I came across the following passages in the Gospel of John:

- I can of mine own self do nothing (John 5:30)
- I do nothing of myself; but as my Father hath taught me, I speak these things (John 8:28)
- The words that I speak unto you I speak not of myself: but the Father that dwelleth in me, he doeth the works (John 14:10)

Jesus here teaches us to simply open ourselves to the inflow of the Divine. We need not do anything but make ourselves available, which is an act of surrender and receiving. In fact, any form of doing will obstruct the inflow of divine wisdom when speaking or performing any action in alignment with one's divine purpose. This openness and making ourselves available is exactly the attitude we need to embody our vision. Be open. Rather than doing, let cosmic intelligence do its thing. There is a passage in the Yoga Sutra (II.27) that talks about freedom from doing, and it is, of course, reverberated in the Chinese term wu-wei, the doing from an inner stance of non-doing, that is, letting a higher intelligence perform the doing through you.

Summarising, the practice is a daily process of
- stating your intention,
- asking your questions
- listening,
- recording the answers,
- afterwards checking for egoic content,
- contemplating the vision and embodying it by being in the vision in real-time without wondering *how* you can *do* it. *You* cannot *do* it. Only the Divine can.

Chapter 4
PSYCHOLOGY OF FINDING ONE'S DIVINE PURPOSE

While the previous chapter dealt simply with the practice, in this chapter we will look deeper into the mechanics, the psychological and spiritual underpinnings of the method before returning again to more practical matters. You need to understand what you are doing to succeed at a deeper level. From this growing understanding, you will also learn how to work out obstacles and blockages and to troubleshoot.

FIVE-LAYERS MODEL (PANCHAKOSHA MODEL)

There is a passage in the Taittiriya Upanishad that describes the human being as made up of five sheaths. Five in Sanskrit means pancha, and sheath means kosha, hence the name of panchakosha model. This is one of the most important passages to understand spirituality in general and yoga in particular. There are direct passages in the Yoga Sutra that refer to this Upanishadic passage. Yoga is a path leading to inner freedom and an inward leading journey. Hence, the outer layers of the five-layers model are very familiar to us, but as we travel inward, we may encounter ground we were not previously conscious of.

The five-layers model enables us to understand how finding one's life's divine purpose is related to all other aspects of our being. It also helps us to understand why the process of finding your life's divine purpose may get off to a rocky start and why its attainment may be a gradual process. The five-layers model also tells us exactly where possible obstacles may be located.

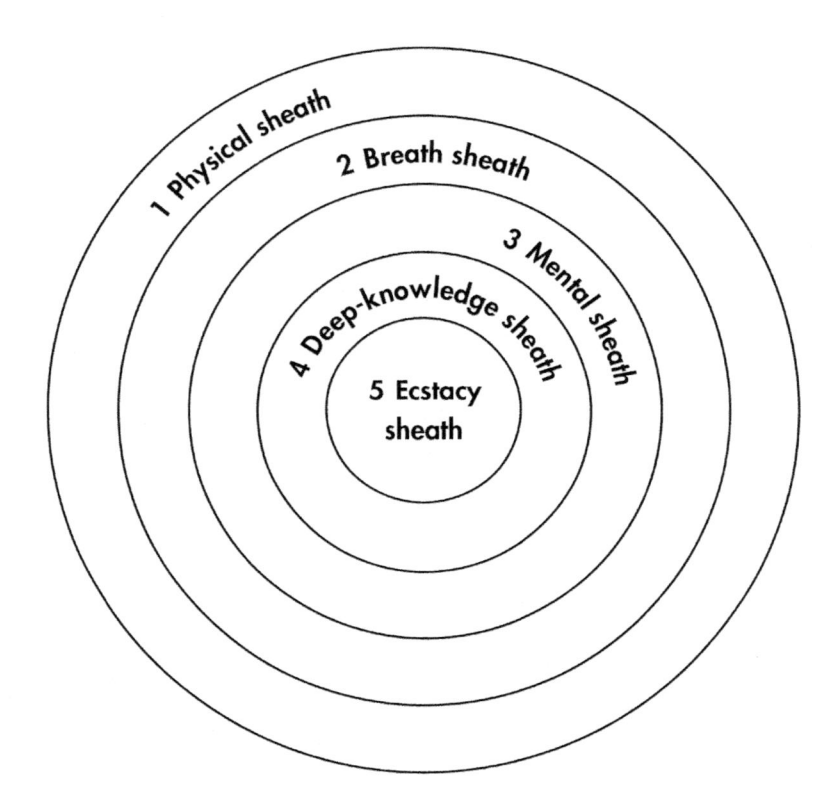

Diagram: Five concentric circles labeled from outside to inside:
1. *Physical sheath*
2. *Breath sheath*
3. *Mental sheath*
4. *Deep-knowledge sheath*
5. *Ecstacy sheath*

I will first give an introduction to the 4th layer, the so-called deep-knowledge sheath in which our life's divine purpose is encrypted. After putting things into perspective, I will then explain the whole model from the outside in starting with the 1st or outermost layer, the body.

The two innermost layers of the five-layers model are direct representations of inner freedom and are related to what the Yoga

Sutra calls objective and objectless samadhi. Our divine purpose is encrypted in the 4th layer, which is called deep-knowledge sheath (Vijnanamaya kosha). There are two different avenues to access this sheath. One is through vision practice, and the other is through classical spiritual practices such as yoga. For maximum effect, you practice both avenues side by side. Vision practice was performed for untold ages by indigenous people. It is hinted at in the Yoga Sutra, the Bhagavad Gita, the Bible, and psychologists like Maslow and inventors like Nikola Tesla practised it. For many modern people, it is somewhat more difficult than for indigenous people, and the reason, which was once aptly described by a Lakota elder to anthropologist Richard Walker, is that we modern people are somewhat thicker. We are thick with conditioning and therefore find it harder to feel nature, to feel the obvious. The conditioning, although a part of it has naturally occurred through the evolution of life, has been largely accrued through the millennia-long process of enculturation that we underwent.

The 4th sheath essentially tells us how to lead a life of divine love and divine purpose. The 5th sheath reveals pure consciousness, and while this is essential for experiencing a liberated death, it can tell us surprisingly little about how to live right. This is because consciousness cannot judge and, therefore, cannot judge what is right or wrong. Nevertheless, this state is profoundly liberating in deep meditation because it removes any fear of death and any uncertainty about where you are going. However, it is overrated in that it can assist rather little when having to make choices that are either right or wrong such as for which profession to train (our svadharma).

When attempting to access the 4th layer, which can tell us what our life's divine purpose is, we ideally employ a dual approach. The first is to try to access the 4th sheath directly through vision practice. This is important because the earlier we get glimpses of the information encrypted in this sheath, the better for the unfolding of our life. It would be a shame if you find out at age 80 what your life should have been about. Even if we do get some information now, it will usually still take us years to implement it. This is what Patanjali means when he says in sutra III.33, "from vision [comes knowledge on] everything".

The second approach, which should be employed parallel, is to gradually purify and decondition the three outer layers until the 4th layer shines through. This is a great method, but if we employ it exclusively and for now ignore the 4th sheath, it may take us decades before we get the first reliable vision from it. This is too long. A vision inspired by the Divine may actually propel us forward on the path of yoga, or whatever else our spiritual practice is, much faster. Our yoga or spiritual practice becomes more efficient if it is spiritually linked to our profession, occupation, to activities that we perform outside of yoga. As sage Yajnavalkya said in the Yoga Yajnavalkya, "Yoga can only succeed in conjunct with fulfilling one's duty to society".

What stops us from clearly perceiving our life's divine purpose is conditioning, incurred through enculturation, i.e., brainwashing through the society in which we live (For example, currently, we are brainwashed to believe in materialistic reductionism and disregard all evidence to the contrary). The difference between subconscious imprint and conditioning is that in the imprint state, we are aware of the fact that we do have a choice. If a particular neurological pathway gets used again and again, the response seems to eventually become automatic, and we believe, then, that we do not have choice anymore. It then is called conditioning.

If we analyse conditioning, we find that it consists of many, many individual subconscious imprints (*samskaras*) that are placed (imprinted in our subconscious) whenever we do, feel, think or say something. Subconscious imprints are similar to a constant recording of our activities. You see them powerfully at work when you learn a new activity like walking or riding a bicycle. You cannot really explain how to walk or cycle. It is basically a vestibular computation whereby the brain learns to brake a forward-falling by shifting our centre of gravity (which most of us don't remember). Once you have learned how to walk or cycle, a neurological pathway is laid, and if you perform the activity again, your brain will simply replay the subconscious imprint pertaining to it (more precisely a series of imprints). If there was no subconscious imprint and conditioning, you would have to learn the same activity from scratch every time you execute it. In other words, subconscious imprint is a very powerful learning method and saves us a lot of time, but it does come at a huge cost, too.

Where it becomes a hindrance is when you would like to learn something new but can't because the same old recording is replayed over and over again. For example, racism or sexism are examples when conditioning goes awry. Other examples would be lack of self-esteem, self-sabotage and self-loathing. These are not behaviours that we consciously choose. We have rather picked them up from family, peers, teachers while being immersed in a social setting. Post-traumatic stress disorder (PTSD), eating disorders, drug addiction and many other mental disorders also are examples of conditioning. With all of these, it rarely is enough if we simply change our minds. Try, for example, telling an alcohol, ice, crack or heroin addict to make up their mind to stop using. That's not how it works.

During an imprint (and every situation is basically an imprint situation) the charge of the imprint, the memory, is seeded simultaneously into body, breath and mind. This means that an imprint has a tissue component, a respiratory/*pranic* component and a mental component. To successfully remove an imprint, we have to firstly delete all three components and secondly replace the imprint with something else (such as a new behaviour we would like to learn). If we do not replace it with something new that is functional, the subconscious will simply keep looking for the old imprint, and chances are, it will dig up a residue of it from somewhere.

An example: If a person has trouble with self-loathing, it is not enough to delete all self-loathing imprints. We also need to replace them with resolutions (sankalpas) along the lines of, 'I love and accept myself whatever happens'.

Additionally, 'deleting subconscious imprints' does not mean that we can pinpoint the location of particular samskaras, go there and delete it. This would be similar to saying that a particular yoga posture fixes a particular disease or problem. Yoga does not work that way. By practicing a large set of yoga postures, which access all areas of the body, we can remove the physical strata of many imprints. The important imprints to delete are obviously the stressful, pathological ones, which we can notice from the amount of tension they place in the body. Yoga will not remove joyful imprints from your body, as joyful imprints do not create tension.

After this brief introduction to the 4th sheath, which is the sheath most significant for our life's divine purpose, let's get now an overview of the entire five-sheath model, working from the outside in. The 1st or outermost layer is the one we are all familiar with, the **body**. The Sanskrit name is Anamaya kosha, which means food sheath, that is, the sheath made up of physical nourishment. Since Rene Descartes, Western culture is firmly based on the body/mind duality. Descartes believed that the body, made up from matter, is entirely separate from the mind or spirit. The body and matter, so he believed, should be subject to scientific investigation, and spirituality should have nothing to do with it. On the other hand, spirit was the subject of religion and was to be completely separate from the body and matter. A bizarre concept at the best of times, if you ask me, but it proved very influential in its day, and we still haven't seen the end of it.

Yoga, to the contrary, is built on the maxim that the body is the crystallized strata of the mind. Thoughts will ultimately become matter and form tissue. This happens similarly to the way that water that freezes and becomes ice. It crystallizes. If the ice is being heated, it first turns into water, it liquifies. In this metaphor, the liquid state represents prana/breath, the life force. If we heat water further, the same material (H_2O) turns into steam, vapour. Vapour, in this metaphor, represents mind.

Looking from an energetic perspective, ice contains the least amount of thermic energy (heat). When you add heat to a substance, its basic building blocks will accelerate, oscillate, and increase movement. That means that water can be looked at as accelerated ice. If you add even more heat, the water particles move so fast that more and more get ejected from the surface and evaporate. The now ensuing steam or vapour is water in a more accelerated state.

In yoga, we use the metaphor of ice-water-steam to explain the relationship of body – breath/prana – mind. Mind is nothing but body in its most accelerated state, and body is nothing but mind in its most crystallized and decelerated state. It is very important that this concept is understood and well contemplated because it will determine how we work with body and mind.

Physical therapy in yoga is called asana (posture). One of the main purposes of posture is to stretch the body in all major directions by taking it through a large range of postures. By conscious breathing in the state of the postures, conditioning, often held as tension, fear and self-limiting beliefs, can be consciously released by letting it go. This is done by becoming conscious of the tension and letting it flow out with the exhalation.

Other objectives of posture practice are to obtain maximum health because lack of health will make spiritual progress and the fulfilling of one's duty more difficult. Posture practice also improves longevity, which yogis try to obtain because it is helpful with fulfilling ones duty. Further objectives of asana are related to particular groups of postures. Cultivating the sitting meditation-postures is important for the practice of pranayama and meditation. Especially postures like lotus posture (Padmasana) and others are pronouncedly influencing one's state of mind during meditation. Another important group of postures are the inversions such as headstand and shoulder stand. They are used to arrest life force, in particular, evolutionary centres (chakras), with the goal to become independent from sensory stimulus. Independence from sensory stimulus is a prerequisite to spiritual freedom.

The most important aspect of postures, though, is the release of the physical aspect of conditioning. Through this release, asana becomes an important aspect of therapy for the mind. If we would only try to change our mind and would never work on the decelerated, crystallized stratas of conditioning that have become imprinted in tissue, conditioning would simply reboot from the physical strata and populate the mind again. This is the reason why mental work that does not include the body is inefficient. I have written about asana in great detail in my first two books *Ashtanga Yoga Practice and Philosophy* and *Ashtanga Yoga The Intermediate Series*.

The second layer of the five-layers model is the pranamaya kosha, and as the name says, it is the pranic sheath or **breath sheath**. If we say breath sheath, we need to keep in mind that the anatomical breath is only the outer, gross manifestation of prana, the life force. There is more to life force than just breath and to believe that they are one and the same is a simplification of the concept of prana.

The breath sheath is the middling sheath between body and mind, and by influencing life force, both body and mind are influenced. In our metaphor of ice – water – steam, prana is the liquid aspect of both body and mind. Water can be relatively easily turned either into ice or steam, whereas it takes longer to turn ice into steam or vice versa. Body and mind, therefore, communicate with each other via prana/breath. This shows the importance of yoga's method to harness the breath, pranayama.

The most important purpose of pranayama is to remove the pranic/respiratory strata of conditioning. Notice when you have any intense experience such as an ecstatic state or a panic attack, that your breathing pattern will change. We need to understand that trauma in the mind cannot be removed simply by working with the mind. Both the body and the breath need to be involved for that work to bear fruit. Modern psychology is coming around to that view, and you can read as much in, for example, Bessel Van Der Kolk's *The Body Keeps The Score*. Pranayama is a methodical approach to changing breathing patterns that thereby influences body and mind. Through pranayama, the respiratory strata and residue of conditioning and subconscious imprint is let go of and removed, and we then become more receptive to working on the mind.

Further effects of pranayama are brain-hemisphere synchronization and equalizing of lunar and solar energy channels. This is a complex subject that I can't deal with here but have extensively written on in my book *Pranayama the Breath of Yoga*. Pranayama also draws prana, which is scattered, back under the surface of the physical body. This means that we are less "out there" and therefore less likely to project onto other people or objects the belief that they are here to make us happy. Pranayama also eventually induces prana into the central energy channel (sushumna), which induces mystical states. Furthermore, via breath retentions (kumbhakas), pranayama helps us to arrest the mind, which also is a precursor for accessing mystical states. Pranayama is, hence, a powerful tool that helps us to cultivate the mind to prepare it for deep spiritual insight. If early attempts at vision practice prove unsatisfactory, pranayama can help remove blockages. Even with a successful vision practice, pranayama is important to accelerate our spiritual evolution.

The 3rd sheath of the panchakoshas is the manomaya kosha, the **mental sheath** or mind. As previously explained, the mind is the vaporized or accelerated strata of both the body and the pranic sheath. This means that any work on the mind must always involve body and breath. Trauma represented in the mind will always simultaneously seed into breath and tissue, too.

CHAPTER 4

The mind has several advantages compared to the body that make it so easy to work with. Firstly, because it is accelerated (compared to the body), it quickly develops and accepts new ideas. Hence, it is easy to change the mind. Like vapour and steam, it will spread into and adapt to any space it can. It is thus gaseous in quality, which is very different to the crystalline, ice-like, frozen quality of the body. The disadvantage of the mind, though, is that it can lose great new ideas as quickly as it adopts them. That's why weekend motivation workshops, after a short while, usually wear off. When the excited, gaseous quality of the mind hits the crystalline structure of the body, it is usually the body that re-seeds and reboots its conditioning into the mind. Hence, asana (to change the body) and pranayama (to change the breath) are essential if one wants to change the mind.

There is another reason that makes working with the mind accessible. And that is that we can become relatively easily conscious of what is going on in the mind. I say relatively because, relative to the body and breath, it is easier to become aware of the programming of the mind. The more gaseous and accelerated conditioning is, the easier it is penetrated by awareness to dissolve it.

The method yoga uses to cultivate the mind is meditation. Yoga has many different meditation techniques, including mantra, meditating on the breath and, of course, the meditation technique central to yoga, the chakra-Kundalini meditation.

A few words on Vipassana meditation, which uses the breath to de-identify with the content of one's mind (creating mindfulness). The method undoubtedly has its benefits, such as destressing and slowing down the mind and becoming more conscious. Unfortunately, in modern spiritual culture, the method has become almost synonymous with the term meditation. It is not. It is only one of many helpful meditation techniques. Other methods should not be neglected.

The most important meditation method when wanting to find one's life's divine purpose is the chakra-Kundalini method, which I have described in great detail in my book *Yoga Meditation Through Mantra, Chakras and Kundalini to Spiritual Freedom*. The so-called chakras are really representations of evolutionary brain circuitry. The lower three chakras, base, lower abdomen, and navel chakras stand for reptilian, mammalian and primate brain circuitry, respectively. It is the heart chakra, representing humanoid brain circuitry and the upper three chakras that are related to our life's divine purpose. This is because the Divine embodies Itself as the spiritual and natural evolution of life on Earth. The Divine as cosmic intelligence and as divine creative force is the driver behind the evolution of life. The evolution of species is nothing but the accumulated evolution of individuals in the aggregate. The Divine drives the evolution of species by flowing into individuals that are particularly open. This openness to the Divine, this making oneself available for divine influx is nothing but your life's divine purpose.

Opening up higher chakras and finding one's life's divine purpose are closely interlinked. We could say that the purpose is driven by opening higher chakras, and the chakra opening enables one to fulfil one's life's divine purpose. Especially these two practices, i.e., vision practice on one hand and chakra-Kundalini meditation on the other, are ideally combined because they do go hand in hand. If more higher chakras are enabled (i.e., higher brain circuitry activated), it is easier to see and fulfil one's divine purpose. If you seriously desire to fulfil your life's divine purpose, it becomes more important to activate higher chakras.

Meditation, in general, is yoga's method of releasing the past and conditioning from the mind. Vipassana, i.e., focussing on the breath and using that to dis-identify with one's thoughts, is here very helpful. By focussing on the breath, we can create distance towards our conditioning and subconscious imprint.

However, chakra-Kundalini meditation should also be employed as it helps us to transcend the viewpoint from a which a particular conditioning seems so important. For example, when in the thrall of the power chakra, competitiveness and ambitiousness seem to be totally natural, as is trying to get limited resources under our control by snatching them away from the control of others (such as in the capitalist marketplace).

Once higher chakras are activated, we see that one common intelligence expresses itself through all of us and that the downfall of the person next to me is my downfall, too. The downfall of the lifeform next to me, similarly, is also my downfall. Life either flourishes collectively or it collectively descends into the sixth mass extinction. It is because we have been in the throes of the power chakra for so long that we only focussed on ambitiousness and competitiveness without understanding that life advances by bio-symbiosis.

Collectively as a species, humanity's divine purpose is to be the guardian, the keeper of this garden of life, Gaia. It is not our purpose to compete with other life forms, to make them extinct, but to equally support the blossoming of all life on this planet. Every time a species becomes extinct, we have failed. There was a time when humans believed that the entire universe, including the sun, was circling around Earth. In the wake of Copernicus, Columbus and Galilei we gave up on this view. Unfortunately, this view has only been corrected in the arena of astronomy. In biology, we still hold on to it. We still believe that the human is the crown of creation and that other lifeforms are here to serve us. Strange, isn't it? People who are confessing to be completely rational and scientific still believe in a dictum that comes from the Bible, i.e., that we have been given Earth to make it our dominion. Genesis 1:28 says, "Be fruitful and increase in number; fill the earth and subdue it". Psalm 8:6 adds, "Thou hast made him to have dominion over the works of thy hands; thou hast put all things under his feet". 400 years into the history of Western Science, science is still dominated by ideas, which its founders never critically examined but unquestioningly accepted. I remind the reader that I have previously shown that the philosophy of Science is actually a brainchild of religion in that regard that the first 300 years of scientists were all religious people. In the light of this, we shouldn't be surprised that Science has been built on religious dogmas such as the one of human supremacy, i.e., speciesism.

It is time that humanity leaves these outdated superstitions behind and evolves to become again a servant of all life (The word *again* here is chosen because indigenous people managed to do so for times immemorable). Because if we do not evolve into that direction, we shall die out like the dinosaurs. Humanity can only fulfil its divine purpose if individuals become open to receiving their divine purpose. The onus today is on us.

A very efficient way of removing conditioning is through the combined application of yogic asana, pranayama and yogic meditation. This prevents that conditioning re-seeds into already purified stratas from others in which it still persists. Once the three stratas, body, breath and mind, are cleansed from conditioning, the fourth strata, the deep-knowledge sheath (Vijnanamaya kosha), can be consistently accessed. The deep-knowledge sheath contains

CHAPTER 4

our divine purpose and the nature gifts and unique talents that we bring to this world. This cleansing of the outer sheaths can be a lengthy process. Because it can be a lengthy process and because accessing our divine purpose and divine gifts is so important, a second form of practice, vision practice, should be used parallel. The disadvantage of vision practice is that it lets us access the deep-knowledge sheath and thus our divine purpose only inconsistently. In other words, it is a hit-and-miss process. But accessing it inconsistently we must, for it would be unreasonable and stunting for our development if we would wait until we have succeeded in yoga and thus enabled predictable and consistent access.

There is a group of yogic methods used to access the deep-knowledge sheath and bring forth its treasures and gifts. The methods are collectively referred to as objective samadhis. I have described them in great detail in my book *Samadhi the Great Freedom*. Vision practice will bring forward some of these benefits at a time when we are not yet capable of formally performing objective samadhi. Additionally, let's remember that Yoga Sutra II.45 says "The power of samadhi comes through placing oneself in the service of the Divine". This means that even Patanjali, the author of the Sutra, believed that the easiest way of accessing samadhi is by serving the Divine. What does that mean in this context? It means that we are using our gifts to serve a greater good, the good of all life, and not just the satisfaction of our personal egotism. So, the acquisition of wealth, goods, property, power, fame, etc. should not be the motivation. Again, Jesus's dictum, "Seek ye first the kingdom of God and everything else shall be added on", states exactly the same principle as Patanjali stanza above.

I will now briefly discuss the fifth and innermost sheath, the **ecstasy sheath** (Anandamaya kosha). The term means ecstasy sheath, and it represents the pinnacle of evolution of life. In yoga, we access it through objectless samadhi, which again is described in my above book. While the deep-knowledge sheath and objective samadhi get us in contact with the God immanent, i.e., cosmic intelligence, the ecstasy sheath and objectless samadhi make us realize the God transcendent. The most important effect is that at the time of death, we can let go of our body with gratitude and without regret and become one with the ocean of infinite consciousness. In yoga, access to the ecstasy sheath and objectless samadhi are seen as results of the other limbs and traversing through the outer four sheaths. There is now in modern spiritual circles this misunderstanding that we should shortcut and go straight to this apex of spirituality, leaving body and society behind to enter nirvana and nothingness. This is not the view that yoga holds and neither does, for example, Mahayana Buddhism. Mahayana Buddhists commit themselves via the Bodhisattva vow to postpone entering Nirvana until all other beings have reached it. Also, serving others is placed into the foreground of spiritual development. It is this attitude that we want to cultivate when following our life's divine purpose. That is because our good and the good of others cannot be two separate things because the same cosmic superintelligence expresses itself through all of us.

But let me try to put a more joyful spin on it because postponing nirvana out of a sense of duty sounds a bit grim. If you would bypass the deep-knowledge sheath and your life's divine purpose, you would cheat yourself of the most fulfilling and joyful section of life. The is no greater thrill than to feel oneself becoming a conduit for cosmic intelligence, touching and transforming the lives of others. It is a great miracle for human beings that we are so wired that we want to make a contribution to each other's lives. Nothing is more satisfying. It is this genuine care for each other, this interest in the evolution of the people around us, that defines our humanity. For that alone, hanging around in the ocean of conditioned existence (samsara) is already well worth it. The truth is that once you are embodying your divine purpose, hanging around in samsara is no problem anymore.

This is encrypted in the following anecdote from the life of the Buddha. A man approached the Buddha and asked, "How many more lives do I have to live?" The Buddha pointed to the sky and said, "As many stars in the sky that often do you have to come back". The man left in abject misery because there was no purpose to his life. Another man came and asked the same question. This time, the Buddha pointed to a massive Banyan tree, a tree with massive spreading roots and multiple trunks, that can grow to 100 metres in diameter, with millions of tiny leaves. The Buddha said, "As many leaves on that tree that's how often you will come back". This man leapt into the air in great ecstasy and, so the story goes, he became liberated on the spot. This man knew his life's divine purpose. For him, every moment was fulfilment, was life spent in the knowledge that he served an intelligence greater than he that expresses itself as the world and all beings. What greater happiness can there be than becoming a vehicle for the expression of infinite intelligence, love and beauty?

But back to the difference between the ecstasy - and deep-knowledge sheaths. When being under the influence of the deep-knowledge sheaths, there is still a sense-of-I. You still experience yourself as an individual, as limited, as, at least in a physical sense, different from infinite consciousness. This is so because infinite consciousness (the God transcendent) has as its body this entire vast universe, and your body is just this small shell, limited in size. While under the influence of ecstasy sheath, this sense-of-I and knowledge of the body disappears. The drop of individual self falls into the ocean of infinite consciousness and dissolves. We attain complete self-transcendence, and no more individuality and personality remain. For how long? This is a surprisingly important question. Because in this state, which Patanjali calls objectless samadhi, there is no identification, nor owning of the body, ego or mind whatsoever. Since there is no identification with body or mind, one cannot drive one's car, nor talk, nor even think in terms of right or wrong. The Shiva Svarodhaya even goes so far as saying, "If one makes material decisions in that state all one's material aspirations will come to naught". That is because no sense of right or wrong judgement, nor any systematic thought is possible in this state.

We all have glimpses of ecstasy sheath. In deep sleep they can last as long as 10 minutes. In daytime, they usually last seconds, and then their significance is often not understood. This is so because during ecstasy sheath-activation, we don't know who we are in the day-to-day sense. If these glimpses last even just a few minutes, brought on by pranayama, meditation, intense grief, ecstasy or an epiphany in nature, they will provoke a breakthrough, a deep insight into the nature of reality. If through spiritual practice, being under the influence of ecstasy sheath can be extended from half an hour to an hour, it will be a life-changing experience. One's sense-of-self may stay, to some extent, permanently expanded, the degree of which depends on one's ability to integrate this experience into one's daily life.

If staying in this state for much longer than an hour, the re-entry into the body, more precisely re-identification with the body, will be noticed markedly. This is because the sense-of-self in the ecstasy sheath is extremely expanded, and the re-identifying with the physical body consists of a profound recontraction. Staying in this state for such an expanded timeframe, also, will not come about spontaneously but only if one's karma allows it; that is, if one's duties in the body are fulfilled. In this case, then, but only in this case, the body will eventually become an obstacle to retaining cosmic consciousness. If there is still karma to be fulfilled in terms of serving others and their evolution, then this should be joyfully accepted. This means that cosmic consciousness, ecstasy sheath and objectless samadhi should not be pursued as a method of getting out of one's karmic debt. It will backfire. I mention this because I have seen spiritual practitioners pursue objectless samadhi out of pain avoidance. It is rather a state that comes about naturally once one's duty is fulfilled and one has given everything one came to give.

The main function of the ecstasy sheath is that it enables you to see yourself as infinite consciousness, which is eternal. Once you have experienced your true nature as eternal, you know that when the body dies, you are simply going home. From then on, all fear of death falls away, and one can live unencumbered. Therefore, the saying, "For as in Adam all die, so in Christ all will be made alive" (Corinthians 15:22). Adam here is a metaphor for the embodied state. Necessarily, the embodied state ends with death and "in Adam we all die". The term Christ is symbolic for consciousness. Because consciousness is infinite, eternal and, therefore, deathless, "in Christ all will be made alive".

THE THREE BODIES (SHARIRAS)

In this section, I will explain the importance of the yogic categories of gross, subtle and causal bodies and their significance for finding your life's divine purpose. I will also place them into the context of terminologies already discussed. This will make things much clearer, and you will feel more confident progressing on your journey of living a life of divine love and service.

Below, you will find a table based on the Yoga Sutra II.19, in which Patanjali talks about the four phases through which the so-called gunas manifest the world. Gunas means qualities or threads of the divine creative force (prakrti), but it is better to understand them as elementary particles. There are three gunas called mass-particle (tamas), energy particle (rajas) and intelligence particle (sattva).

THE UN-MANIFEST STATE OF THE QUALITIES (GUNAS)

In sutra II.19, Patanjali says the qualities initially rest coiled, in equilibrium, in the state of deep reality or unified field. Patanjali calls this state un-manifest. If you look in the first row of the table, you will see that the sheath relative to the un-manifest gunas is the ecstasy sheath. During the un-manifest state of the qualities, there is no world projected forth, nor was there a body and your consciousness was one with the consciousness of the God transcendent. That's your original state. You are originally one with the Divine, that's the original covenant of God that cannot be revoked by whatever you do or what you have done. And that's where we all go back to. The questions are only: how long does it take us, what difference do we make on the way and how much pain do we all cause each other on the way?

If you go further to the right, you see that the yogic technique relative to the un-manifest qualities (gunas) and the ecstasy sheath is the objectless samadhi. That means your core, your origin, and your original state is objectless samadhi. That's great news because most spiritual practitioners think it's really difficult and unattainable, and it is but only because we spent 10,000 years of enculturation on burying it. It's simply like coming back home. When you die your last death, once you have done all you came for, you are going back home. It's not something to fear but something to really, really look forward to.

STATE OF QUALITIES (GUNAS)	SHEATH (KOSHA)	YOGIC TECHNIQUE	EVOLUTIONARY CENTRES (CHAKRAS)	Aspect of BEING
UNMANIFEST (unified field)	Ecstasy sheath (Anandamaya kosha)	Objectless Samadhi (samadhi on consciousness)	Crown (Sahasrara)	Consciousness
MANIFEST	Deep-Knowledge sheath (Vijnanamaya kosha)	Objective Samadhi (samadhi on the objective world)	Third-eye (Ajna)	Causal body (Karana Sharira)
SUBTLE	Mental sheath (Manomaya kosha) & Breath sheath (Pranamaya kosha)	Meditation, Pranayama, Kriyas, Mudras	Throat (Vishuddha) Heart (Anahata) Navel (Manipura) Sacral (Svadhishthana) Base (Muladhara)	Subtle body (Sukshma Sharira)
GROSS	Physical sheath (Anamaya kosha)	Asana	No chakras	Gross body (Sthula Sharira)

Go further to the right, and you see that the chakra relative to the ecstasy sheath and the objectless samadhi is the crown chakra, the Sahasrara. When life force (prana) is concentrated in the crown chakra, you are in objectless samadhi. There is no sense of time, space, future, past, or body. You are in the state prior to the Big Bang, you are in the God transcendent, nirguna Brahman, the Dao, Yahweh. You may ask how can you be prior to the Big Bang? In the Bible, Jesus says, "Before Abraham was, I AM". Jesus was referring to a crown chakra experience, to an ecstasy sheath experience. The same statement was made by Krishna in the Gita.

Go further to the right in the table, and you find consciousness under the aspect of your being that relates to crown chakra. In the crown chakra, you experience only pure consciousness, and that is what you abide in when practising objectless samadhi, which again is the essence of the ecstasy sheath. In the state of unmanifest qualities (gunas), one is only aware of consciousness.

If you imagine, for a moment, the state before the Big Bang. In that state, there is no time and no space, only unified field. Time and space are dimensions of Big Bang. Only once change and movement occur can we start to measure distance and time spent to travel from point a to point b. Because there is no time and space prior to the Big Bang, the state prior to the Big Bang called Unified Field, ecstasy sheath, Brahman or consciousness, can be accessed from any point or time within space/time. That's really important to understand because we feel so separated from it. It is right here, wherever you are and wherever you go. You carry the Brahman/Dao/Yahweh/ God transcendent in you wherever you go because you cannot go anywhere where the God transcendent is not, because the Big Bang, the entire projected universes takes place within consciousness, within you.

CHAPTER 4

Before we go on to explore the manifestation of creation, let's keep in mind that there is a place in your physiology (the crown chakra) where you experience via objectless samadhi an aspect of your being (the consciousness) that is, was, and will be, forever one with the God transcendent, and that state is the content of the ecstasy sheath.

THE MANIFEST STATE OF THE QUALITIES (GUNAS)

Let's look now at the second row in the table above that starts with the qualities being in the manifest state, which is representative of the Big Bang, the creation of the universe. From the manifest state onwards, the entire table refers to the God immanent, cosmic intelligence, whereas the top row refers to the God transcendent, infinite consciousness. The psychological sheath representative of the manifest state of the qualities (gunas) is the deep-knowledge sheath. Encrypted in the deep-knowledge sheath is all information relating to how the God immanent expresses and evolves Itself through us. Yes, that's right. The God immanent is not a permanent, solid-state type affair like the God transcendent, but it evolves and develops, it is a process not a state. This has been confirmed and explained by British mathematician and philosophy professor Alfred North Whitehead in his seminal *Process and Reality*.

The dynamic evolution and process-nature of the God immanent can easily be confirmed by looking at the expansion of the universe and the natural evolution of life, which are both process-like. The manifest universe, including all matter, energy and beings, is nothing but the crystallized body of the God immanent. The interaction of the individual with the God immanent is, in many ways, more thrilling than the more muted and metered realization of the God transcendent.

Up to the evolutionary step of the humanoid, lifeforms unconsciously co-created with the Divine. The term co-create means that our future is not written down in some holy book, it is not fate. Our choices, decisions, tendencies, the way how we work out our karma, do matter and impact who we will become in the future. Beginning with the human being, life-forms do have the possibility to become aware that the power and force driving their spiritual evolution is the immanent aspect of the Divine, that is, cosmic intelligence.

We could look at it this way: For a long part of their evolution, life-forms have been unconscious that the Divine was powering their spiritual evolution. That state is called unconscious co-creation. Now, we have the choice to be conscious about this divine influx, and this state is called conscious co-creation.

The Divine cannot create evolution entirely on its own. It needs to develop suitable life-forms first. For example, we can assume that the Divine knew about electrical engineering and quantum mechanics during the Jurassic and Cretacean periods, but no suitable life-forms were available to download that knowledge, to become conduits for it and to embody it. It took the arising of characters like Nikola Tesla and Max Planck to receive this information. And even then, during that download-process, Tesla and Planck would have moulded the theory and practice of these branches of physics through who they were. If other scientists would have played these roles, the history of science would have been different, therefore the term co-creation.

All knowledge initially exists in the intellect of the Divine. In the Gita, stanza IV.1 Lord Krishna says, "This ancient yoga I have previously taught to Manu and Vivashvat [the ancestors} …and it was lost through the long lapse of time. I am now teaching it to you [Arjuna]." In the Yoga Sutra the same is said in stanza I.26.

In order for us to know how we can serve the Divine and the evolution of life and embody the divine, we will need to access the deep-knowledge sheath. This should be done initially through vision practice, which will become easier once we have started to embody divine will. It will also become easier to the extent to which we have purified the outer sheaths.

If you look further to the right in the table, you will find that the yogic method to access the deep-knowledge sheath is objective samadhi. Objectless samadhi is well known in Vedanta and Buddhism, but objective samadhi is peculiar to yoga. Objective samadhi is a way to make new knowledge manifest by downloading it from the intellect of the Divine. Great artists like Bach, Beethoven, van Gogh or Dali, great scientists like Planck, Einstein or David Bohm and great civil rights leaders like Gandhi or ML King were actually practising objective samadhi, whether they were aware of it or not. The Yoga Sutra states in stanza VI.1 that one can have the ability to do so by birth, i.e., through one's karma earned in previous life times.

If you go in the second row of the table one step further to the right, you find that the Ajna, the third-eye chakra, is the one on which we need to focus when attempting objective samadhi and accessing Vijnanamaya kosha. The third-eye chakra is the seat of the God immanent in the body, and it is also the place in which prana must be held when wanting to hear OM, the background radiation in the universe and the vibratory residue of the Big Bang. During vision practice, it can also be helpful to focus on the third-eye chakra.

Going one column further to the right, you find under the Aspect of Being heading the causal body (Karana Sharira).

In contemporary spiritual culture, you often encounter the simplistic belief that we do have consciousness (purusha, atman) and a physical body and that's it. It is important to realize that that there are two mediating layers between those two. If you look, for example, at the Christian concept of soul, it does not just consist of pure consciousness/awareness. When we are told that after their resurrection the righteous ones will sit to the right of Jesus Christ (although aspects of this phrase are metaphorical), some important information is conveyed here. Your consciousness or purusha cannot be separated from that of another person, that's why the Vedanta correctly insists that there is only one consciousness (atman) that we all share. However, the Christian soul includes not just the consciousness but also the causal body (Karana Sharira). While in consciousness, we are all the same, in our causal body, we are all different, and that is beautiful. Through each of us, the Divine embodies a different part/aspect of Itself. There is no hierarchy in this, it is rather that the sum total of all causal bodies (Karana Shariras) makes up what the God immanent wants to embody as. The causal body is the sum total of your highest aspirations and potential. It is the highest vision of yourself and can only be embodied over many, many lifetimes.

We could say that the God immanent is not complete unless all of us have reached their highest potential. That is correct in that the God immanent yearns for us reaching that highest potential, but it is incorrect in that the God immanent is a process and, therefore, does not have an endpoint. If it had, creation would come to an end. However, creation cannot come to an end because the God immanent is limitless creative potential.

In the Bhagavata Purana, we find a passage where Krishna says, 'The greatest thrill for me is if the devotee recognizes Me.

CHAPTER 4

In this case I cannot but rush and embrace the devotee". If you strip the metaphor and anthropomorphism away, this passage is clear in describing the attitude of cosmic intelligence towards localized embodied intelligence. The causal body is the sum-total of God's ideas about you. Your consciousness is one with the God transcendent. Your causal body is one with the God immanent. To the extent to which we are embodying the Karana Sharira, we will live *in the zone*, are free of internal dialogue, have complete certainty, and feel how the divine creative force comes through us and embodies itself as us.

THE SUBTLE STATE OF THE QUALITIES (GUNAS)

Let's look now into the third row of the table which starts with the subtle state of the qualities of nature. The definition of subtle means non-perceptible to the senses, or non-empirical. It is, however, feel-able to the extent that an indigenous person would be able to feel and listen to the spirits of mountains, rivers, rocks, animals or plants. The subtle strata is less of an abstraction, less removed from the empirical than the manifest/causal strata. There is a Sanskrit term describing the subtle sphere as madhyama. Madhyama means middling or in between, and it refers to the fact that the subtle strata is the communicator or middling agent between the gross/empirical and the manifest/causal.

The subtle strata contains both the mental and pranic (breath-related) sheaths, listed in the panchakosha-model. All processes that take place in your mind (rather than in your brain) and in your vital airs (collectively referred to as prana) are subtle processes. You may say that what is happening in your mind is empirical, but if you talk to a neurologist, they would only refer to the biochemical and bioelectrical impulses in your brain as empirical. Some neurologists, therefore, consider Freudian or Jungian psychology as quackery, a view that the current author does not share.

Because both breath and mind are part of the subtle strata, most yogic processes and techniques are related to this strata. Apart from the physical ones, all yogic obstacles stopping you from recognizing, expressing and living your life's divine purpose are related to this subtle strata, that is, they play out in your mind and in your vital airs. For this reason, you will find the bulk of yogic techniques, including meditation, mantra, pranayama, mudra, etc. in this row. They are designed to remove the obstacles from the mental and pranic sheaths. The obstacles are conditioning, subconscious imprint, varieties of suffering and karma. To the extent to which we can remove the obstacles from the subtle strata, we will be able to embody our life's divine purpose. This is a theme recurring in this chapter over and over again. Vision practice and general yogic practice are really supporting each other and are ideally practised side-by-side. Vision practice does support general yogic practice by confirming to us that "on the other side" there actually is a cosmic attractor (the God immanent) pulling us towards It.

Go over to the third column in the subtle row, and you will find the chakras related to this strata. Here are the chakras from the base (1st chakra) all the way up to the throat (5th chakra). The lower three chakras are, of course, where the basic human urges are located from survival over intimacy/ procreation to acquisition of wealth and territory (including real estate, number of friends on social media and intellectual territory). The more reduced the obstacles are, the freer can we embody the lower three chakras without being defined by them. To the extent to which we do not let us be defined or limited by the lower three chakras (but rather just utilizing them), we are ready to embody ourselves via the heart and the throat chakra.

Both these chakras are related to our life's divine purpose. To activate the heart chakra (both through vision practice and through formal yogic practice) means to see all human beings as embodiments of divine love and treat them with the according respect. This chakra teaches us that it is not enough to experience everything as pure consciousness. It is not enough to see that consciousness in everybody and then to not do anything about it. In fact, it is more important to treat everybody as if you could see God in them than to actually be able to see that and to still not change your behaviour. That means, how one stacks up in action is more important than what one professes to have realized or seen. Our life's divine purpose often pushes us into this direction by being a dispenser of divine love to all we meet. It wants us to protect, nourish and bring about the unfoldment of all people and lifeforms we meet. To be able to do that, we need to call off conflict within ourselves and love ourselves, too, because it is not possible to love others while one hates oneself.

The theme of protecting, nourishing and bringing about the blossoming of all life is brought to its logical extension in the throat chakra. While in the heart chakra the focus is on humanity alone, in the throat chakra it is extrapolated to the larger community of life, all living things including animals, plants, fungi, microbes but also to things we consider inanimate like mountains, rivers, oceans, the atmosphere, etc. For these are spirit, too. This is sometimes difficult to comprehend for members of an estranged, de-naturated consumer society but ask any traditional, indigenous person anywhere in the world, and they will confirm that this is what they see. Modern humanity has lost much in that regard, and it is only because we do not recognize plants and animals as our brothers and sisters, and mountains, rivers, forests and oceans as our mothers and fathers, that we can metre out so much pain and destruction to them and not feel their pain.

In the fourth column of the third row, you will find the subtle body (Sukshma Sharira), the location in which all described in the last paragraphs takes place. To live in a gross, physical body and then suddenly become aware through vision practice of what the Divine sees us as (encrypted in the causal body), can at first feel as if we are divided into two stratas that don't meet. It is as if we could see our highest potential, but we can't embody it in real life. It is here where it becomes important to understand the subtle body. The subtle body is the connector, the transmitter, the relay between the causal body (the locum of our divine destiny) and the physical body. If you have difficulties drawing your divine purpose down into your physical body, i.e., to embody it, it is because your subtle body is underdeveloped and blocked by obstacles. It is here where our karma is located, and it is dependent on the subtle body how much we can embody our life's divine purpose in our day-to-day physical life. That's where general yogic practice such as pranayama, yogic meditation, mantra, mudra, etc. come into their own.

The ancient Brhad Aranyaka Upanishad states about the subtle body that like a caterpillar once coming to the end of a blade of grass reaches out and draws itself across to the next blade, so the subtle body at the end of a lifetime of the gross body reaches out and draws itself across into the next gross body in the next lifetime. The subtle body is thus a store and transmitter of karma from one gross body to the next. At the same time, it is a constant recipient of new karma incurred by

CHAPTER 4

the gross body and recipient from the causal body of our divine purpose, divine potential and divine gifts. Both these influxes meet in the subtle body and play themselves out as our spiritual evolution across the sum total of our embodiments. The subtle body is, therefore, an important meeting point receiving input from both below and above. The more evolved it is, the more can we draw down divine purpose into our physical body and embody it in our daily lives. That's why most yogic techniques focus on cultivating and evolving the subtle body.

THE GROSS STATE OF THE QUALITIES (GUNAS)

We are now coming to the 4th and final row in our table representing the gross state of the qualities of nature. What is important to understand about the states of the gunas is that the chronological order is from the top down. In the unmanifest state, the gunas are resting in equilibrium beyond time. Beyond time because we cannot measure time, since there is not time unless there is change, and the qualities (gunas) being in equilibrium means there is no change. The qualities then enter the manifest state with the Big Bang. In the first moment of the Big Bang, all matter is compressed into a space the size of a pinhead. With the subtle state of the qualities there is already more differentiation, but the full manifestation and manifoldness of creation we reach only in the gross state.

Go one field to the right in the table and you find the physical sheath (Anamaya Kosha), called the food-sheath, but it is referring to the body. Although, when practising, we generally first deal with the body and thus encounter the five sheaths from the outside in (a process called involution), you need to understand that the sheaths originally appeared from the inside out (a process called evolution). The innermost, 5th sheath (Anandamaya kosha/ecstasy sheath) is eternal and uncreated. The 4th sheath, Vijnanamaya kosha, or deep-knowledge sheath, may be eternal, too, but it will at least gradually evolve. There is a crystallization process from here outwards via the mind (3rd sheath) and pranic sheath (2nd sheath), and the physical sheath (gross body, 1st sheath) appears last.

Please note that the yogic technique for the body is asana (posture). As I have shown in my previous books, in the long history of yoga, the emphasis was first on samadhi, then on meditation, later on pranayama and only rather recently (last few thousand years) on asana. The main reason we practice asana is to remove the physical layer of conditioning from this gross strata. This is a process that will also help you to conceive and embody your divine purpose because conditioning holds you in the past.

Further benefits of asana are general improvement of health and increased longevity. The inversions such as headstand and shoulder stand will help you to arrest prana in the third-eye and throat chakras respectively. This makes you independent from sensory stimulus, which creates inner freedom. As long as we are dependent on sensory stimulus, it is more difficult to fulfil one's divine purpose. Finally, asana practice helps you to sit in high-quality meditation postures such as lotus posture, etc. Meditation postures and inversions are an art in themselves which I have described in great detail in many of my previous books. Please do not attempt them unless you know exactly what you are doing. Meditation postures enable us to place the spine in exactly the right double-s curve so that we are open for divine influx. It is, of course, much easier to have a divine vision in a high-class meditation position than when sitting with a round back. Also, from that angle, vision practice and formal yogic practice are ideally undertaken side-by-side for maximum benefit.

One field further to the right in the table above, you find the gross or physical body (Sthula Sharira). While, for most of us, it is the only part we know or are aware of, it is actually the last and final part to appear. Because it is the densest, and our being crystallizes from the inside out, it takes the longest to appear. In the early days of our spiritual search, we may think of us as physical beings having spiritual experiences. We are not. We are spiritual beings having physical experiences. Do not think of your divine purpose as something disconnected from your physical strata, high above or far away. No, it's the other way around. Your divine purpose was actually here first, and your gross body only exists so that you can fulfil your divine purpose. Your subtle and physical bodies are results of your divine purpose as encrypted in your causal body. Although you may now think of your physical body as being your self, your inner bodies are much older than this outermost, peripheral strata of yours. It is simply the case that you forgot. Remember Krishna's saying in the Gita (IV.5), "You and I are ancient beings oh Arjuna and have both lived many lives. I do remember all of them, but you Arjuna, dost not". While discovering your life's true purpose, on one side, is an exciting discovery, in truth it is a rediscovery of what was there all along, a coming home.

THE THREE TYPES OF MIND - THE CONSCIOUS MIND

The terms conscious, subconscious and superconscious minds are modern terms that we find in psychology, but they are nevertheless very helpful for us to explore as they will deepen the understanding of the subject matter.

The mind is vast, and we are consciously aware of only a minute part of it. Because our mind, according to yoga, is made up of the same elementary particles (tamas - mass particle, rajas - energy particle and sattva - intelligence particle) as the rest of creation, it can know almost everything and perceive a vast number of phenomena. However, this is not necessary and even downright unhelpful for one's survival. If your mind were really completely open to everything it could perceive, you would be incapable of going about your daily life and dealing with necessities such as procuring food or earning your livelihood.

From the point of survival, important is not how much can we perceive but how much of that is useful for us right now. For that reason, our mind has various perceptual filters that filter out about 99% of what we could perceive as currently useless. Through mystical practices such as yoga or psychedelic substances, these filters can be temporarily suspended. We may then be able to perceive a much vaster bandwidth of sensations, which can result in ecstatic states or very fearful ones. When Arjuna asked Krishna to take back the celestial eye he was given (Bhagavad Gita XI.45-46), he did so because he was frightened and weighted down by suddenly seeing everything.

Schizophrenia or other mental disorders may be due to a person's perceptual filters becoming reduced or inhibited for various reasons, which will lead to behavioural changes. Our Western society has very little tolerance for behavioural changes. Sometimes, a person who simply sees more than most of us gets admitted to the mental ward because their behaviour does not conform with the very narrow standards our society unfortunately has. Indigenous societies tolerate a much wider variety of behaviour, i.e., their norms are not as rigidly defined.

CHAPTER 4

During the 1980's and 90's in India, I experienced there also a much less punitive attitude towards neurodiversity.

It is absolutely essential that we take responsibility for the contents of our conscious mind. In Yoga Sutra II.34, Patanjali says that if we become aware of thoughts in conflict with our evolved view of self, we need to counteract them by contemplating the opposite. Practically speaking, this means that if we experience hatred towards anybody, we need to transform that into love, which was also stated by Jesus.

The reason for this is that all actions begin at the level of thought. If we think hatred for long enough, our actions will become hateful and poison the world. Even if you can live with that, then consider that this hatred will also manifest in your own body as self-hatred and disease. Anything that we put out into the world will eventually come back as a karmic boomerang. Patanjali says that we usually don't notice this due to the time delay between cause and effect. But the longer the karmic boomerang will take to return, the larger its trajectory and the greater its velocity upon impact.

People are often concerned about the fact that they need to love their enemies. Jesus was absolutely correct when stipulating this, but note that he did not hold back when expelling the money changers from the temple of David, and he often severely chastised the Pharisees and scribes. Let me explain: If you critique somebody's behaviour from a position of hatred or resentment, your actions will carry a severe emotional charge that the critiqued person will sense. They will feel your upset and know that your anger is tied to your previous emotional baggage, which has nothing to do with their present actions.
In other words, they will feel that you are upset because you are processing your own emotions by projecting them outwards.

In this case, you are just using your current opponents as a projection screen for your frustrations, independent of how right or wrong they are in the present situation. In other words, part of your reactions towards them will entail a projection of your past onto the present. That's what the critiqued will pick up on, and it will make them resist your suggestions and arguments. If, on the other hand, you suggest, correct and communicate from a position of love and respect for the other, you can still be earnest and stern, but there won't be unconscious content and projection in your message. It can therefore be accepted more readily.

To give a contemporary example, environmentalists often despise corporate executives for making decisions destructive to the environment. Although those decisions may look reckless, the executives themselves are often caught up in a system that forces them to create profits for shareholders, and if they fall short, they will simply be replaced by somebody else. The decision makers often think that, given the circumstances, they are doing their best rather than being hardened evildoers. If we do project hatred towards those people, we make it less likely that they will inquire into our ideas. They are more likely to blanket-reject all of our suggestions because they come parcelled up with hatred, and who could blame them? If, however, our critiques and suggestions come atop our basic emotion of love, corporate decision makers are much more likely to have a close look at what we say.

THE SUBCONSCIOUS MIND

What is it, then, that tinges the messages we send out with things that we are not aware of? It is the subconscious mind. The vast majority of our mind is subconscious and for good reason. When learning a new skill, we start from conscious incompetency. That means we know that we don't possess a particular skill. When acquiring the skill, we move first to conscious competency, that is, in order to perform it, we have to think and be present with what we do. Typical examples would be learning to ride a bicycle or car, fly a plane, speak a new language, etc. In the beginning, you translate your first language into your second, and you can hear yourself thinking in your first language while you translate. Once the skill is perfected, we can do it without diverting conscious awareness towards it. We call it now subconscious competency, which is a much higher level of skill. You can now drive a car or speak a new language without having to think about it. It happens as if automatically. This is important for several reasons. Firstly, it means you can do it much faster, which is particularly noticeable when speaking a new language. Conscious competency means you can speak it correctly, but you need to speak slowly, which will make you sound clunky. Subconscious competency means you can speak at or close to the speed of native speakers.

Another reason why subconscious competency is important is because it frees up the conscious mind to deal with something else. Remember, for example, when you were working on something, and upon being asked a question you said, "Hang on a moment'. You do this because your conscious mind cannot deviate from the task without making a mistake. Compare that to being able to drive a car while talking to somebody and giving them your full attention. The driving is done by your subconscious mind.

You would be surprised to find out that most tasks we do all day long are performed by your subconscious mind with it needing little or no conscious attention. This frees up your conscious mind for other things. You could, for example, compute formulae related to Black-Hole-formation or inquire into the nature of reality while sleep walking through most of your daily life.

During childhood, the predominantly active part of the mind is the subconscious. We are basically in a hypnotic state that allows us to absorb everything quickly without filtering it through the conscious mind. This means that, as children, we can learn languages and many other skills much easier, but it also means that we can be effortlessly manipulated.

The subconscious mind cannot say no. This is both its grandeur and downfall. Because it cannot say no, which the conscious mind can, it can quickly soak up whatever there is to learn. During childhood, we are learning by being immersed into our social and familial setting, without critical analysis. But with that immersing and subconscious accepting also comes the unchecked acceptance of psychological malware, that is, we are downloading the hang-ups and emotional toxicity of those around us, our parents, siblings, relatives and peers.

Children cannot protect themselves against physical, verbal and sexual abuse from their primary carers because the subconscious mind can only say yes. The reason we find it hard to learn languages later on is because they are now processed through the conscious mind, which is usually critical. It does not just absorb. The subconscious mind simply absorbs everything directed at it, and this means that a child can absorb up to four separate languages spoken to it simultaneously. When the behaviour of caregivers and peers is damaging, however, the subconscious mind is helpless. It can only absorb the negativity; it cannot reject it. Because of that, we end up with an enormous amount of negative, subconscious content that we pick up from primary carers, etc. To express it in simple terms, if our parents experienced self-loathing and self-hatred and a lack of self-esteem, we would automatically pick this up together with the valuable skills simply by being exposed to them.

Around the time of entering puberty, the conscious mind switches on, and we suddenly become self-conscious. Due to that, we are initially going through an awkward phase because being self-conscious has not yet crystallized into a permanent sense-of-self. A grown-up has developed a permanent sense-of-self, which makes life much easier compared to a teenager. We have been long enough in situations where coming from a permanent sense-of-self was required.

Having a permanent sense-of-self, however, does not mean that this sense-of-self is healthy. In fact, unless our parents, peers, siblings, etc. were superhuman, we can be sure to have acquired at least some destructive and dysfunctional aspects to our identity. As adults, our partners or other people close to us may alert us to such aspects of our psyche. Other destructive aspects are so internal that only we ourselves may notice them due to self-reflection. An example here would be self-sabotage. We may have a certain skill, which we have successfully performed when being alone, but when having to perform it in front of an audience, we may lose all confidence. This may be due to the fact that, deep down, we do not really believe in ourselves or that we are deserving of success.

In a situation when we are under pressure, such as an audition, the subconscious mind may revert us to an infantile state prior to us learning the particular skill at hand by simply remembering not being good enough. Situations like these will repeat themselves over and over until the content of the subconscious mind is changed. This can take a very long time, decades even. It can also lead to the fact that somebody who is, by all means, very good at something, underperforms for most of their life without ever changing the behavioural pattern of self-sabotage. What can we do in this situation?

In this situation, we need to re-condition the subconscious mind. How is this to be done? Firstly, we need to become aware of what kind of programming is at the core of our failure. In many cases, this is lack of self-love, self-acceptance and self-esteem. This often even leads to downright self-loathing and self-hatred. I would go as far as saying that most people have experienced moments of self-loathing and self-hatred whether they are conscious of it or not and whether they allow themselves to remember it or not. In all of these cases, we need to revert the feeling and contemplate the opposite, as Patanjali says in Yoga Sutra II.33.

Practically, this means that if we recognize self-loathing or its result, self-sabotage, we would instead contemplate a resolution along the lines of, "I totally love and accept myself". It is, of course, not enough to consciously think this thought while at the same time subconsciously feeling the opposite. You will recognize this by the fact that the thought will remain a mere dry thought with no feeling, colour or sensation attached to it, or in extreme cases, you will even feel repulsed to think this new thought. In either of these cases, you need to ask yourself, "How does it feel to totally love and accept oneself? How does such a person feel and experience themselves? What does it actually mean to love and accept oneself? How can I truly embody self-love and self-acceptance?"

Through such inquiry, you come eventually to understand that you need to let the thought of self-love and self-acceptance sink down deeply to the bottom of your being until you stand in self-love and self-acceptance, until you are self-love and self-acceptance, until you fully embody it.

In order to do this, you need to close your eyes, sit still and sit in self-love. Use all exhalations to let negative judgements about yourself leave, and with each inhalation, let love penetrate every cell of your being. Sit in that state until you have completely experienced it. This does not usually happen in a single sitting, and there may be serious subconscious resistance to let that feeling take place. Don't worry about this subconscious resistance. It usually is not even personal, not about you. Most subconscious resistance is ancestral; it is ingrained in you because, in your ancestral lineage, people were used to thinking in these terms about themselves. It is time to change this now.

It might be helpful if I fill in here a personal account. In my family history, serious self-depreciation and self-loathing was handed down. Most things that I touched in my life went pear-shaped. I didn't realize at first that this was due to me believing that I didn't deserve any better. I simply didn't know any better than that. I believed that the state in which I walked around, that is, believing that I was worth nothing, was normal. Maybe it is normal, but it's certainly not natural. One day in my quest for mystical experiences, I accidentally happened to catch a glimpse at myself through the eyes of the Divine. The Divine looked at me with complete love and knew me only as created by Herself in eternal perfection. The Divine looked at me as an embodiment of Divine Love.

It took me a while to understand the implications of that. I began to ask myself, if the Divine can look at me with pure love, why can't I? My way of looking at myself as handed down by my family and ancestors definitely had a strong religious component, although neither of my parents confessed to being religious. But the underlying attitude was that we are a sinful, rotten lot, stained by original sin, probably condemned to eternal damnation and not worth a second look.

It was only after I had a glimpse of looking at myself with pure love through the eyes of the Divine that I understood the religious origin of my lack of self-esteem and self-love. I understood that my family and ancestors received their self-loathing and lack of self-belief from a misguided religious belief. It came from the belief that the Divine has an ego to judge from and the misunderstanding that the Divine could look at you with anything but pure love. The Divine is pure love, and whatever it looks at, it cannot see anything but itself. The Divine can only see from an already established premise, i.e., divinity. Therefore, everything that the Divine looks at it sees as divine and pure love.

I then asked myself if the Divine could look at me with pure love, why couldn't I do so, too? This had far-reaching consequences. In the beginning, I found the process very difficult. Whenever I proposed the above statement, my subconscious mind reacted violently by throwing up all its disgust, judgement and vitriol that it had accumulated through the ages. Whenever it did that, I simply stood in the experience of pure love and did not judge my mind. Of course, there was an invitation to judge and to feel repulsed by what my subconscious mind displayed, but this would have perpetuated the original pattern. I simply let the subconscious mind vomit up its anguish, and without judging it, I calmly let its reaction pass. It is important to do so while remaining established in the new proposition, in this case, that I am pure love.

After some time, the reactions of the subconscious mind became less violent. This was due to two reasons. Firstly, the subconscious mind didn't get a reaction to throwing up its vitriol. If I had reacted with vitriol and self-loathing to what it was showing me, I would have further emboldened the pattern, i.e., rewarded the subconscious mind for bringing up negative judgements about myself. But because there was no reward, no "my subconscious mind's depravity knows no limits", there was no incentive to continue beyond what was necessary.

Secondly, by continuing to be established in the feeling of self-love, new subconscious imprints of self-love were constantly sent into and embedded in the subconscious mind. Your subconscious mind will throw up its established beliefs about you (and, in fact, about anything) until newly entered imprints related to your new sense-of-self have reached a critical mass. At that point, the subconscious will flip its message around and now throw up your new self-image, i.e., the one based on self-love.

How long will this take? That depends on a few factors. Firstly, how long and with how much conviction have you played the previous game? For how long have you entered more imprints based on self-loathing and how intensely have you held them dear? Of course, that is not something that we can truly know, and that's why it's best to not really worry about how long it takes. Simply accept that you have been at this game for probably a very long time, many lifetimes even. For that reason, we shouldn't expect immediate results. You will not extinguish the pain, loathing and misery of the ages in a fortnight.

Secondly, the subconscious mind's acceptance of your new paradigm depends of how real and strong your new imprints are and how regularly you place them.

Let's deal with *how regularly* first. I suggest that you take time at least twice per day to experience your new way of seeing yourself. This does not have to take ages. Usually, five minutes is enough. Five minutes sitting in deep self-love will be much more powerful than half an hour of superficial contemplation. Which brings me to the second factor of change, the authenticity and depth of your contemplation.

The most important factor determining change will be how real and how authentically you can experience self-love, self-acceptance and self-esteem. One way of doing that is to integrate as many sensory components as possible, such as "How does it look, how does it sound, how does it feel", etc. Another aspect are the resolutions that you use. For example, if "I am an embodiment of Divine love" gets your hair standing, you may have to look for other ones more appropriate for you. In my case, probably related to my partially heavy-handed Catholic upbringing, I needed divine permission to be able to think in this new way. It was only when I had seen myself through the eyes of the Divine that I could own this stance myself. And that is even considering that, for parts of my life, I would have called myself an atheist. Still today, I consider myself a sceptic in that I do not believe anything unless I have tested it over and over again. However, that is not how the subconscious mind works. The subconscious mind is an amalgamation of your past and often believes something totally contrary to what the conscious mind does.

The most important aspect determining success, then, is the depth of your contemplation, the authenticity of your feeling. Unless you can really feel that you love yourself, the subconscious probably won't change much. However, there is, of course, an evolution taking place, and the new way of relating to yourself may not come suddenly but may have to be developed.

CHAPTER 4

During your contemplation of self-love, do not just go through the motions but ask yourself what you have to do, what you have to change in order to really feel it. Part of that is that you get the phrases right. The ones that I am suggesting are:

I am Divine love.
I am an embodiment of divine love.
I am pure love.
I love and accept myself.
I accept whatever thoughts and emotions come up.
Every breath I take the Divine is breathing love into every cell of my body.
I live life as divine love.
I let the Divine speak and act through me and communicate only from the divine love in my heart.
I give unconditional love to all and truly love all beings as children of the Divine.
My heart radiates divine love to all beings.

Take these ones to start with and then explore which ones work better. If you can come up with some of your own resolutions in your own language and terminology, then do so.

We need to explore now what it means to love oneself and to experience self-love. Some people have asked whether this makes you selfish? Should it even be allowed to think something like that? Is it really healthy to have a high self-esteem? Does it not make you an egotist?

From my experience, the exact opposite is the case. I have seen that people who act arrogantly, proudly, ego-inflated and self-grandiose, do so because, deep inside, they feel like small, scared children frightened because of their unimportance. The less a person believes in themselves deep inside, the louder they will be banging their drum and singing their song about their own greatness. A person who has a healthy self-esteem will not think about themselves a lot. In fact, the higher your self-esteem, the less you will be fazed about humiliation. Reacting violently to humiliation actually shows that you yourself believe the narrative that is offered to you. You react intensely to humiliation only if you yourself believe that you are worth nothing. To a person firmly established in high self-esteem derogatory, depreciating and insulting comments will be like water on a duck's back. You will simply note that they are not consistent with your sense-of-self, and that's where the story ends. You react violently and intensely only if the negative judgement sounds a chord, pushes a button, rings a bell.

Similarly, the case with self-love. Selfishness exists because we don't love ourselves. Self-love is a fire that warms your heart from the inside. If that warmth is not there, we seek gratification on the outside. A heart full of love will never say, "Because I love myself, I deserve to have this or that". It will never say, "As a proof of my self-love, today I will afford myself this or that, or I will treat, pamper, and spoil myself". It will never say, "Because I love myself, I am better or deserve more than others".

Spoiling, treating, pampering ourselves, affording ourselves that bit extra becomes necessary if no self-love is there. It becomes a replacement for self-love. If you truly love yourself, nothing else is needed because you have everything already. True self-love needs no external stimulus, and no external stimulus can make us truly feel loved. External stimulus is used to cover a lack of self-love. And that includes the need to be loved by others. We are hungry to be loved, accepted, appreciated by others to the extent that we do not love ourselves. Think about it for a moment, to what extent would you fall in love with somebody else who does not love themselves? Possibly to the extent to which you do not love yourself? Additionally, the extent to which a person does not love themselves marks the degree to which they can be manipulated from the outside. If you truly love yourself, you do not seek the approval of others. If approval comes, you welcome it, but if it doesn't come, you welcome that, too. You are not dependent on it.

Selfishness and greed, then, are caused by lack of self-love and low self-esteem. I hold back my gifts and have a controlling personality ultimately because I am afraid that I could end up with less or even nothing. This perception of shortage and lack of supply on the outside is due to an emptiness, a lacking on the inside. Consider, for example, the economy of many indigenous tribes. On the occasion of spiritual festivities, each member is making gifts to many other members of the tribe. If at the end of the festival, you end up with nothing; because you have given everything away, you have the highest status in the tribe because you are a giver. When the next festival comes around, everybody will try to outdo you by showering you in gifts. Tribal people can do that because each of them has a personal relationship to spirit. Spirit has informed them of what their divine purpose is, and it certainly is not hoarding and keeping essential goods locked away from being accessed by others. Traditional indigenous people feel an inner fullness and connectedness that is very different from the separation and estrangement that moderners feel. Modern people feel disconnected from the world around them. They believe in the discreet self that feels frightened and must protect itself by hoarding limited resources, lest we run out. Imagine for a moment what the indigenous method of circulating goods would do to the economy of a tribe (measured in velocity of circulation) and also to the fabric of relationships. The indigenous system creates a close-knit community whereas the modern, western, industrial method creates loneliness and separation.

RESOLUTIONS SUITABLE FOR RECONDITIONING THE SUBCONSCIOUS MIND

Theoretically, you can project into your subconscious mind anything you like. However, progress in your spiritual evolution depends on the quality of the material that you project into your subconscious mind and not just what we can externally measure as success. Let's look, for example, at the case of Adolf Hitler. Hitler had projected racial hatred into his subconscious. He was very serious about it and believed that he had an important role to play in cleansing the world and civilization, which without him would come to no good. During the mid-1930's, it didn't take him long to sell over 30 million copies of his book Mein Kampf. During his rallies, he was often adored by over a million people. At the eve of World War II, you would have been forgiven to call him the most successful person of the decade. But his success quickly became unravelled as the toxicity of his agenda bore fruit.

What we need to learn from that is to not measure ourselves in terms of ambition, power and success, etc. There are lots of self-help books which suggest to visualize your future in terms of ambition, power, success, influence and wealth. In terms of the material suggested in this book, we would ask, "Who do you want to succeed over? Whom do you want to obtain power over?" Whenever there is comparison in our goals, we must realize they are tainted by ego, fear and belief in lack. I want to have power over something or somebody because I want to pre-empt their attack, that is, I want to conquer fear by giving myself more power. A recipe for conflict. I am ambitious because, deep down, I believe in my own insignificance and worthlessness. A recipe for disaster.

Another mistake self-help books often make is to suggest you visualize the type of wealth and goods you want for yourself. Some of these books even quote certain sayings of the Bible to further their point. But they do not understand Jesus's, "Seek ye first the Kingdom of God and everything else will be added on". The "everything else" is your reward, your material wealth. It is what you receive. Jesus suggested to develop your giver-nature, to develop what you have to give, rather than worrying what you want to receive.

Think about it for a moment. Do you think a relationship in which you first define what you want to get rather than thinking what you have to give will work long-term? Relationships which work are the ones in which we joyously give out of a feeling of abundance and don't worry about what we get in return. Again, exactly the way indigenous tribes are organized.

You need a red light coming on whenever you think about your future and goals in terms of "having". We are not to worry about "having" but expect supply simply by finding our way of "being". That means that all of your affirmations that you project into your subconscious mind should relate to your way of being who you are. By concerning yourself only with what you give, you create a vacuum into which creation will then automatically pour all you need.

Wouldn't it be hypocritical confessing to a philosophy that we are all sharing the same consciousness but then go and visualize a million dollars or two in your bank account? The habit of visualizing riches is based on the very philosophy of separation, that is, the belief that this world is a hostile or at least indifferent cosmos that has no interest in you. By trying to manifest wealth, you are actually confessing to yourself that you are worthless. Why would you have to spend time visualizing wealth unless deep down you are worthless?

The teaching in this book says that you live, you are alive, because you are a vital aspect of God and that the Divine has created you to express itself as and through you. All of the world's inventions, all art, all science, all love, all beauty have come out of the intellect of the Divine. Reward, and that includes material reward, will come automatically as a by-product to the extent to which you embody your divine purpose. All of this will be added on if we first seek the kingdom of God. How do we do that and where do we get this information from?

THE SUPERCONSCIOUS MIND

I will now introduce a third aspect of mind, the superconscious mind. Like the subconscious mind, it is not conscious, but rather than beneath, it is above the threshold of your conscious mind. Our conscious mind represents the present, it deals with day-to-day problems. The subconscious mind represents your past, it is a crystallization of your entire past, thoughts and feelings. For you to be able to evolve, to move forward, we need to delete negative, self-depreciating, subconscious content that holds you in the past.

The superconscious mind is your future. Right from the beginning, the very inception of you as a being and all information pertaining to your evolution came from your superconscious mind. When I'm saying from the beginning, I do not mean the birth or conception of this body. I mean the very beginning of you as a being. Probably, this was when you started your journey as a single-cell organism billions of years ago. Right from that beginning, your potential, what you could be, was encrypted in the superconscious mind.

The superconscious mind is really the intelligence of the Divine, but your superconscious mind is where your mind overlaps with the mind of the Divine. All this information of what you could be was there right throughout your biological evolution. A new upgrade was downloaded every time when you were ready to make an evolutionary step. Principally, this would have been the junctions when going from archaeon to bacterium, later to multicell organisms, possibly fungi, plants, fish, amphibian, reptile, bird, mammal, primate and eventually humanoid.

Even as a humanoid, you would have, from time to time, received brain-software-upgrades, but the difference from what is happening now is that there was no conscious collaboration from your part, no co-creation. You were merely driven by the evolutionary force of nature which is embodying herself as life in the process of what Shri Aurobindo called the uplifting of all matter to the state of divine consciousness. The difference now is that you are conscious and aware of this process, and you can contribute to it and accelerate it.

If we would simply let our ego choose our resolutions and goals, they would obviously entail the idea of the separated, discreet self because that's what the ego does and is. The ego's job is to create a limitation of consciousness in space and time and, therefore, identification with a body. By definition, the ego then must experience itself separate from the Divine and, therefore, must be afraid. Because it is afraid, it must suggest you to be stronger, better, more advanced, more beautiful, more intelligent or even more spiritual than others. It does this in an effort to get limited resources under its control and influence. In order to do so, it must snatch them away from others. The ego tells you that you are a selfish-gene-powered flesh robot separated from its environment whose job is to outcompete other flesh-robots by bringing limited resources under its control.

The ego tells you that you need to do this to pass these limited resources on to your genetic progeny so that they flourish and everybody else's progeny dies out. It tells us that humanity is the apex of creation, and amongst humans we ourselves are the apex.

Unfortunately, this is exactly what is happening. Everybody else's progeny is dying out, and it's called the 6th mass extinction of life on Earth. Unfortunately, our extinction is at stake, too. What I have just paraphrased is the most miserable and debased philosophy that humanity has ever created. If we really go on and annihilate the biosphere, then this justification of competition and the belief that humanity is the apex of life are to blame.

But luckily, now we can do better. We know that the ego has its job and it's great at what it does. It makes us capable of identifying with a body in time and space. But this is not life's purpose. For purpose, we must go beyond ego by asking the superconscious mind. Our purpose is giving and contributing to the lives of others so that the entire web of life, the biosphere, increases its flourishing and blossoming.

It is important to realize that the ego itself is not a bad thing. Without ego, we cannot identify with a body and a limited mind. Without it, no biological and spiritual evolution of life would be possible. But the ego is not the right door to knock at when looking for a philosophy of life. The superconscious mind is. It is the superconscious mind that tells what we ourselves can contribute to the larger web of life, to the family of life-forms, to the superorganism Gaia.

In order to learn from the superconscious mind, we must bring ourselves into a receptive position. We must accept the superconscious mind, the intellect of the Divine as something that is capable of giving instructions.

If you believe that the universe is a dumb, entropic machine heading for heat death, the planet a dead rock, and you the result of random mutations, natural selection and bioelectrical and biochemical occurrences in your brain, then you are headed for extinction. And this is so because this philosophy prevents you from receiving instructions from the only considerable source of intelligence in the Cosmos, the intelligence of the Divine.

In this regard, the indigenous people were and, to some extent, are still far ahead of we modern, western, industrial people. Indigenous people understood that everything, every plant, animal, human, rock, river, the wind, fire, lightning, thunder, the oceans are manifestations of divine intelligence and capable of giving instruction if only we listen.

ALIGNMENT OF ALL THREE MINDS

Ultimately, what we are looking for is the alignment of all stages of mind. When we are setting out on our journey, the content of the conscious mind is almost entirely determined by the programming of the subconscious mind. We could say the subconscious mind is leading the conscious mind. At the same time, the conscious mind is disconnected from the superconscious mind, i.e., it cannot receive instruction from it.

At some point now, our conscious mind wakes up to itself, it realizes that it is conscious. But that is not the end of our evolution, it really is only the beginning. The conscious mind then realizes that the subconscious mind contains vast amounts of programming that is not congruent with the new aims of the conscious mind. The conscious mind now starts to recondition the subconscious mind by thinking into it, over and over again, new programming that is consistent with the new direction in which the conscious mind wants to go. Gradually, we can say that the subconscious and the conscious mind are brought in alignment, that is, the subconscious mind has in its majority accepted and supports the programming that the conscious mind chooses.

The conscious mind's chosen programming, however, is not collected willy-nilly just because it sounds nice or amazing. It is not as if the conscious mind is going through the aisles of a supermarket and picking out, amongst many displayed destinies, the one that appears to tickle the conscious mind's fancy. The conscious mind chooses its new programming based on bringing itself into alignment with the superconscious mind. The first step in achieving this is to notice the presence of the superconscious mind. Yogic meditation and yogic pranayama can go a long way here. Near-death experiences or recovering from a deadly disease are other instances in which we become aware. Sometimes, it can be the death of a loved one, a terminal disease or a crisis brought on by a relationship breakdown. Often, it takes a deep crisis for us to revaluate our lives and to look for more.

CHAPTER 4

In the next step, then, the conscious mind begins to download its destiny from the superconscious mind. The method to do so is vision practice. The three types of mind are now coming into alignment. The term alignment here is, of course, metaphorical. Because the intellect of the Divine is everywhere, you need not bring yourself into a special location to listen to it. Having said that, there seem to be locations where it is easier. This is very much confirmed in many ancient religions, such as Shinto (Japanese state religion), Daoism, and Hinduism, but also in the Bible we find references to it.

Alignment, rather, is a state of mind. It is important is to profess to it, that is, to verbally state, that one is now in alignment with the mind of the Divine. It is important that the conscious mind does so with complete congruence and without doubt. This is a state that can easily be achieved by somebody who practices yogic pranayama and meditation. If the conscious mind states, "I am now open to influx of the superconscious mind", or "What do You want to become as me?" the transmission of divine intelligence will now start. If it does not start, the problem is not to be sought in the superconscious mind, the intellect of God. Remember that divine intelligence cannot withhold because it is pure giving-ness, unlimited potential, and it does not have an ego.

Yes, I know, most of us, even if atheistic sceptics, still think of God as the white, bearded male sitting up on a mountain scowling down on us, saying, "Well, if you work a little bit harder, you may become worthy of my communication." However, that's not God, it's an extrapolated human psyche. That's how patriarchs and tribal chieftains acted 6-8 thousand years ago when religion was created. We can now evolve from outdated, tribal forms of religion. We now know that the Divine has no ego and is pure love, giving-ness and intelligence. We now know that the message of the Divine was clear even before time started, is clear throughout all ages, and will still be clear after time has ended. And because there is nothing but the Divine, the message cannot but be heard everywhere and in all places.

So, where is the problem if the message is still not coming through? Now, this is really important to understand. If you still cannot hear the Divine speak to you although you clearly have given with your conscious mind the command that you are ready to hear, then the problem is still in your subconscious mind.

I know, people will say, "Not the subconscious mind again", but the subconscious mind is always the weakest link in the equation. I believe that one's conscious mind can be polished for this work in relatively short time, that is, two years give or take. However, the subconscious mind can take much longer. And to be realistic, the work on the subconscious mind never really stops; that's why one has to go daily through one's cultivations and resolutions even if one believes one has already embodied them.

A case in point is dreaming. There are different types of dreams. Some of them are relating to the future and are giving us knowledge pertaining to decisions we have to make. But many dreams are simply chopped up, regurgitated subconscious content that we go through because we couldn't come to terms with and compute it in daytime. If you have at least sometimes disturbing or annoying dreams, then there is still subconscious work to be done. We could go as far as saying that as long as there is a body, there is probably still subconscious work to be done. In order to maintain alignment of superconscious,

conscious and subconscious mind, we need to daily practice a cleansing regime of the subconscious mind.

DAILY CLEANSING REGIME OF THE SUBCONSCIOUS MIND.

The most important aspect of the daily cleansing regime of your subconscious mind is to understand its importance. The above paragraph did show that any blockage or difficulty in accessing the superconscious mind is based on your belief that you are incapable of doing so. There is nothing else to intercept your conscious and superconscious mind. If your subconscious mind is compliant and coherent with the approach chosen by the conscious mind, then download from the superconscious mind will start automatically. This state will take some time to develop, and the reason is that our modern Western-Scientific culture is hostile towards any brain-software (i.e. belief systems) that are not built on empiricism and materialist reductionism. Once you have understood that you need to replace a lot of these beliefs, you basically need to overwrite a significant amount of existing programming. This will take time.

The present author had the great fortune of being introduced to these concepts almost 40 years ago and can vouch for the fact that progress in reprogramming the subconscious mind is usually not measured in years but in decades.

Don't get me wrong, some progress is noted very quickly but usually to be interspersed with setbacks. Because of these setbacks, people often give up. Don't! Expect and know that setbacks will come and then practice your daily cleansing routine with renewed vigour. Understand that it took us centuries and millennia to put our current selfish-gene-powered flesh robot paradigm into place, and it will take some time to overwrite it with programming that is based on bio-symbiosis, i.e., software that is based on all lifeforms forming a superorganism for mutual benefit.

Every day, once or twice, sit still, breathe slowly, close your eyes and take yourself through the following affirmations:

Everything that comes up is okay.

With every breath, I let go of negative judgements about myself.

With every breath, the Divine breathes love into every cell of my body.

I see God in every lifeform I meet and in everything I look at.

The Divine, through me, is touching and healing everybody I meet.

I am open to communication from the Divine.

The Divine is letting me know what It wants to embody through me.

I am now so still that I can hear the Divine expressing itself through me.

I completely surrender to the influx of divine intelligence.

I am open to the descent of the Divine and consecrate myself to It.

I am aligned with cosmic intelligence and infinite consciousness.

I receive divine revelations and express divine love.

I am in service to the Divine and all life.

I see divine order and perfection everywhere.

CHAPTER 4

I understand that it is the intelligence of the Divine that is manifesting Itself as my life.

I understand that my thoughts are thought by divine intelligence.

You can use as many of those resolutions as you like or focus on just one or two. Make sure that you contemplate and cultivate all of them at least a few times. Take your time to really feel them and become them. As you become ready, add to or replace these resolutions with ones phrased in your own language and terminology. Your personal ones may be more effective.

Chapter 5
IMPLEMENTING YOUR LIFE'S DIVINE PURPOSE

After the last chapter introduced a lot of background information to improve your understanding of the subject matter, the remaining three chapters of the book deal with consecutively deepening layers of practice. You can read ahead through this material, but it is important at some point for you to sink the ideas presented in the previous chapters systematically into your subconscious. Especially this fifth chapter will present a list of what I call "principles of consecration". These principles should not just be read and then set aside. I suggest that you write them down and regularly contemplate them so that they gradually replace possibly existing malware in your subconscious. When creating a list, my choice of words is not definitive and authoritative. You may be able to find better words in your own language.

HOW DO I HAVE TO CHANGE MY SENSE OF SELF TO EMBODY THE VISION?

So far, we have mainly dealt with various ways of making yourself open and receptive to a vision, outlining how the Divine wants to embody Itself as you. We now need to turn towards what you need to become, who you are to become, to embody this vision. In your meditations, you need to ask yourself in what way do you have to change to be able to embody your vision.

While closely related, the actual vision and how the vehicle has to change to embody the vision are different. I will give you a couple of examples. Before I gave in to my life's divine purpose, I hated flying. I was considering myself as a serious yogi and yoga researcher, but for a long time, I gave airports and aeroplanes a wide berth. I believed that if people wanted to learn from me, they needed to fly themselves to come to me. My own comfort stood in the foreground. Once the vision of my divine purpose fully got hold of me, I realized that I would have to be ready to go way out of my comfort zone and carry my teaching to whoever wanted to receive it (within reasonable means). Aeroplanes always had made me deeply uncomfortable, partly because of the fact that I am a recluse and needed to suddenly mix with a lot of people, but also, I do enjoy a certain amount of control over my movements. When you travel a lot, you have to surrender and trust that a lot of other people are doing a decent job in guaranteeing your safety. I had to learn to talk myself into the idea that I am at home in airport and aeroplanes. Using some of the methods described in this book and understanding that more was at stake than my own comfort enabled me to do that. Needless to say, that part of this understanding entailed the fact that it would produce a whole lot less greenhouse emissions if I flew to my students than having large groups of them constantly fly around the world to see me.

I had a similar problem with speaking daily before differing audiences. The problem wasn't so much with speaking and teaching as such, but I was used to the same students staying with me for a long time. To be able to teach before quickly changing audiences requires a different skill level in creating rapport. It is not something that I felt comfortable with doing. Again, understanding that I needed to change to fulfil my vision and that I needed to be open to receiving a new skill set that I thought was beyond my capabilities enabled me to do so. It was also necessary for me to accept that I had to forsake a big part of my treasured recluse-level-introvert personality if I was taking on the challenge to fulfil my life's divine purpose.

The key in those examples is that you need to be open to change your definition of who you are, that is, you need to expand your sense-of-self. Think of your sense-of-self functioning like a radio station on a radio. Thoughts are not created inside of your brain. Your brain is simply a receiver. Your sense-of-self (i.e., who you believe you are) will determine what thoughts, beliefs and also skill sets you will be capable of receiving. The station to which our inner radio is tuned is largely determined by how our parents, siblings, teachers and peers have programmed us. It is not something that we ourselves have done. At this point, therefore, your sense-of-self is determined by your past and your subconscious mind, meaning we could say that humans walk around like (usually badly) programmed robots. This is exactly the view that mystics like G.I. Gurdjieff had.

It is time now to let your sense-of-self be determined by your superconscious mind rather than your subconscious mind. This will enable you to download the skill sets to fulfil your vision. Include now daily into your cultivation of thought patterns aligned with the Divine the following resolution (sankalpa):

How does my sense-of-self have to change for me to be able to download the skills to fulfil my vision?

Note that even after you have downloaded a new skill blueprint, the honing of a skill through practice may be required. This is not disputed here. But if you prevent yourself from downloading the skillset in the first place because you believe it is beyond your capabilities, you will never get to practice it. We will now look into a series of principles which, when understood and integrated, will enable you to progress more deeply with the subject matter. Here they are:

ANY SET OF BELIEFS CONSISTENTLY HELD WILL PRODUCE CORRELATED OUTCOMES.

As previously discussed, whichever set of beliefs you are choosing will produce outcomes that correspond to them. A set of beliefs built on competitiveness and vindictiveness will produce its correlated outcomes as will a noble set of beliefs that places yourself in the service of all life. Most of us take a very long time to realize that we are free to choose any belief system we like. Our initial belief system we are, in some ways, born into (to that regard, that we are programmed by those around us), but all of us will change it to some extent. The important thing to realize is that you can choose to modify beliefs as much as you want. The only consideration should be ethics and what behaviours a new set of beliefs will create. A set of beliefs cannot be proven or disproven either way. For example, you cannot prove or disprove if the world is ugly or beautiful or if people are good or evil. It depends on your perspective, which is another way of saying it depends on your belief system. But your set of beliefs will create the world in which you live in that your brain will always highlight the data that corroborates your existing beliefs, and it will supress the data that is conflicting with your existing beliefs.

Why is that so? For the purpose of survival, our minds are equipped with perceptual filters that filter out most data apart from the one that supports our existing reality tunnel. We have a tunnel view of reality because to (permanently) see the full reality would make us dysfunctional (however, it can be helpful to get occasional glimpses of the totality of reality to increase your horizons). Our perceptual filters let us see just enough so that we can function and survive. For this purpose, the mind will highlight all data that supports already existing beliefs. This function exists so that you do not have to invent the wheel every single day. You wake up, you know who you believe yourself to be, and you can start your day right away without having to make a 10-hour inquiry into the nature of reality before you can brush your teeth (which, in itself, could be fun, but we leave that to another day).

If you, for example, chose to believe that the world is ugly and people are evil, your mind will simply highlight all data that supports these beliefs, and they will become further entrenched. This means that your mind will cherry-pick all data that supports the belief that the world is indeed ugly and people truly are evil. The outcome will be that you are in a very unfortunate and painful state. Our principle, "Any set of beliefs consistently held will produce correlated outcomes", says that we should not choose sets of beliefs according to their level of truth (which is a question of perspective and previously established premises) but according to their outcomes. We are attached to our belief systems because we consider them true. But their truth consists only in the fact that we first implemented them and then cherry-picked data to support them. Choose another set of beliefs, and your brain will cherry-pick a different set of data to support the new belief system.

If the outcome of your belief system is to make you miserable then choose a different one. Once you do have a workable set of beliefs, you need to now consistently maintain it. If you change your set of beliefs every few days (it is possible to even change them every few hours), then the outcomes will be so mixed that they cancel each other out. Consistently maintaining your beliefs means that you do write down a set of beliefs consistent with your vision and contemplate and cultivate them once or twice per day. Once you have internalized them you may do this less frequently. But you need to check what sort of data your mind cherry-picks. Let this be the test for how deeply you have internalized your chosen beliefs.

Before you install a new system of beliefs, check that they are in alignment with divine intelligence. This will be discussed in much more detail, so here is only a quick check list. Beliefs should be based on:

- Bio-symbiosis, the harmonic cooperation of life forms for mutual benefit
- Non-competitiveness, non-comparison and non-ambitiousness
- Respecting of the sacredness of all life forms, natural and geological formations
- Bringing about the flourishing and blossoming of all life
- Supporting the spiritual development and evolution of all beings
- Being instead of having
- Respect for indigenous people and cultures, minorities and all those we consider "others"

THE DIVINE IS THINKING MY THOUGHTS AND IS MANIFESTING THEM AS MY LIFE, BUT I CAN CHOOSE WHAT TO THINK.

This is an important principle to understand. It is based on Krishna's "All actions are performed by my divine creative force (prakrti). Only fools believe to perform them themselves".

CHAPTER 5

You are aware of the fact that your heart beats by itself, your breath moves by itself, your digestive systems digests your food and turns it into locomotion, speech, thought, etc. without your conscious involvement. If you cut your skin or break a bone, they heal by themselves. Your immune system defends your body without your doing, and your genes are there ready to function without you having knowledge of DNA. This all seems to be obvious, yet somehow, we have talked ourselves into the idea that we are the active faculty, the doer, the agent in our life. Even the driver behind your thoughts is not you. Have you noticed that it's almost impossible to turn your thoughts off, to stop them? How so, if you are doing the thinking? You are not, the Divine is the motor behind your thoughts.

But most importantly, how is it that if you focus on something really intensely, it is more likely to take place? For example, you happen to think about somebody; the next moment, the phone rings, and there they are. Amongst hundreds of people, you look at somebody in the departure hall of the airport reading a book. Then, they lift their eyes and, without looking around, they look you straight into the eye although you maybe 50 meters away and there are hundreds of people around. You walk on the street and feel that sensation as if you are being stared at from behind. You turn around, and there is that pair of eyes.

It is obvious that our thoughts do have an influence on the world around us, although most of us do not think consciously and concentratedly enough so that this influence would be consistent. But it is not we who are manifesting this influence. Our mind is a small part of a collective, cosmic mind, the mind of the Divine. It is the same mind that the Divine uses to think the sum total of all universes and life into existence. It is this mind that, via the divine creative force, crystallizes into matter.

None of that is done by us. It is the Divine that does everything, and there is only one mind.

What we can do, though, is to choose what to think. Of course, initially, we seem to be like an unconsciously programmed robot, but as we start to wake up, we notice more and more that we can change our thoughts and are free to think pretty much anything we want. But with that comes great responsibility. Our thoughts should not be chosen haphazardly and willy-willy. Beware what you wish for, as the old adage goes. Because whatever we chose to think, the Divine will manifest as our life. Think any thought consistently and long enough, and it will turn into reality. Therefore, be mindful of what you think.

YOU DON'T NEED TO KNOW HOW YOUR VISION IS GOING TO BECOME MANIFEST.

When creating their new sense-of-self and new reality, people often get stuck thinking about how they can get there. You don't need to understand how to get there. There is a power greater than you that moves and does everything. We don't know at all how this power is doing what it is doing, nor will we ever, and neither do we need to know. What we need to do is to visualize ourselves in real time in the state which our vision outlines. Through this mental attitude, we create an openness to receive. But it is not we who are doing the creating, we are only receiving. It is important to look away from the how towards the state we want to reach. By visualizing ourselves in present time in this state, we become open to receiving.

CHAPTER 5

I TOTALLY ACCEPT THAT I DETERMINE MY LIFE THROUGH MY THOUGHTS AND THAT IT IS DIVINE POWER THAT MANIFESTS MY THOUGHTS AS MY LIFE.

Somehow, we brainwashed ourselves into this belief that our thoughts have nothing to do with how our life turns out. In fact, everything that we do or that does happen to us starts on the thought level. We cannot change reality and create the reality that we choose unless we accept that our life is indeed determined by our thoughts. And there is no point in looking back and wailing how much damage we already have done to our lives. It is important to understand that, with our thoughts today, we will determine the life we will live tomorrow. This is also the meaning of the term *kriyamana karma*, karma we are creating now that will manifest in the future. All *kriyamana karma* (in fact, any karma whatsoever) starts on the thought level. We are first thinking ourselves into doing something before we take action.

Again, it is important to realize that this ability to turn thoughts into reality is not related to our brain and not related to our power. There is a cosmic superintelligence, which we could call the operating system of the universe. This software is not localized but runs decentralized on all brains, minds and actually on all matter, including black holes, galaxies, etc. We could say that this software uses the sum total of all matter and all beings as its hardware. I know it sounds crazy, but that's the truth. Both hardware and software together are what we commonly call God. You do not have to turn thoughts into reality, but the Divine does.

Understanding this awakens us to the necessity of mental and emotional cleanliness (shaucha), the first yogic observance (niyama). Cleanliness, in this context, means to abstain from toxic thoughts, emotions and speech. If you think about it for a moment, if we are engaging in toxic thoughts, emotions and speech, we are actually emitting this into the collective mind. This is why the public discourse in times of fascism, xenophobia, racism, etc. turns so toxic, because we are all poisoning each other's intellects with the fear-based thoughts we think.

FREEDOM IS ATTAINED BY LIVING YOUR DIVINE PURPOSE, BY EXPRESSING ITS WILL AND EMBODYING ITS NATURE.

I often get asked whether I thought there was free will, and then, often, facts from neurology are quoted to claim that we don't. To begin with, I think the question is wrongly worded. It should be whether we have choice or not, and the answer is obviously yes, we do, but it is subject to how much our conditioning will allow. Will is a completely different problem. I believe in our current state we do not have will but only choice. There is only one will, and that is the will of the Divine. And that is the will for life, for free expression of all lifeforms and the will to live in harmony with all species and bring about the blossoming of more life, importantly, including non-human life because it is mainly non-human life that supports us and makes sure that *we* are blossoming and can continue to live here.

In this current context, another question often asked is, "How can God allow there to be so much misery?" The misery is entirely of our own making, it is human-created. If we end up making ourselves extinct, and there is about a 50% chance that we might, then it has nothing to do with God, it is our own great creation. And one of the reasons why that is possible is because we do have choice.

In the Bible, it is said that the human being is created in the image and likeness of the Divine. I have already explained that we have misunderstood that and created a Divine in the image and likeness of ourselves. A humanlike, egotistical god that becomes jealous if we believe in somebody else and then punishes us with plagues, locusts and floods. Then it gets even more bizarre. The giant, bearded, white male in the clouds has second thoughts and sends us his only begotten, beloved son, in whom he is well pleased. We murder the son, get cleansed by his blood, and the giant white, bearded male forgives us, and everything is fine again as long as we do not again cease believing in him. Is there anybody else out there to whom the story doesn't make sense or am I alone?

Why has this so-called god only one begotten and beloved son? Who are the rest of us then? Why are our mothers considered sullied because they begot us with our fathers naturally? Is that not insulting to our mothers? How can somebody be cleansed by the blood of the victim they murder? Why does somebody forgive only after we have murdered their only beloved son? Why not before?

I could keep piling up the questions, but let's look into what it actually means to be created in the image and likeness of the Divine. The main quality of the Divine is that It is unlimited in space, time and potential; It is free. Because we are made in the image and likeness of the Divine, we are created free, too. If we let somebody be free, it means we have to let them make choices of their own even if we consider them wrong. Unless you let somebody make choices independent of your own views, and that includes choices that you consider poor, they cannot learn. That is our drama, the drama of humanity. We are free to make our own choices, but we also have to live with the consequences of our poor choices. But once we have made poor choices, there is no point in accusing the Divine to have let it come to that. We make the wrong choices, and we have to deal with the consequences. There is no point, after centuries of us ignoring divine law (such as that homeostasis, the fluctuation of the bio-parameters within a narrow band, is maintained by biodiversity, which itself is a function of bio-symbiosis), to now try to dump the results of our flawed actions on God.

The whole situation reminds me of having teenagers. As your children grow up, you have to give them more and more freedom. The only way to empower them is to gradually step back, watch them make wrong choices, hit the canvas (or possibly harder surfaces), and if necessary, help them to get back on their feet. It is through the making of wrong choices and the having to get yourself off the canvas that empowerment takes place. There is no point in trying to overprotect others because we cannot truly learn other than through having made wrong choices ourselves. There is no faster learning than having to realize that one's own choice was flawed, one's own evaluation of a situation having led to a disastrous outcome. The humiliation alone of having to live with flawed choices is well worth making the experience. Making bad choices and having to live with the consequences hones one's capacity to make better choices. There is nothing that makes one mature faster than having the freedom to decide from an almost unlimited variety of choices how to go about one's life. How else are we going to grow up and live successfully? By listening to the advice of others? In most cases, this advice is wrong anyway or at least based on the needs of a completely different person.

Choice we do have, and we have it because the Divine is not a heavenly dictator that created us like little robots having to adore It like a narcissistic autocrat. However, we have to go even further in stating that the Divine does not even know about our misery. The Divine is absolute beauty, love, freedom and intelligence. Everything that the Divine thinks comes automatically to pass, i.e., passes into reality, because apart from the Divine, there is no reality. There is nothing to oppose or limit it.

The Divine cannot perceive anything not in alignment with its own nature, which means the Divine can only reason deductively. Deductive reasoning means to think from an already established premise. That is, the Divine can perceive the world and the beings only in line with its own perfect love, beauty, freedom and intelligence. Any misery that we can create for us, due to the fact that we have choice, cannot be perceived by the Divine. If the Divine could perceive our wrong choices and their results, it would mean that the conditions created by our choices would automatically become real and part of the true world. They cannot and do not because they are outside of the perception of the Divine. Our many miseries will always be an artificial creation not enshrined in natural law.

Secondly, because the Divine can only ever see us in the eternal perfection in which it created us, It will always welcome us back into Its embrace, whatever we have done. That is the message of the parable of the prodigal son. The son believed to have squandered his inheritance, but he never did because it was not within his exertion to do so. But the father embraced the son as soon as he saw him because, in the view of the father, the unity, the original covenant, had never been broken. The very fact that the Divine can reason only deductively is what guarantees our return to Divine Love and to spiritual liberation and freedom.

Spiritual liberation means to become free from the tyranny of our own mind, conditioning and enculturation. We become free by uniting with the divine presence felt in our hearts. It is then that we can align with divine will. Divine will is the flourishing of all life and its co-existence in bio-symbiosis. By embodying this will, by becoming again the guardians of all life on this planet, we become free from the darkness and destructiveness within us.

THE DIVINE CANNOT BY ITSELF INITIATE A COURSE OF ACTION ON THE LEVEL OF THE INDIVIDUAL.

This means that the Divine cannot impersonate as an avatar, come down to Earth and change history. The idea according to which the Divine can embody as an individual that is entirely godly is a theological error that has caused huge damage. Instead of us taking our responsibility into our own hands, for ages, we have believed in or waited for avatars and messiahs who never came and never will come. The Divine cannot turn Itself into an individual because the Divine does not have an ego to limit Itself in time and space. It cannot become a human body because Its body is already the sum total of all matter and all beings. It is all bodies. Whatever the Divine is to do here on this plane, It can only do through us. God cannot turn Itself into a human but can act on our level by individuating through us. If we want our society and our actions to become more divine, we have to stop waiting for God to do so. The Divine is doing

CHAPTER 5

Its part and has always done so. It is up to us to download the Divine into us and embody Its will now. There has never been a better time to do this, and if we don't do it now, it probably is up to another species that will rise from the dust of the 6th mass extinction, after it has settled.

What the Divine does for us, It must do through us. It can act through us only to the extent to which we realize It. It is an illusion to believe that it is the duty of the Divine to change our lives. The Divine is doing all It can, but it is we who fall short. In order for the Divine to fully come through us into this reality, we must realize that the Divine has the capacity to inform us, to teach us. The extent to which the Divine can work through us is determined by the degree to which we realize It. This degree can, of course, be increased through yogic pranayama and chakra/Kundalini meditation. For the Divine to become human, It must do so through us, and we have to provide and cultivate the conduit by consecrating ourselves to the Divine. This consecration happens first through spiritual practice of the yogic limbs and later on by daily confessing to the Divine the intention to become Its conduit. The sincerity with which we confess this matters.

If the Divine cannot initiate a course of action on the level of the individual (i.e., It cannot decide by Itself to embody as Jesus, Krishna, etc.) what can It do then? It can initiate a course of action on the level of the cosmic! That means It projects forth knowledge and qualities, but these have to be embodied by individuals ready for that, and the choice is theirs to make. And this projecting forth is what the Divine does and has done and will do in eternity. The Divine is the force that projects forward the sum total of all universes, beings and knowledge. It cannot, however, limit Itself to a particular individual.

THE DEGREE TO WHICH WE LET THE DIVINE EXPRESS ITSELF THROUGH US, WE ARE LIVING OUR DIVINE PURPOSE (SVADHARMA).

To live one's svadharma is the ultimate experience in life. It feels as if we are pushed onwards and enlivened by an infinite intelligence rather than by our own small and feeble intellect. And it does feel so because this is truly what is taking place. The two terms, "living our svadharma" and "the Divine expressing Itself through us" are, in fact, synonymous. Our svadharma is what the Divine wants to express through us. And to experience that, to live that, is the greatest experience we can have. You can then feel how this cosmic intelligence is coming through you and expresses Itself as you. Nothing else is needed to live a great life.

For that to happen, two things are required. One is the realization of the Divine as being capable of expressing what It wants to do through us. It is capable, and It is doing Its best to express Itself through us, but It is limited due to our lack of realization and cooperation. The more we grow spiritually, the more we realize the Divine, which in turn spurs us onwards on the spiritual path. This realization is, of course, not something that comes spontaneously but is produced through spiritual practice. Divine realization is always natural, and there was a time when it was normal, which was when indigenous civilizations spanned the globe. This epoch in the Bible is metaphorically called The Garden of Eden. However, a long time has passed since then, and as Krishna says in the Gita, stanza IV.2, "This ancient yoga was lost through the lapse of time". Well, it wasn't just through the mere lapse of time but more through our ignorance and corruption, which the Puranas (a class if Indian mythological texts) call The Four Yugas (world ages) and the Bible calls, "our eating from the Tree of Knowledge of Good and Evil". It is the ten-thousand-year long process of enculturation during which humans settled down, developed agriculture and started to believe that they could own the Earth, own other human beings and become the masters of creation rather than its guardians and servants.

The second thing that needs to happen is our call to action, our will to consecrate ourselves to let the Divine come through us, to embody It. This can often take us way out of our comfort zone and is likely to go contrary to what our society today considers normal. Normal it may be, but what is today normal is not any more natural in that it acts contrary to natural and divine law. The destruction of nature, of species and of human beings may be normal, but it is not natural. If we are ready to let the Divine come through us, we will again be called upon to become guardians of the Earth alongside today's remaining indigenous people.

Important is that realization and embodiment go hand in hand. There is no point in sitting in a cloistered atmosphere while the world is burning and needs you. Divine realization and divine action are two sides of the same coin. To just realize and not enact on it means to remain in a position of one who receives but never gives back. To follow up on the call of the Divine is to fulfil its will. To simply listen to the realization as if it was a psychedelic experience is akin to consumerism, entertainment. The point is to follow up on it and embody divine will. It is for this reason that the indigenous people say, "Don't tell us about your realization. Simply by watching your actions we will see what you have understood."

HOW TO FIND YOUR LIFE'S DIVINE PURPOSE

DILIGENTLY WATCHING YOUR THOUGHT PROCESSES, YOU HAVE TO TRANSFORM CONFLICTING THOUGHTS INTO ONES THAT ARE SUPPORTIVE OF YOUR NEW SENSE-OF-I.

Success comes from accepting this process, whereas failure comes from non-diligence. This principle is based on Yoga Sutra II.34, which says, "If there is conflict due to discursive thoughts the opposite needs to be cultivated".

The first step is that you do receive a vision of how the Divine wants to embody Itself as your life. Gradually, over the years, you work on refining this vision. An essential part of this is removing erroneous egoic content from the vision including statements defining you in terms of what you have instead of what you are. Also, statements describing what you are in comparison to others such as greater, more powerful, more beautiful, etc., need to be eliminated. Another important aspect of refining the vision is through beginning to embody it. Only as you begin to embody superficial layers of the vision will deeper ones be revealed to you. This is because you cannot see more advanced aspects of the vision from the vantage point from which you begin.

During the early days of implementing your vision, probably the most important work is in the conflict of your highest potential and noblest aspiration (as embedded in your vision) and the sense-of-self still contained in your subconscious mind. Your vision may tell you something along the line of being a servant of all beings by contributing to their spiritual evolution while your subconscious mind still tells you that you live in a hostile or indifferent cosmos where others need to be controlled and their attacks pre-empted. There is bound to be a conflict between the new and the old.

The important work here is that we are diligently watching our mind, and if we find thoughts of competitiveness, self-loathing, low self-esteem and putting ourselves and others down, we need to consciously reverse these thoughts. This is an ongoing process, and there is no time limit on it. We may be initially enthusiastic in this task, but our efforts may be flagging because there is no quick success. But think how long you simply regurgitated the programming of your subconscious mind and how long it took to acquire and cement your current conditioning. For each of us, it is obvious that this process took at least as long as our current body is old. On top of that, our conditioning contains ancestral, collective and biological layers that we share with members of our family, tribe, community, caste, profession, nation, species, genus, etc. Additionally, even we as individuals have an ancient history that is veiled from the conscious mind.

Summarizing we have to accept that this transformational work of changing our mind cannot be completed on a weekend or even within a year. It is an ongoing process that will span your entire embodiment.

This process can easily be likened to the cleaning of our body by means of shower, washing, etc. It is a daily task that is not ever completed but is an ongoing process. Similarly, the process of removing emotional and mental toxins is an ongoing cleansing process that, like cleaning the body, has to be undertaken daily. There are bound to be lapses in this process and then periods where we return to it with renewed enthusiasm.

For this purpose, it is best to create a more and more detailed description of your new self-image, of who you need to become to fulfil your divine purpose. By reading this description at least once a day, it becomes obvious when you are engaging in self-depreciating thought patterns, which are violating your new sense-of-self. Self-depreciating thought patterns are also likely to self-perpetuate. If you do notice prominent ones that are recurring, it is helpful to write them down in a separate list. This list will contain everything that you need to leave behind, that you need to surrender, let go. There is no need to re-read this list daily, but it can be helpful to read it through every time you add a new pattern to the list. The purpose of this let-go list is so that every time you unconsciously repeat a destructive thought pattern that a red flag goes up or a red light goes on. You then consciously reverse the destructive thought pattern and think its opposite. For example, the classical pattern would be if you notice hatred (remember, hatred of others equates hatred of yourself as the subconscious mind cannot differentiate), to turn that hatred into love.

A note of caution: Thought reversal is a process by which we reverse self-depreciation thoughts into those that empower us to embody our divine vision. It can be misunderstood to be applied to anything negative if, when acknowledged, would take us outside of our comfort zones. For example, it is obvious that neo-colonialism, white supremacism, sexism, racism, inequality and destruction of the biosphere are ongoing problems in today's world. Tackling these problems and finding solutions start with admitting that we have these problems. Thought-reversal is sometimes used to deny the existence of these uncomfortable truths, in which case it turns into spiritual by-passing.

Spiritual by-passing means that we are using our spiritual path to deny the existence of problems or to deny the importance of acknowledging them. We would say something along the lines of "I just can't go there", or "that's not me" or "always focus on the bright side", because it is too confronting for us to acknowledge those truths. But a spiritual path or discipline that enables us to silence or override our conscience is just like taking a drug to escape our common reality. That's why Karl Marx said that religion is opium for the people. It is a trap that we must not fall into.

We need to differentiate whether the thought that we are considering reversing is a damaging program thrown up by our subconscious mind, inhibiting our unfolding, or whether it is current feedback we are getting from the world in present time. For example, we should feel uncomfortable for driving fossil fuel vehicles or burning fossil fuels for any other purposes. And we should use that discomfort to push public policy and multinational corporations towards using renewables such as wind, solar and hydrogen. Until we have achieved that goal, we must live in an in-between state that includes the tension stemming from being involved and implicated in something that is not right. It is easy to find spiritual arguments that the world is perfect as it is and that everything is exactly as it should be, but at close examination, these statements out themselves as a white, middle-class fairy-tale. Tell the story of the perfect world to a colonized person living in a ghetto, a child suffering from paedophilia or to women enduring domestic violence. We would hold such positions simply because to see ourselves implicated would be unbearable. But bear it we must, and the tension must be felt so that we can harness it as a force for change.

THE DIVINE IS ABSOLUTE POWER, LOVE OVERCOMES HATRED, AND LIGHT OVERCOMES DARKNESS.

If you have read this book to this point, then you may have understood that there is a cosmic intelligence that turned Itself into matter through the power of thought. It then created an infinite amount of energy contained in the multiverse in various processes leading, for example, to light. It then animated this matter and energy and became millions of life forms in an ongoing process of evolution and life-affirmation. These life forms can now even develop a personal devotional relationship to this cosmic intelligence as It clearly loves us.

It is one thing to understand this theoretically and occasionally think this as an uplifting, lofty thought. But we must go further than that. We must ask ourselves whether our day-to-day life is reflective of the fact that the Divine is absolute power, that love overcomes fear and hatred, and that light overcomes darkness. Because if our day-to-day life does not reflect this choice of values, then these values amount to mere lip service, to theorizing. There is a saying amongst Native Americans, and it is probably reflective of indigenous culture worldwide, "Do not tell us about your realizations. We will see merely from watching your actions what you have understood." Spot on!

I may hold the belief that there is no real power outside of the Divine as a beautiful thought, but that's how far I take it. That is not enough. I have to actually apply it in day-to-day life, and that means that in my day-to-day life, I have to be a messenger of the Divine. This means that I cannot go on to live according to the Darwinist maxim of survival of the fittest and treat the biosphere as something that is our dominion and can be exploited, coerced and dominated at will. My daily life must incorporate the new maxim that everything I see and sense is part of a super-intelligence computing itself through us and the world. That means my life must be one of practising the principle that all life benefits and flourishes by living together in the state of bio-symbiosis. That is the concept that we are not cut-off, separate from each other and the environment but that one spirit expresses itself through all matter and lifeforms. This leads us to a new approach of cooperation, where problems are seen as the whole falling out of balance, rather than looking for individual culprits that must be locked up, punished and wiped out, whether they be viruses, bacteria, pests, weeds, criminals, wolves, sharks, corrupt bankers or politicians or ethnic or religious minorities.

The absolute power of the Divine is something that no individual hero, white alpha-male, strongman, superstar or leader can claim. It is only something that can be expressed through the whole community of beings including all members of the human and non-human society, including plants, animals, microbes, fungi, and geological and natural formations such as rivers, mountains and forests.

WE MUST COME INTO DAILY CONTACT WITH THE ULTIMATE SOURCE OF INSPIRATION, THE DIVINE.

A truly divine life can only be lived with daily contact to the Divine. I'm using the term the Divine here as purposely ambiguous, as incorporating both cosmic intelligence and infinite consciousness. The truth is, despite our apparent greatness and our ambiguous claim to being the crown of creation, we humans appear to not know what is right or wrong and what is the right thing to do. We can learn this only through inspiration and vision from the Divine (On a side note, please consider that all codes of civil law have originally been inspired by mystics such as the Vedic rishis, Hebrew prophets, etc. It was the mystics who first told us to not kill and steal). That is the reason why we need to make a daily effort of getting into contact with the Divine.

By the same measure, we should also be cautious of persons or systems that claim that they are the only ones in contact with the Divine. Any such person or system, in the long term, can only be destructive, as one person can only express one aspect of the Divine, not more. It is only by all of us daily practising access to the Divine that power grabbing of individuals and movements/groups can be halted. A truly free and egalitarian society is only possible if we teach everybody how to get into contact with the Divine. It used to be that way in indigenous societies. That way, power is equally shared around and no one group can control enough of it so that it can do serious damage.

KNOWING THAT THE DIVINE EXPRESSES ITSELF AS US, WE MUST DAILY, CONSCIOUSLY INVERT OUR POSITION IN COSMIC MIND, MAKING OURSELVES FREE OF SUPERSTITIONS AND COLLECTIVELY HELD BELIEFS OF SEPARATION, UNFULFILLED NEEDS, LIMITATIONS AND FEAR.

There is only one mind, the mind of the Divine. Each individual is only a centre of awareness within this ocean of cosmic mind. Although we believe to be separate, this is a kind of deception that is being maintained by identifying with the ego. The ego is nothing bad but simply a piece of software whose introduction became necessary after the Divine became embodied as an infinity of individuals with seemingly separate bodies. The program ego was written to connect some part of cosmic mind to an individual body to enable its survival. The trap our modern culture fell into (but not most of the world's indigenous cultures), was to identify with ego and, therefore, create the myth of the discrete, separate self, pitched in competition with countless other separate selves. This collectively held superstition made it necessary to introduce such concepts as social Darwinism, materialistic, reductionist empiricism and the bizarre belief that consciousness and mind are produced inside of our brains, whereas the truth is that the brain is nothing but a filter that reduces cosmic mind so that it can be downloaded for use by an individual body.

The ego then does nothing but reducing an infinite bandwidth of cosmic mind to a single radio station that we can listen to and consult to aid the survival of our body. The ego is a tool to be used for survival of the body but has no use beyond that. Especially, we should not identify with it. We must realize that we and all beings are nothing but centres of awareness within a cosmic mind that contains all beings and all multiverses. Within this mind, there is nothing discrete and separate, but everything is interconnected, entangled and without clear boundaries. The idea of a boundary came by extrapolating the skin surface of our bodies into the spiritual realm. My soul/atman is no different from your soul and the soul of the world or, as Lord Krishna said, "who see me in all beings and all beings in me, sees indeed".

With this being established, we must accept that cosmic mind is like a giant matrix into which every being is thinking. Due to that, we are all subject to outdated superstitions which we unconsciously pick up from the collective. Even if we know them to be untrue, they seem to be coming back, and for that reason we give them more credit than they deserve. Especially the 20th century was a century in which humanity held on very strongly to outdated superstitions such as the one that the human being is a skin-encased, selfish-gene-powered bio-survival machine that needs to outcompete others, which equates to reducing the human being to empirical, materialistic processes such as neuroelectric and neuro-chemical processes in the brain.

Nothing is further from the truth. However, rather than getting all despondent that we are living in an age of confusion and ignorance (in India called the Kali Yuga), we need to calmly restate the original proposition stated by mystics of all cultures and traditions down the ages. That is that there is one supreme intelligence and reality, which we may call unified field or infinite consciousness. This intelligence has crystallized itself as all matter and all beings. Each being, whether human or otherwise, is a localized expression of this cosmic intelligence. This cosmic presence flows through and enlivens all of us. If we accept the invitation of this presence and let it flow through us, we can then consciously co-create reality with It and all beings, thus leading to a state of bio-symbiosis where all beings flourish and collectively create more life. The downfall of one of us is the downfall of all of us.

Realizing that we are all connected, we must understand that the current dominant philosophy of materialistic reductionism is responsible for the destruction of 80% of the world's wildernesses, of 66% of wild mammals, 75% of insects and of the depletion of 80% of the world's fish stocks. In 2030, we are expecting to have more plastic in the oceans than biomass, almost half of all children are now experiencing some form of chronic inflammation in their bodies. The WHO expects depression to make up 25% of all health expenditure, and soon 50% of all children to be born on the autism spectrum. Combine that with rising of oceans, melting pole caps, thawing of permafrosts releasing methane (a much more dangerous chemical than CO_2), 1 million species nearing extinction, acidification of oceans, rapid erosion of topsoils, depletion of drinking water supplies and desertification of arable land, we must understand and accept that this materialistic reductionism that sees us as the crown of creation with the mandate to make the Earth our dominion, rather than equally share it will all species and organisms, is indeed destructive. It is destructive not only on a physical level but also on the level of mental health, hence, the rise of mental diseases, suicide, depression, etc.

For this reason, we must daily, consciously invert our position in cosmic mind and calmly state that all belief in separation and a discrete self is a confusion. We must state to ourselves that there is one consciousness, one intelligence, the Divine, flowing through us, all beings and all matter. All life is holy, and all sites are sacred. There is no single place on this Earth that can be desecrated as a nuclear waste dump because the whole planet is a sacred site. The Divine is computing Itself by expressing Itself as all beings and all matter in a way that collective life, the biosphere, acts like an incubator for more life via bio-symbiosis. An individual in alignment with the Divine will feel the Divine's presence on Earth as divine love and divine beauty. Being in service to that means that we constantly listen to the Divine and are open to It regarding how to bring about more balance on Earth between all lifeforms and organisms.

WITHOUT COERCING OR CONTROLLING OUR MINDS, WE ARE LIVING OUR LIFE'S DIVINE PURPOSE SIMPLY BY CALLING UPON COSMIC INTELLIGENCE TO EMBODY AS US.

Mind is eternal and infinite and cannot be controlled. Mind is the intelligence of the Divine and is thought into by all beings.

How, then, could we as individuals control mind? And what, apart from creating mental strain, would trying to control mind do? In the words of Abraham Maslow, "What one can be one must be" or as Lord Krishna said in the Gita, "All actions are performed by my divine creative force (prakrti) and only a fool believes to be the doer".

This means that we are acting counter to nature if we do not follow our divine purpose and impulse. Hence the strain, the meaninglessness, the emptiness, the purposelessness and the anxiety and depression that many of us feel as we follow the mainstream narrative of our society of competing and measuring our life's success by acquisition of material goods. Living our life's divine purpose means right the opposite. It means letting go of resistance to our calling and letting us fall into this cosmic intelligence that carries and moves everything. Once we do surrender to that calling, we need not control and coerce the mind anymore because the Divine will now speak and act through us.

There is a huge misunderstanding in literature dealing with this subject, that success is obtained by pushing or coercing the mind into a certain direction and by restraining or suppressing certain aspects of our self. Then there are suggestions that thoughts must be held in the mind. All of these are misunderstandings based on suggestions that we first choose what we want to have similarly to walking down the aisle of a shopping mall and picking out consumption objects based on our haphazard preferences. This implies that the Divine would have modelled creation based on the template of a shopping mall. What a consumerist, capitalist pipedream! It also implies that we are picking out what we want to have based on some willy-willy desires that we happen to currently entertain.

But this process is not about having and receiving. If it was, then no wonder that we would have to strain, coerce and control the mind into holding certain thoughts, such as visualizing bags of money standing in the corner. But it is not! This process is about being and giving, about embodying the aspect of the Divine, which you were created to embody. This means simply going back to the Divine masterplan from which we have strayed. We are going back to our own source, which is called our divine will. Your divine will is in alignment with the Divine and the fulfilment of your life's divine purpose.

Once we have a rough idea what this is, we need to remember that this is not something static but a process that keeps evolving as the God immanent (cosmic intelligence) is not static either but a dynamic process. Once we know the general direction of our vision, we only have to call onto the Divine to embody Itself as us, and It will do through us what It wants to become as us. The only thing we then need to do is to keep bringing the subconscious mind (by means of purification) in alignment with the superconscious mind, our divine vision. Once this is achieved, obstacles in your life will move out of the way, and success comes by itself. This is why the Nazarene said, "It is not me doing the works but the Father in me who is doing the works". He also said, "The works I have done you shall do, too, and greater works than I you shall do". How is that possible? It is because the carpenter knew that what he did was not due to his personage and personal power but that he had made himself into a conduit of divine will. And he knew this was not something exclusive to him but a technique that he could teach to others and that others could replicate.

THE RELATIONSHIP OF YOUR MIND WITH THE DIVINE CREATIVE FORCE IS IN EXACT CORRELATION TO WHAT YOUR MIND UNDERSTANDS IT TO BE.

We would all like to be able to summon an infinite power to be at our disposal. And yet this is exactly what we have. The divine creative force is executing divine will without questioning it. It will automatically bring it into effect. The divine creative force breathes us by uttering the mantra Soham 21,600 times per day (the average number of breaths per minute is 15, multiplied by 60 seconds, multiplied by 24 hours). This process takes place automatically and unconsciously without our participation. However, for us to be able to embody our highest potential, to fulfil divine will, and to live our life's divine purpose, it is necessary that we consciously understand the power of the divine creative force so that it can consciously co-create with us. This is because people like Gandhi, Einstein, Van Gogh, Mozart or Nikola Tesla became so adept at what they did. They realized that there was only one power in creation, of which everything else is an expression.

The divine creative force is the source of the sum total of all parallel universes, the number of which may be infinite. And it is the source of trillions of black holes, stars, galaxies and beings, all of which are projected forth from their seed state, are manifest for some time and are eventually reabsorbed, upon which they enter the residue state. This takes place in an eternal, ongoing process without beginning and without end.

To the degree to which we understand this unlimited power, to exactly that degree, it can unfold itself through us and become the motor through which our divine purpose is implemented and becomes reality. This means that if your understanding of creation is fractured, if you believe that it represents a senseless jumble of conflicting forces that randomly enact upon each other and accidentally have created you, then your capacity to implement your life's divine purpose will be a reflection of that understanding. That means it will be fractured and very limited.

If, however, your understanding is that there is one power that expresses itself through everything, including you, and that this power wants to embody itself as you, it will be able to do so to the degree to which your ego can step out of the way and let it do its bidding.

DIVINE GUIDANCE IT POSSIBLE ONLY TO THE EXTENT TO WHICH YOUR MIND RECOGNIZES COSMIC INTELLIGENCE OF BEING CAPABLE OF GIVING THIS GUIDANCE.

Everybody would like to be guided by a higher intelligence, even if that is not the exact wording they would give to this process. And why wouldn't we? The amount of certainty and inner peace that we could derive from such an apprenticeship is comparable to nothing else in life. The problem is, side-by-side with this wish or idea, we hold concepts in our subconscious that sabotage the very possibility of receiving such instruction. We believe that life is a purposeless accident brought about by random forces such as a lightning accidentally striking a primordial cocktail of amino acids, bringing about our DNA and life. Really? What's the likelihood of that to happen? Apart from bearded-white-guy-in-the-sky, that's about the tallest story I've ever heard. The problem is that, so far, there weren't a lot of alternatives offered to those two outlandish narratives. This fact alone should already have us thinking.

If our species is to flourish on the planet and to build a global sustainable civilization, it cannot be driven by the agenda of competition, coercion, separation and domination, an agenda that we assert against each other, men assert against women, whites against blacks, industrial people against indigenous people, neo-colonialists against the colonised and, most importantly, humanity against all non-human life on the planet.

A different agenda, the one of cooperation and bio-symbiosis of all life, must come by recognizing and realizing that cosmic intelligence expresses and computes itself through all matter and life. This means that the process of finding and implementing your life's divine purpose should take place parallel to a form of spiritual practice to foster direct contact with the Divine. That's the reason why I recommend combining the content of this book with formal yogic practice. I have, however, taught this method successfully to members of the Christian, Hindu, Sufi, Buddhist, Daoist, Shinto and Jewish faiths. It works also very well combined with shamanic/animistic practices. It does seem that people who have an existing spiritual/religious framework in place find it much easier to obtain instruction from the Divine. And this is simply for the reason that, while the Divine is always communicating with each of its children, we cannot always hear and understand the language and messages. This is, however, entirely due to us, our conditioning and not because of any lack on behalf of the Divine.

Remember that the entire indigenous spirituality is based on the premise that pretty much every single individual can/will get in contact with the Great Spirit/Great Mystery. If a single individual would fail to do so, this was seen as a danger to the entire tribe. This goes some way for us to understand how our entire Western civilization could push life on Earth to the brink of extinction. It has cut us off from the very source of life, the source of all information that makes up this cosmos.

I want to encourage you to do some form of formal practice to make contact with the Divine easier. If you have one (an existing faith), use that one, great. If you don't, try yoga based on the books that I wrote previously. There is a perception in some quarters that contact with the Divine should be automatic, easy, effortless. It may be so in the case of a traditional, aboriginal person who has never left stone age hunter/gatherer culture. But as the old Lakota medicine people told the anthropologist Richard Walker, for modern white people, it is more difficult to have visions because we are "thicker". We shouldn't be surprised. Isn't our entire way of life based on separation, alienation? Look at the artificial, de-naturated living spaces we created in modern cities. Personally, I find visions much more difficult to obtain in Faraday-cage-like, modern steel and concrete buildings, far away from nature. Accept, then, that you may have to do some form of spiritual practice to transform yourself to become a conduit or conductor for divine intelligence.

There is another aspect to this that is not easy for me to put into words. The process of yoga is somewhat complex because it is an undoing of a complex process of enculturation/conditioning that started with us exiting ourselves from the Garden of Eden, called in scripture "the eating of the Tree of Knowledge of Good and Evil" and continued right through to Noah's ark and Cain and Abel (symbolizing the war of agriculturists against nomadic herders). The same process is described in the Indian Puranas as the myth of the four yugas from Golden Age (Satya Yuga) to our current Age of Darkness (Kali Yuga). We can say, then, that yoga is a complex set of practices because it needs to undo the complex activities that separated us from nature over thousands of years. But even if we go back all the way to the so-called Garden of Eden or Golden Age, which are nothing but fancy metaphors for our past as indigenous people, we see that indigenous people, too, usually do serious work to get access to the Divine. Australian Aborigines did send their pubescent youths on walkabout, a month-long process from which some would not come back. The African shaman Patrice Malidoma Some, when describing his own initiation process, said that it was normal that each year, some in each cohort would die. It was considered unavoidable. Lakota youths had to spend three days on a hilltop without clothing, food, drink, shelter or contact. The reason why I am mentioning all of this is because there is a white, neo-colonialist attitude that you can have divine vision and realization right now without having to do or give anything in return. "I wanna have it all and I wanna have it now", do you remember that slogan?

I do think that we modern, industrial people, many of us white, do have to go back to this ancient knowledge, otherwise we'll continue to do what we are good at, which is destroying the world and nature. But when we do go back, we should acknowledge that this option is still open to us because ancient cultures like the Aborigines, the Native Americans, indigenous Africans, ancient Indians, etc., have kept the door open for us, have held space for us while we were busy destroying their civilizations. They did that for us because they knew eventually, we had to come back. They do, therefore, deserve our respect and gratitude.

Now, we clever white folks finally have realized we need to go back to ancient wisdom, so the latest clever scam we are pulling is that it's totally easy, you have to do nothing, it's just flipping a switch or two in your brain. That is again the same old story that we modern folks are supposedly smarter than ancient, traditional societies. Now we think we can just get without effort and work what those traditional people had to work for. Do you see the modern sense of entitlement in that? Do you see the neo-colonialist attitude? We have to accept the fact that it will be work and, most likely, more work than traditional, shamanic people have to put in because they never departed from living in harmony with nature. I am afraid that modern people who believe there is no work required are only switching their words but not their actions, not their consumption habits. Brothers and sisters, if we then get back to this business of divine inspiration and vision, let's hold in deep respect those who have held this space while we focussed on conquering, dominating, manipulation, coercing and destroying nature. For all that to work out, we have to give something back, put some work and energy into it. It won't just happen all by itself simply by us stating that it does.

WE KNOW THE DIVINE TO SUCH DEGREE AS WE CONSCIOUSLY PERMIT IT TO BE INCARNATED IN US.

This principle follows directly from the previous one. First, we have a somewhat hazy vision and idea about the Divine. We can glean this from epiphanies brought about by spiritual practice, fasting, meditation, prayer, isolation in nature, etc. This must be followed up by allowing the Divine to incarnate in us, a process called consecration to the Divine. At this point, obstacles will manifest, as the Divine will take us necessarily out of our comfort zone. The Divine's vision of us is vast, perfect, but our view of ourselves is dim and incapacitating. The two collide.

At this point, we need to work on our subconscious to allow more of the Divine vision to penetrate our heart and soul. Our subconscious will try to hold us back and often, for good reason. It is afraid that we get criticized, judged, ostracized, persecuted, burned at the stake, crucified, which in the past often happened.

To the degree to which we transform our subconscious, a gradual process involving practice, we can consciously permit more of the Divine to incarnate as us. It is only then that our knowledge of the Divine increases. Before that, we know nothing. Consecrating ourselves to the Divine will change our actions and possibly not in a way that makes life for us more convenient and comfortable. If we dare to allow that, we will learn more about the Divine, we will know more about It.

That's why the neo-colonialist attitude described above where people, after their first 15-minute practice, have epiphanies and consider themselves healed and transformed, does not stack up. These epiphanies may be a beginning. And they must be measured not by how good they make us feel about ourselves, but to which degree they enable us to place attitudes such as giving, serving and making a contribution to the lives of others (including non-human) at the centre of our lives.

Ultimately, we must admit that we can never fully know the Divine. How could a small organ weighing a few pounds (the brain) understand an infinite intelligence that embodied itself as the sum total of all multiverses and beings? This is why the Lakota call the Divine the Great Mystery, which we can never fully know and comprehend. Similarly, Shankaracharya says in his Brahma Sutra Commentary that the Brahman (the Divine) cannot be fully experienced.

We can, however, get glimpses and a growing understanding of the Divine, (which ultimately will still fall short). And our understanding will grow to exactly that degree to which we allow previous glimpses of It to transform ourselves, to transform our surface-self, the part of us that comes in contact with others and the environment. That means we need to allow It to change our actions, our values, ethical standards and the degree to which we hold ourselves accountable for our actions. Only then we can expect to learn and know more.

THE DEGREE OF REALIZATION OF THE DIVINE DETERMINES THE POWER OF OUR THOUGHT.

All of our actions lead to karma, whether good, bad or mixed (Yoga Sutra IV.7). But actions do not appear in a vacuum. They all start on the level of thought, the thought-stage. Before we swing into action to do something, we have thought about it often, even if only subconsciously. By repeatedly thinking about something, we do change our psyche, we adapt it so that it eventually becomes capable of acting. By going through this process over and over again, we have become who we are today.

Let's say we have now woken up to the fact that we are a more or less badly conditioned and programmed robot. We now want to break free. For this, we need to change our thoughts. This text has outlined ways of obtaining a new programming, i.e., via vision and spiritual practice. But even then, it is obvious that during the long timespan of our evolution, a lot of energy has gone into creating and establishing our present programming, our enculturation. In order to change it, we need to either spend a long time doing so or we need to concentrate our thought. With a very concentrated thought, just ten short years of practice can undo and change a lot of what eons of conditioning have put into place.

This is the reason why the bulk of yoga methods are essentially concentration exercises. Yoga says that all actions lead to results, but usually, they do so in the far future. By the time the results come around, the effort that has caused them has taken place such long time ago that we don't seem to see the connection. For this reason, we are not aware of, or forget, the power of our thoughts.

Once we have learned which thoughts to think, and how to make the mind itself concentrated rather than dispersed, the next step is to realize the degree to which the Divine is driving the power of our thoughts. If you think about it for a moment, there is an infinite intelligence, and we manage to download thought-software from It. If we could manage to change our subconscious mind so that it would align itself with our consciously chosen, divine thought patterns, what would that do to the impetus and power by which these thoughts are thought?

Ultimately, there is only one power in the cosmos, the Divine, and equally, there is truly only one intelligence. Everything lives from that, through that and in that. Because there is only one power, all of our thoughts, even our unconscious thoughts that may be in conflict with us being in service to the Divine and all life, are still essentially powered by the Divine. There is nothing else to power thoughts. This process is then called unconscious co-creation. It is limited because, although the Divine is the power behind our thoughts, our thoughts themselves are subconscious and not aligned with divine intelligence.

Imagine what would happen if the power behind our thoughts and their intelligence would be one and the same? It is then that we enter the sphere of conscious co-creation. Once we do know, through vision practice (and through some thought-vetting that I have previously described), that our thoughts are in alignment with the Divine, we need to now focus in our meditation practice on realizing the Divine. And that means realizing that the Divine, in fact, is all power there is, and that It is what is manifesting our thoughts and even thinking them. This is so because there is only one mind, the mind of the Divine, which is like an ocean, and we are only a wave within it. Once all of that is realized, the flood gates open, and an incredible amount of power can be channelled through our thoughts. That's why individuals like Jesus, Krishna or Buddha could do what they did.

A disclaimer: Please note that this mechanism will work only if your thoughts are, in fact, in alignment with the Divine. We cannot use this power to the satisfaction of our personal egotism, such as using it for manifesting riches or personal power or qualities that make us excel before others. These are thoughts alien to the Divine. It is only when our vision is in service of all life, is life-affirmative and in the spirit of making a contribution to the life of others, that Divine power will come through it.

BECAUSE THE DIVINE CREATES VIA CONTEMPLATION, WE MUST DO THE SAME.

In a passage attributed to the 1st century church father Origen, he says, "The story goes that the Lord planted two trees in the garden of Eden, the Tree of Eternal Life and the Tree of Knowledge of Good and Evil. Do you think the Lord rolled up his sleeves and grabbed a spade? No, it is meant metaphorically." Most of us who heard these passages telling of the trees as children would have automatically visualized the Father as a gardener and agriculturist. When growing up, by the time we become more critical, passages such as these then make us sceptical against religion, with good reason. The reason being that, in the footsteps of St. Augustine, the literal interpretation of the Bible became common ground, whereas the metaphorical interpretation favoured by St. Jerome was widely abandoned. If we follow the literal interpretation, we are back at visualizing the Divine as a male, white, bearded farmer and warlord, which we can easily identify as an extrapolation and projection into the sky of the back in those days en vogue alpha-male, Zeus-inspired, tribal chieftain.

It begs the question, then, if we do side with Origen and Jerome and see the statements of the Bible as largely metaphorical (with historical content interspersed), how does the Divine plant trees or create anything for that matter?

To understand this, let's firstly remind ourselves of the meaning of the sacred syllable OM as being omniscience, omnipresence and omnipotence. This means that the Divine is everywhere and in everything, and that all knowledge and power is in and comes from the Divine. Let's look at an example to see how the Divine creates, and a good example is simply the entire multiverse. All information pertaining to the multiverse is, like anything else, contained in divine intelligence. The multiverse comes into existence simply by virtue of the Divine contemplating "multiverse". Because the Divine is unlimited power and intelligence, the contemplation of multiverse is simply being implemented by the divine creative force. This divine creative force (i.e., the God immanent) is the only real power there is. For that reason, there is no obstacle that can prevent the arising of the multiverse.

CHAPTER 5

It is exactly the same mechanism that we must use when we are fulfilling our life's divine purpose. We must simply receive the vision and then regularly visualize and contemplate the vision. This contemplation will then be implemented by the God immanent, the Divine creative force. It will do so without any strain and exertion on our behalf. In fact, strain and exertion on our behalf often create an obstacle and also lets us know that we may have strayed somewhat from the vision.

Important for us is that true creating and creativity comes from bringing ourselves in alignment with divine will and then regularly contemplating what the Divine wants us to do. This contemplating will then activate the divine creative force. We are not to coerce, control or strain ourselves or our minds in any way but are to surrender to Divine power, which will do everything.

It's important here to realize that it is effortless for the Divine to contemplate an infinite number of universes into existence. There are no obstacles for the Divine on the level of the cosmos, because the Divine is the cosmic. On the level of the individual or the particular, though, the situation is different. The Divine cannot reduce Itself to the individual or particular unless introducing an ego. Because the Divine is the cosmic, the general, the universal, It cannot have an ego because ego means limiter in time and space. For that reason, whatever has ego cannot be the Divine. Because the Divine is the cosmic, limiting/reducing Itself in time and space to something particular is contrary to Its own nature. For this reason, the Divine on the level of the individual can only act, be and become Itself, through and as us.

This process is called individuating through us. In colloquial language, we could say that each of us is a miniature form of the Divine compressed in space and time via the software called ego. We must realize this, put ourselves into the service of the Divine and all life, and apply the same method that the Divine uses for creating. The method is to simply contemplate what is to be created, and the Divine creative force will enact it.

A clarification: A few paragraphs above, I used the statement, "The multiverse comes into existence simply by virtue of the Divine contemplating multiverse". This statement is, of necessity, shorthand. Hearing that statement, one could ask when does the Divine do so and what causes it to start the contemplation? Remember that the Divine is not subject to time but is infinite and eternal. Lifeforms are subject to time because our minds use time as its operating system. We could say that our mind is written on the operating system of time. The Divine is in a different situation. It can neither stop nor begin contemplating anything. Everything that exits in Its intellect is forever real and eternally projected forth. The Divine cannot stop or withhold the contemplation of anything because that would again require an ego, a limiter in space and time, from which to withhold a contemplation. In reality, everything that is in the intelligence of the Divine is eternal and infinite. It only appears to us as if things had a beginning and an end because our minds compute things by placing them on a timeline. Our minds do so because they are limited. If you would want to compute everything independent of space-time, you would have to temporarily dissociate from your body and mind and enter cosmic mind/consciousness. This is what yogis do in samadhi. It is not feasible to do this permanently while still in the body because the body requires for its survival a mind that can compute limited data within space/time.

For example, those of you who have had peak experiences/samadhis, you may remember that, at the time, you felt removed from the body and its survival needs. Only upon return, you would have felt that the body was cold, hungry or needed to change its position due to discomfort. This is indicative that during the peak experience/mystical state, identification with the localized egoic body-mind ceases, the sense-of-self expands, and we are now partaking of cosmic mind, the extent of which, as a rule of thumb, is determined by the length of the mystical experience.

TRUST AND CONFIDENCE COME FROM KNOWING THAT THE DIVINE IS PURE LOVE (I.E., IT IS LIFE-AFFIRMATIVE), THAT IT IS OMNIPOTENT (I.E., THERE IS NOTHING TO OPPOSE IT), THAT WE ARE ITS "CHILDREN" (I.E., WE ARE VITAL TO IT AS CONDUITS OF EMBODIMENT) AND THAT WE CAN CO-CREATE WITH IT BY PLACING OURSELVES INTO ITS SERVICE.

Trust and confidence are things very important in today's life but hard to obtain. There is such an enormous flood of information, the vast majority of which is irrelevant and confusing, that many people walk through life insecure and suspicious. Ultimate trust and confidence that we are capable of and living up to the task ahead comes from knowing and understanding the Divine and Its qualities. The cosmos around us is mysteriously constructed as a giant incubator of life. There are an infinite number of universes imaginable with physical parameters slightly different to ours, and in them, life would have been impossible. Again, if we look at lifeforms, their diversity, creativity and beauty is breath-taking. It is something we have come to take for granted because we happen to have developed it on this planet. However, look for example at the beauty of tropical rainforests or coral reefs or the mass migration of large mammals on the African savannah and compare this to the emptiness of the Moon or Mars or the toxic atmosphere of Venus. Life does make everything incredibly beautiful. In mystical states, watching this incredible abundance of life, we can feel the love of the Divine, expressing Itself as life, directly. The ever-increasing abundance and complexity of the biosphere is the crowning success of divine intelligence. We need to realize and feel that we are a direct creation of this divine intelligence and so are all other creatures. It is our duty and purpose to create ever more levels of harmony and abundance on this planet.

In moments when this mandate feels overwhelming, we need to place ourselves in the heart chakra and feel this pure love of the Divine for us directly. It helps to remind us of Krishna's words in the Shrimad Bhagavatam, "When the devotee realizes me I cannot but rush to the place and embrace the devotee. There is no greater thrill to me." It is for this reason that Jesus said, "A new commandment I give to you, that you love one another; as I have loved you, that you also love one another. By this all will know that you are my disciples, if you have love for one another" (John 14:34-35).

Through misguided religious education, many of us grew up with the concept that the Divine is hovering far above in the heavens, and our earthly realm is a godless one. As the sky-religion myth goes, only when we have shown ourselves to be worthy here can we ascend to a place that is actually ruled by God. The truth, however, is that there is no place where the Divine is not. Everything you see is the Divine. The entire cosmos, all matter and all beings are nothing but the crystallized body of the Divine. But humans have incredible minds, which they unfortunately can use to talk themselves into all kind of strange philosophies. The sooner we realize that there is nothing but the Divine and no power to oppose It, the faster we can heal, and the sooner we will stop hurting our biosphere, our sacred Mother Gaia.

Many of us grew up with a feeling that our life is meaningless and purposeless and that we are superfluous in this world, that it might just exist quite as well without us. This is a sad state of affairs. Every being has been thought into existence by the Divine because it constitutes a conduit, a bandwidth the Divine needs to express Itself. One of my Vaishnavite Bhakta teachers explained to me that the Divine needs every single one of us, and if the Divine did not make any efforts to reveal Itself to me, I should start to call It out and scold It. Coming from a heavy-handed Catholic upbringing, this was baffling to me at first but eventually had a profound healing effect. The worst that a devotee can bring into the fray is a lack of self-worth. Your core, the atman/consciousness/self, is of the exact same essence as the Divine. The difference is only that the crystallized body of the Divine is the totality of all universes containing an infinity of beings, whereas our body is only this five to seven-foot frame. This teaching is called beda-abeda, identity-in-difference doctrine, from the Indian acharya Ramanuja. If, then, we are in essence the same as the Divine how can we be worthless or purposeless?

The greatest glory, the greatest freedom and the greatest feeling of fulfilment a human being can obtain is by placing herself into the service of infinite consciousness (God transcendent), cosmic intelligence (God immanent) and all life (God as life), the holy trinity. It is then that all avenues of life are suddenly opening themselves up to us, and what previously seemed like struggle now takes on the form of joy.

Chapter 6
PROCESS OF IMPLEMENTING YOUR LIFE'S DIVINE PURPOSE

It will be helpful for you to regularly go back and study the principles of consecration, described in chapter 5. This will help you to find out in what way you have to change and how you have to transform. It will remind you into what you have to convert yourself, where you have to grow to embody the vision of yourself as seen by the Divine. Remember that, already in the Gita, Krishna stated that it is better to live your life's purpose (svadharma) in a mediocre fashion than to excel in somebody else's svadharma, which is foreign to your spiritual development and growth. There are powerful implications here. Your life's divine purpose is your path of spiritual development and growth. It is not something that is set once and for all, but it is a dynamic process, the very path on which you can live up to your highest potential. In this context let's look at some areas of life where that growth is likely to occur.

RELATIONSHIPS - CONFLICTS

Human beings are interconnected. The whole web of life, the biosphere, is one of interconnectedness. No being can exist in an isolated fashion. Even if you are a hermit on a mountaintop who never talks to anybody, the air you breathe is exhaled by plants, every atom of your body is welded together by consecutive supernovae (exploding stars), your DNA has been contributed to over billions of years by millions of different lifeforms, which in some form or another have become your fathers and mothers. A major part of your body and its functions are not even cells pertaining to it, but are your microbiome, a multitude of microorganisms that contribute to almost everything you do. Even a hermit is a living and walking bio-symbiotic community, if he admits it or not.

The purpose of our spiritual journey is not the ecstasy that we may experience in moments of divine revelation, although that sure is a bonus. The purpose of our spiritual journey and all that we experience is to make a contribution to the life of others (human and otherwise) and that we help others to fulfil their highest potential. And while that may sound like a burden to some, there is actually no greater joy and nothing more rewarding than that.

When we are new to this path, there may be an initial reluctance to serve others, born of our society's accepted philosophy of social Darwinism, i.e., that you do best to serve your own interest. But social Darwinism is based on a huge error and that is the belief that there is such a thing as the discrete, separate self. Because in our development, we start out on our journey as bodies, we believe the body to be our self. But as the indigenous people for 100,000 years have taught, and what has been confirmed by all religions in one way or another, as we mature and evolve our sense-of-self gradually increases. On the reptile level (in yoga called the base chakra), we are only concerned about the survival of our bodies, whatever the cost. As we develop into mammals (in yoga represented by the sacral chakra), we may be happy to sacrifice our bodies so that our spouse or progeny survive. Suddenly, our own survival is not anymore in foreground but has been superseded by a greater good, the survival of the family or greater family.

As we then mature to the primate level (represented by the power chakra), our sense-of-self increases to take in an entire social structure that today includes nation states, and our wealth and status. For thousands of years, millions of humans chose to put their lives down to defend their nationhood, or their position in society or simply their possessions. From a mere vantage point of survival, most of this is largely absurd, but because wealth, status and nationhood are part of primate consciousness, they are now suddenly worth defending and dying for. If our previous selves as reptiles and mammals could witness such behaviour, they would simply shake their heads in disbelief.

As we mature to humanoid consciousness (reflective of the heart chakra), our sense-of-self again increases to see the whole of humanity as family bound by love. Somebody under the sway of the heart chakra is incapable of seeing another person as an enemy. It was in this spirit that Jesus exhorted us to "turn the other cheek". Let's inquire here for a moment how it is possible that luminaries like Jesus, Gandhi and M.L. King happily laid their lives down for people who ultimately hated them. In the Gita, Krishna says, "I am the self in the heart of all beings". In the Bible, Jesus says, "It is not me doing the things but the Father in me doeth the things", and "Greater things than I you also will do"' and "ye all are gods, ye all are children of the most-high". Krishna and Jesus both knew that the centre of our being is the Divine. Because the Divine is indivisible, all of us carry the entirety of the Divine in our hearts. Because the Divine is everywhere the same, it is the same infinite, eternal, pure love, freedom and beauty that we all carry in our hearts. We do share the same self. There is only one self, the Divine, which we all share.

I think we all can agree up to this point, but the next step is not quite so obvious, it is all too easily overlooked because our bodies seem to occupy different places in space. However, this is only on the gross, material level, which is only the outermost level of our being. This has already been explained in chapter four, in the section on the teaching of the five layers (panchakosha doctrine).

On our deepest level, the heart (Sanskrit hrt), the consciousness, we all share the same self, the one and only self. Because of that, any concept of otherness dissolves on the level of the heart. There is no other. Everybody you meet is nothing but a slight modification of your own self, is you. I don't mean to say that they are an illusion, or an outward projection of yourself, no. All beings you meet have the same divine core you have and, in that core, are identical to you. Only on the surface, they embody a different path of computation of the Divine. Because of that, when a human being has reached the state of development of a Jesus, Gandhi or Martin Luther King, no enmity exists anymore since the sense-of-self has expanded to include the whole of humanity. At this point, one feels the downfall of any person on Earth as much as it would be one's own child or mother. We must reach this stage collectively, otherwise there will be no future for humanity. Our technological and scientific development has jumped too far ahead of our spiritual development. To look at only a single example, nuclear power would be no problem if we all realized that we all partook of a single self. Nobody could even conceive dropping such a device on human beings because, although

CHAPTER 6

there may be people on the other side of the world that we have difficulties communicating with, they would still be included in our sense-of-self. You would feel their incineration as if they were your mothers and your children. Until we have reached this common culture of spiritual realization, we must be on our guard towards science and technology because, currently, we do not have to spiritual maturity to use it, and as a result of that, science and technology are instead using us (as currently seen with artificial intelligence).

In order to deeply implement your life's divine purpose, you must understand, you must realize that there is no other. The whole of humanity partakes of the one self, the one and same atman, our consciousness. The more you contemplate this and the more you can embody this realization, the easier it will become to follow your divine calling.

It begs now the question, if we do all partake of the same self, how come some of our relationships are more fragmented, are more conflicted, than others? If you do have a negative, conflicted relationship with somebody, it is because they represent a rejected, unowned, lost aspect of your own psyche. I am not talking about the divine self here, the consciousness which we all share. It is a spiritual misunderstanding to believe that we consist of nothing but the body and the divine self. As discussed in chapter 4, there are several layers in between. If necessary, please review this important material.

All of us are on an ancient journey. As Krishna stated in the Gita, stanza IV.5, "You and I are ancient beings who have lived many lives. You, oh Arjuna, do not remember them but I remember them all". On this ancient journey, all of us have made many experiences, and some of them have traumatized us. Because of traumatization, we have rejected certain aspects of our psyche, which we find now hard to own. Our conscious mind finds it hard to admit that darkness exists within us (i.e., our subconscious), and therefore, it projects everything it experiences as conflicting on others, i.e., the mind externalizes conflicting material. We externalize conflicts that are raging deep in our subconscious and project them onto others. It is easy to point our fingers on others, who must be brought to justice, who have to be confronted and exposed and made to pay for what they did, whoever they are.

If you are going through really intense negative emotions regarding work colleagues, family members or other people close to you, people which you cannot avoid, then this is usually due to externalized and projected subconscious content. Because it is difficult for us to own conflicted and painful parts of our psyche, we are externalizing those conflicts by projecting them on suitable targets in our environment. If there are no suitable targets available, we actually go looking for them and draw them into our lives. Often, the people that we draw into our lives are there so that we can project our inner conflicts on them, which is an unconscious way of dealing with our trauma in the hope of healing it. In this case, the people we are projecting onto have little to do with the actual conflicts. They are more akin to pawns on our inner chess board on which we enact our suppressed drama.

How can you find out whether this is the case? Let's look at an example. Let's say you work under a mean, narcissistic boss with a sadistic streak (this is completely hypothetical, not that such things happen in real life). In scenario one, the actions of the boss have nothing to do with your past, they will only provoke feelings related to the present time. You would then, for example, be free to feel sorry for the boss that they are in such a terrible traumatized state, that they have to let it out on their workforce. Or you would be free to express your anger at the boss, simply leave and get another job. In this case, you would quickly let go of the anger, and if somebody asked you a week later, you could barely remember it. In scenario one, no projection takes place; hence, there is freedom and choice of reaction and the personage of the boss has no psychological significance for you.

In scenario two, the actions of the boss would trigger a lifetime of agony, and you feel that neither can you maintain your dignity, nor do you feel that you can get out of the situation by simply leaving. Here, the actions of the boss trigger you to project subconscious content related to your past onto the present situation. You feel that you become so emotional that the situation is completely out of your control. You feel that you have no choice in regards to reacting, and your freedom is impinged on by your emotional reaction.

The same is often to be found in intimate relationships. Let's say after a difficult day, my partner gets home, and she treats me in a snappy way. If I have only feelings pertaining to the present moment, I will have the choice to be extra nice to her to get her out of her predicament. Or I will be able to communicate to her what she is doing (i.e., she is projecting onto me), and this feedback may get her to change her behaviour. There is choice and emotional freedom in my actions. Compare that to a situation in which I had a primary carer (usually a parent) who has treated me abusively and manipulatively and humiliated me. If a similar situation now occurs with my current partner, I will not just feel the present, but I will project all past abuse, manipulation and humiliation onto the present; I will thus emote. The situation may result in a huge emotional outburst where I shower my partner with the agony of decades and lifetimes of humiliation and despair, and they will wonder what hit them. As this is playing out, I feel as if I have no choice to withhold that outburst and my freedom of expression is severely limited. If that happens regularly, the outlook for our relationship will be dim. In such a case, I need to ask myself which part of the sensation (the present-time feeling) is related to my partner's present behaviour and which part of it (the emoting of the past) is related to past hurts, which have little to do with my current partner.

To make matters a bit more complex, our sensations do have something to do with our partners (or other likely screens of projection) but not in the way it appears. The reason why a partner with such behavioural patterns would appear in my life is because I need them to display a certain behaviour (colloquially called "pushing my buttons") so that I can become conscious of my projection and then let go of it. In our present example, it would mean that I become conscious of the fact that I do hold a primary hurt, imprinted by a primary carer or parent, which now stops me from living my life and fulfilling my highest potential. In other words, we are entering relationships to overcome our own traumas and to emotionally and spiritually mature in the process.

Often, however, these primary hurts are much older still. In the Yoga Sutra, Patanjali states that all types of experience are due to karma, i.e., things we have done in past lives. But that does not mean that we have to just silently suffer and not change anything. It means the opposite. It means that we must understand patterns of imprint that lead to the suffering and let them go. Unless we let them go, we will simply keep repeating the pattern, causing future suffering.

How do we let go? We let go by releasing the energy and effort used to hold on. In order to understand that, hold any object in your hand (let's make that a non-breakable object). Now, hold it tight. Do you realize how holding it requires effort and energy? Now, let go of the object (drop it) and feel what changes. It is simply the release of the effort and energy used to hold on. But you may say, "But I try to let go". Okay, let's do another exercise. Take the object and try to let it go. Try for some time to let it go. Do you see what happens? Nothing, you are still holding on. Do you realize how *trying* to let go is an anathema to really letting go and how *trying* to let go is actually holding on? *Trying to let go is simply a reworded refusing to let go.* You can only *try to let go* by not releasing the energy required to holding on.

The reason why we have conflicted relationships is because they show us that there are dark spots in our psyche, areas where we have internal conflicts, which we externalize by projecting them onto others. To the degree to which we heal those internal conflicts, their external equivalents will disappear.

A clarification: this does not mean that we have to let ourselves be victimized if somebody does something wrong. To stand up to the wrong, to protect victims is our dharma, our duty, it is the right thing to do. But after the giving up of inner conflicts, we can now do so without inner, emotional charge. We can do so much more effectively. Imagine, for example, you were an environmental activist with serious emotional hang-ups meeting a hedge-fund manager, trying to convince them to stop investing in activities damaging the biosphere. If you think of the financier as "one of those fat-cat bankers who are raping, pillaging and looting our sacred mother Earth", very likely, this attitude will be subconsciously picked up by them, and they will act adversarially, in order to protect themselves. If, however, you do manage to include the financier in your sense-of-self, they will experience your presence as basically beneficial, and they will listen to your proposals more openly. This way, we will be more efficient environmentalists and social activists.

Please note, the knowledge according to which our life and relationships play out according to our subconscious hurts should never be weaponized. It is designed for us to look at our own life and understand how our own actions (often executed in the remote past) have informed who we are today. This reasoning ultimately empowers us to create the person we will be tomorrow via our thoughts and actions today, through accepting that we have created who we are today via our thoughts and actions of the past. The two go together, and one cannot be without the other. You cannot hope to be free to create your future unless you accept that you have created your present self, through your own actions performed in the past. What we should not do is to use this knowledge to analyse others as in, "They are being abused because they carry abuse in their subconscious" and by extension "They had it coming to themselves" and "Therefore, it's their own fault". That constitutes weaponization of knowledge. We cannot learn from analysing others as, ultimately, we cannot see their thoughts and do not know what got them to this point. We can use this knowledge only to analyse ourselves and then treat others with support and compassion. If in doubt, always protect the victims.

HIGHER CHAKRAS

Because I explained our spiritual and biological evolution up to this point, I will quickly sketch out the future and coming evolution as it pertains to the subject of this book. With the opening of the fifth chakra, our sense-of-self expands further to take in all human life and the entirety of the biosphere, including geological and natural formations. We will see that animals, plants, microbes, coral reefs, forests, rivers, mountains and ocean are spirit, and they are crystallizations of consciousness. It is better to say *are* rather than *have*, because to have implies possession, and you are always separate from your possession. But in this case, *are* or *be* implies an essentiality, as in being of one's own nature.

The philosophy according to which all creation is spirit is, of course, not new. It is called animism, and it is what the indigenous people have believed since time immemorial. It is something that modern humanity has lost by means of separation and estrangement. It is something that we need to regain if we want to again thrive in bio-symbiosis with all life on Earth.

The next step when expanding the self is when we commune with the God immanent, cosmic intelligence. This is the function of the third-eye chakra, and we could say that vision practice is an epiphanic activation of the third-eye chakra. Accurately, it is called third-eye because we are obtaining a vision of some sorts (even if it is non-visual), and the practice of visualizing is connected to the third-eye. Whereas on the level of the throat chakra we behold the effects of cosmic intelligence, the cosmos into which cosmic intelligence has crystallized, on the level of the third-eye chakra, you are directly communicating with this intelligence itself.

At the level of the crown chakra, our sense of self expands into infinity and eternity, we are beholding the God transcendent, the infinite consciousness. Time, space, limitation, and identification with the egoic body-mind here come to an end, and we become one with the ocean of infinite consciousness.

This stage is largely beyond words, but I have tried as much as possible to describe it via metaphor in my book *Samadhi The Great Freedom*.

An important note about the chakras is that they do not constitute a hierarchy, as the concept of hierarchy and authority is left behind after the power chakra. For creation to function, there need to be beings that fulfil each of these seven separate functions. Spiritual evolution is not a race to nirvana, but it is about becoming able to embody each of these seven functions freely coming from choice rather than programming and conditioning.

However high we are going in chakra activation, we must return to the heart because it is from here that we can make a contribution to the life of others and serve. Even an activation of the crown chakra provides valuable only to the extent that we realize that all of this evolution is not about ourselves, it is not about us having far-out spiritual experiences, it is about us becoming able to serve all life.

FORGIVENESS

We previously looked into the importance of transforming our relationships for implementing our life's divine purpose. We also looked at how to deal with conflicts and how to transform them. A big part of that is forgiveness practice. We have a tendency of going through life entertaining righteous anger (sometimes called holy anger), and holding grudges against people who have slighted us or outsmarted us is a big part of that. And we believe that we are entitled to hold those grudges and that, somehow, they enrich us and we would come up short if letting them go. We are afraid that letting go of grudges would mean we are letting others off the hook. About this, Jesus says,

CHAPTER 6

"Judge not, that ye be not judged. For with what judgment ye judge, ye shall be judged: and with what measure ye mete, it shall be measured to you again" (Matthew 7:1-2). As so often, so also here Jesus displays a profound understanding of spiritual psychology. Unfortunately, he has been mistaken to have said that there is a heavenly judge that has nothing better to do than listing and judging every single of our shortcomings on judgement day. How could that be when God has no ego from which to pronounce judgement?

Remember also that Jesus was the one who explained in the parable of the prodigal son that the Father (the Divine) did not judge the son who returned. Additionally, it was Jesus who, when faced with the adulteress, said, "Then I too, shall not judge you". No, the meaning of Matthew 7:1-2 is something entirely different. During our life, we judge ourselves and others by two different metres. We are seeing the speck in the eye of our brother but not the mote in our own. It is due to this that we can hold grudges. If only we saw clearly, we could see that we, too, need forgiveness.

The situation changes entirely, however, when we die. During death, the barrier between our two different value systems (an inner for ourselves and an outer, harsher one for others) breaks down and merges into a single value system. Suddenly, for the first time, we are not blind anymore to all the many little ways in which we ourselves have cheated and come up short. And now, we are judging ourselves by the same unforgiving meter by which we have judged others all our life. The judge does not sit in heaven, but the judge is part of our own mind, our superego, as Freud called it. And there is no escaping those merciless, prying eyes because we carry our mind wherever we go, and our mind has recorded in every minute detail we have ever thought, said or done.

There is no way escaping that judgement, because in death, it is ourselves who are the judge. The judgement we pass on ourselves is resulting in future lives, their types of experiences depending on our actions in past lives (Yoga Sutra II.12-14). The way now to improve our situation is to not exert judgement on others. Alternatively, if we have to exert judgement (as dharma may require it), then to do it compassionately according to the same set of rules by which we ourselves would like to have judgment metered out to us. If we train ourselves all life-long to not judge and instead exert compassion, then it is by this metre that during our death we ourselves will be judged (by the judge residing in our own heads). This mystical teaching of Jesus forms the basis for forgiveness practice.

Ideally, we daily ask ourselves who it is that we currently hold the strongest grudge against. We then let go all of this grudge on our exhalation, we breathe it out, and in our imagination, we tell that person, "Brother, sister, I set you free. Go in peace". This is a practice that we perform ourselves in our mind. In most instances, it is not advisable to call people with whom you have a difficult relationship to tell them you that you forgive them. What is important, however, is that you cleanse yourself from any negative sentiment you have towards anybody because this festering, negative sentiment in your subconscious will ultimately turn against you.

Another reason why we find it hard to forgive is because we believe it to be our job to hand out payback for the perceived wrongs that others have committed. But is that our job? In Romans 12:19, we find the statement, "Dear friends, don't try to get even. Let God take revenge. In the Scriptures the Lord says, 'I am the one to take revenge and pay them back.'" This passage is a rehash of Deuteronomy 32:35, that says, "'Vengeance is Mine, and retribution, in due time their foot will slip; For the day of their calamity is near, And the impending things are hastening upon them." If we take out the usual anthropomorphism that lets us see the Divine as a wrathful tribal chieftain (who in days of yore, before the separation of powers, was tribal judge, too) extrapolated into the sky, this passage simply says: an aspect of the Divine is divine law, of which the law of cause and effect is part. When looking at human behaviour, cause and effect is nothing but the law of karma. The above statement does not imply that there is a deity that personally goes after transgressors. Similar to the laws of gravitation and thermodynamics, the law of cause and effect does not need an enforcer. It automatically applies impersonally to all of us in all situations at all times. For example, if you step off the windowsill in the belief that you can walk in thin air, it is the law of gravitation that strikes you down not its hypothetical enactor. Similarly, the law of karma, law of cause and effect will enact itself independently without the need of an enforcer. That's why Jesus points out that we should not carry grudges and ill will around with us. The law of karma will catch up with all transgressors in due time whether or not we hold grudges. In the meantime, however, holding grudges damages no one but us, their entertainers.

If we carry around a deep aversion against somebody, our subconscious cannot even differentiate whether the aversion is against us or somebody else. It will apply it equally in both directions. For example, our conscious mind may say, "I hate so and so," but the subconscious mind will translate that into "I am hatred" and gradually poison you by doing so. Combine that with the fact that, at the moment of death, our mode of judging will turn around and be applied to us, then letting go of one's grudges and negative judgements is one of the healthiest decisions we ever make. It is basic mental hygiene.

Forgiveness practice as described above should be done whenever we feel that we hold negative sentiments towards anybody. That means that we daily soul-search whether we carry negativity against somebody. This is not as straightforward as it seems. It happened in my own forgiveness practice that every day when asking whether there was a grudge against anybody, that the face of a particular male appeared who, so I believed, at some point in my life had tried to deceive me. Every day, I forgave him and exhaled all negative sentiments, but again the next day, his face reappeared. I was puzzled how often I would have to repeat this, and the practice became more and more shallow, obviously because I already had forgiven him. It was months later that I realized that behind his face was hiding the face of an ex-partner, who I really did not want to forgive. My subconscious simply placed a face that held little emotional charge on top of the one that I should have worked on but resisted. If forgiveness practice appears shallow and without emotional charge, we always have to ask ourselves whether there is something hiding underneath that we do not want to look at.

A note: Forgiveness practice is a spiritual cleansing method. It has nothing to do whether or not the civil code of law should be applied or not. It does not mean that we don't stop perpetrators. If somebody has injured, abused, threatened or damaged you in any way, it is your right to enact the civil or criminal code of law. In some cases, it may not just be your right but also your duty as you may protect future victims by stopping the perpetrators. But this is not the subject of our investigation here. Whether or not you do have to put somebody behind bars is completely independent of the fact whether you forgive them or not. A point in case is the fact that sometimes family members publicly forgive the convicted murderers of their loved ones. Forgiveness practice is a method of maintaining emotional hygiene independent of a societal course of action.

A good example here is Nelson Mandela. Mandela was 28 years in jail for armed resistance (in his day called terrorism) against the white-supremacist, apartheid regime of South Africa. After president Willem De Klerk released him, Mandela understood that, although his body could walk free of jail, he would carry jail within him wherever he went unless he forgave his captors and tormentors. The focus of the act of forgiveness was not so much his captors and whether what they did was forgivable or not. The focus was on Mandela himself and his realization that in order to become truly free, he had to let go of the past. Forgiveness is really a letting go of the past so that you can move into the present and future unimpeded by what happened. In order to fulfil your highest potential and to truly become the new you, you need to be able to let go of the past, and forgiveness is nothing but letting go of our interpersonal past.

GRATITUDE

Another important quality when pursuing your life's divine purpose is gratitude. Gratitude has a mysterious power that charges your thoughts and turns them into reality. In order to fully appreciate the power of gratitude, we need to again resort to that master of spiritual psychology, the Nazarene carpenter.

In Matthew 15:36-37 we find, "Then he took the seven loaves and the fish, and when *He had given thanks*, He broke them and gave them to the disciples, and they in turn to the people. They all ate and were satisfied." Whether or not you believe if Jesus really did feed 5000 people is not the decisive fact here. But if you analyse the statement above, you will notice that whatever Jesus did was encapsulated in the phrase "He had given thanks". An even more astonishing episode we find in John 11:42 when Jesus reputedly raised Lazarus from the dead. I tend to read the Bible and other ancient texts metaphorically, so I'm not too concerned whether or not the events happened exactly as described. I am interested in understanding the metaphysical principles and applying them. After Jesus had them remove the stone, he said "Father, I *thank* You that You have heard Me." Please note that Jesus hasn't done anything yet, nor has the Father, but Jesus acts as if everything is already done and dusted. The degree of certainty here is both astonishing and crucial. In the next stanza, we then find, "I knew that you would always hear me". Here, Jesus displays unification with the Divine. Because he knows that he fulfils divine will, he knows that the Divine will always hear him. Jesus is entirely congruent. Please note, you cannot artificially produce true congruence, authenticity. Jesus can only do so because he knows he is fulfilling his life's divine purpose. You cannot use this method to further your own egoistic goals. If you try to use this method for your own advantage, whoever in your audience is switched on will notice the lack of congruency and authenticity. Only after Jesus has pronounced the first two formulae does he now utter the command, "Lazarus come forth". What is shown here is that the phrase, "come forth" was previously charged with gratitude and unification with divine purpose.

We also notice that, at the Last Supper, Jesus *thanked* God for the bread and wine (Luke 22:17,19), which took place at a time he knew that his end drew near. He demonstrates here that when our end comes, we should not complain that we already have to die but we should display gratitude for what we were able to experience. This gratitude transforms our lives and certainly our deaths. In order to die freely, we need to die in gratitude.

The important pattern in all these passages is that Jesus uses gratitude to purify himself to be a conduit for divine intent, divine will. In most of our day-to-day actions, we erroneously believe ourselves to be the source of our power. For this reason, only a small, limited amount of energy is available to us. If we realized that, alone by ourselves, we can do almost nothing but that an unlimited wellspring of divine power is available to us, everything would change. That is what Krishna means when he says in the Gita to surrender the fruits of all actions to him. In truth, they are his anyway, but he wants for us to realize this and remember it at all times.

A totally sincere gratitude, an authentic gratitude, is born of the realization that we are not the agents in our life, but life is enacted upon us by the Divine. That means that, in moments of utter gratitude, our day-to-day mind breaks through to this greater reality, and we unify with the Divine. Every breath you take is not taken by you, but you are breathed by the Divine. Your thoughts are not turned into actions by you but by the Divine. Your food is not digested and turned into tissue by you but by the Divine. Your body has not been created by you, nor has your DNA, nor your cells nor your organs, but they are all created for you by the Divine. The more we realize that nothing happens by ourselves, but all is done by the Divine and give thanks for that, the more are our actions energized by divine power. Gratitude towards the Divine turns us into a conduit for divine power. Whatever we become conscious of and give thanks for, the Divine will create, as long as it is in alignment with divine will. Divine will means life-affirmativeness and creation of life. It wills good for all lifeforms and also good for the superorganism Gaia.

ACCEPTANCE/RECEPTIVITY

During this entire process, we must ask ourselves who do we have to transform into to embody our vision(s)? Who do we have to convert ourselves into to fulfil our life's divine purpose? As we are taking first steps to embody the vision, certain qualities become apparent to us that we do not yet seem to possess. Once we have identified them (and it is a good idea to keep a journal about this process), the question is how to we go about obtaining them?

The answer is not by hard work but by acceptance. I'm not saying that there is no place ever for hard work, but what I'm saying is that clenched teeth and furrowed brows are usually in the way of downloading what is inevitably ours already. It is more efficient to have a receptive attitude and ask the Divine to supply these new qualities whenever they are needed.

We need to understand that, in truth, it is not we who are creating these new capacities, but they are available because the Divine already sees us with these qualities in eternal perfection. Remember that the Divine cannot see us in any other state as eternal perfection because the Divine is eternal perfection and cannot see in a way contrary to its own nature. If the Divine could perceive things contrary to its own nature, this entire vast cosmos would have never come into existence. This is what is meant with the statement, "A house divided against itself cannot stand" (Matthew 12:25, Luke 11:17, Mark 3:25).

What we then need is not effort but acceptance and receptivity to become who we need to be to embody the vision.

CHAPTER 6

The Indian saint Paramahamsa Ramakrishna, who had a great propensity for samadhi (yogic ecstasy), was once asked how he so effortlessly managed to get into samadhi. Ramakrishna's answer was, "By totally accepting it". That is exactly the attitude we need to display for obtaining divine gifts. Yes, divine gift is an accurate terminology here. Usually, we like to see ourselves as the architects and builders of our successes, but it is more accurate to see them as divine gifts that we need to make ourselves receptive and accepting towards. Please note that the quality of receptivity and the term divine gifts here refer to qualities of your "being" and not to things you may wish to "have". Do not try to develop a receptive attitude towards what you like to have. The having comes naturally as a quid pro quo for you fulfilling divine will. That is the true meaning of the often misunderstood, "Seek ye first the kingdom of God and His righteousness and all these things shall be added unto you".

WHAT DO I HAVE TO SURRENDER?

This question is closely related to the one about receiving and accepting. To the degree that we invite the new, become reborn in the new, we must let go of the past, die to the past. Often, we are so busy with wanting to become, striving, bringing about the new that we don't realize that we are too full with the old that needs to be left behind to be able to receive something new. There is a Zen anecdote of a student who climbs up on a mountain to visit a teacher. Upon finding him, he bursts out with stories how he wants to change and what he wants to achieve. The master suggests they should first have a cup of tea. When filling the cup, he keeps pouring tea into it until it overflows and even then keeps going. The student calls out, "But wait, the cup is too full to fit anymore in". At this point, the teacher says, "Exactly like you. Too full to fit anything in".

To not fall into this trap, we must let go of old behavioural patterns that keep us so full to the brim that nothing new can enter. We must continuously ask ourselves which parts of us, which behaviours, need to be surrendered? What do we need to leave behind? This could include our entire past hurt, our entire history of fear, inner conflict and self-loathing. We need to become aware of self-judgements, doubt, unworthiness, limitations and lack of trust that impinge on, prevent or slow-down our spiritual evolution.

OVERCOMING OBSTACLES

In this section, I will use an abundance of technical yoga terms. If you are not familiar with them, please skip straight to the next section "Further resolutions to implement your life's divine purpose". However, you may wish to come back to this obstacle section for troubleshooting later on. It is important for you to have a reference guide when obstacles do manifest. Stanza I.30 of the Yoga Sutra contains a list of obstacles to yoga, which are also obstacles to implementing your life's divine purpose. They are sickness, rigidity, doubt, negligence, laziness, sense indulgence, false views, failure to attain a state and inability to maintain it. Let's have a quick look at them, case by case.

The yoga master T. Krishnamacharya believed that sickness was often caused by non-alignment with the Divine. We are called into this life for some purpose. There is something we came here to do, and deep down, we know it. As we grow up, by means of enculturation, our materialistic society drags us more and more away from this knowledge. Eventually, we give up and leave our path. But deep down remains this thirst, this yearning. We know and remember how it feels to have a calling, to be called upon. We have a memory of being in alignment with cosmic intelligence because that is where we came from. And this thirst, this yearning, always keeps calling from within, and there is nothing that can quench it but to enact divine will, to return to the path of our divine purpose.

Eventually, and often because there is not much encouragement within our social field, we settle for drowning out this thirst with something else. We are looking for secondary satisfaction to drown out this primary desire. Typical secondary satisfactions are drugs, sex, power, money, wealth, success, fame, more likes on social media, academic achievement, consumption, etc. These will work for some time, but the effect wears off quickly. It is then that the stimulus has to be increased, for example, we have to have more success or fame for the same degree of relief.

Due to this pattern, we are doing things which are not in alignment with our values and are damaging to our bodies. For example, we may drink heaps of coffee to stay awake, work through the night to deliver that thesis or report in time for the deadline. Because of all of these stresses, eventually the body develops disease symptoms to show us that we need to change our behaviour. Note that it is the mind that is forcing the body to perform actions that are unhealthy, thus bringing about disease.

An alternative method to forcing ourselves through will power to achieve things is acting in alignment with our life's divine purpose. We are then able to access a source of energy outside of our individuality, we are tapping into something greater. This prevents us from having to force or goad ourselves to do the impossible, which likely leads to burn-out. It also means that many secondary gratifications, which would otherwise lead to our undoing, will fall away. I'm not saying that Western medicine or any other systems of medicine should not be consulted. By the time strong symptoms are displaying, it is good to go to the doctor. The way of life suggested here is to live life holistically and in harmony with one's divine purpose prior to symptoms developing, so that no undue stresses are placed upon body and mind. Yoga counteracts sickness through the yogic limb of posture (asana). By practising, daily, a wide range of postures, the body is kept healthy. Sickness is also related to an imbalance of the three humors (doshas), vata, pitta and kapha (these are complex Ayurvedic terms that lose their depth when simply anglified). Pranayama is the prime method for bringing the humors back into balance, with various pranayamas available for different effects. Surya Bhedana pranayama is used to reduce an aggravated vata, and Ujjayi pranayama is used to alleviate aggravated kapha, while Shitali, Sitkari and Chandra Bhedana pranayamas are employed to decrease excess pitta.

The next obstacle listed in the Yoga Sutra is rigidity. Rigidity implies that there is a clear system of values and rules applicable in all situations and, importantly, that we have a copyright on it. When doing the work proposed in this book, it is good to avoid such beliefs as they prevent us from learning new things. Rigidity almost always means that we are not open to receiving and accepting because we believe that we create things out of ourselves. It also makes it harder to forgive as we believe in clearly established rules that everybody should know, and if somebody transgresses them, the solution simply is their punishment.

CHAPTER 6

Rigidity closes us off to the fact that our sense of self is on a journey of expansion. It tells us that, somehow, we know everything already or at least that there is not much new that needs to be learned. Related to rigidity is the mental attitude of fundamentalism. It means that from the many vantage points from which we can look at a situation, there is only one worthy of embracing. It is a closing off against others with different values and a denial of our interdependency with all life. Interdependency also means to be constantly open to change.

Rigidity is related to too much life force (prana) flowing through the solar energy channel, relating to the right nostril. Rigidity means to see only your truth and being unable to accept other truths outside of your understanding, which is a solar attitude. Generally speaking, Nadi Shodhana is the pranayama to correct this state, but if solar predominance is strong and persistent, it needs to be tackled with Chandra Bhedana pranayama, i.e., taking all inhalations through the left nostril and exhaling through the right. This diminishes fundamentalism and increases relativism, i.e., being ready to accept the views of others.

The Yoga Sutra then lists doubt, which is diametrically opposed to rigidity. Doubt comes from the fact that our mind is in relativistic mode, that is, the belief that there are no universally accepted rules for defining right or wrong and particularly that we cannot know them and are, therefore, at a loss what to do. The opposite of doubt is certainty, and certainty comes from the knowledge that there is cosmic intelligence, that we can access it and are capable and worthy of doing so. Doubt is then a result of the failure to realize the Divine, or at least the belief that, for whatever reason, we are incapable or unworthy of accessing It or implementing Its advice. The more we bring ourselves in alignment with cosmic intelligence, the more doubt disappears because we are in service to the source of all knowledge and power, which is present everywhere (infinite) and at all times (eternal). Yoga treats the pair of rigidity and doubt by means of pranayama (breathing exercises). Pranayama balances the pranic load between the lunar and solar energy channels, an imbalance of which (depending on whether the lunar or solar channel is favoured) will cause either doubt or rigidity.

Doubt is the mirror image of the previous obstacle, rigidity. It means that too much prana is flowing through the left nostril. This causes a lunar attitude, which means that one sees truth in everything, starts to believe that truth is a relative thing and, in the end, becomes so paralysed that one cannot make a decision what to do any more. This obstacle is removed through Surya Bhedana pranayama, which lets us take every inhalation through the right nostril and all exhalations are done through the left. This increases fundamentalism, i.e., being sure about one's own choices, and decreases relativism.

The next obstacle is negligence. Negligence comes from an I-don't-care attitude and works like a crab-like shield, a hardening that we carry around us to stop ourselves from getting hurt. We believe that the more we harden on the outside, the less we have to care about what happens. "Toughen up', as the saying goes. This is a misconception that is built on the notion of the discrete self, the idea that our self is encapsulated inside of our skin and what happens outside doesn't need to bother us as long as it doesn't involve our family or asset portfolio. This is an erroneous belief. There is a stanza in the Shrimad Bhagavatam where Krishna says, "He who feels the pain of all beings is a yogi indeed". The more our sense-of-self increases, the more we feel everything around ourselves and, by extension, also the pain of everything that goes wrong. To try to protect ourselves by trying to crawl back into our crab-like shell won't work. It's what we have done for so long, and it has never worked.

We need to let ourselves be disturbed and pained by injustices and the destruction we metre out to the biosphere and use this pain as a motor for change. We need to overcome the need to numb ourselves. As our heart opens and we evolve beyond internal conflicts, our capacity for love, understanding, compassion and forgiveness increases, and we can become agents for change in this world without despairing. Negligence is cause by excess tamas (mass particle, inertia) in the mind. Yoga treats excess tamas through Nauli (a kriya exercise), Kapalabhati and Bhastrika (both pranayama exercises).

We now come to the obstacle called idleness, sometimes also called laziness. Our modern world is hyperactive, frantic, maddening. It is understandable that we want to retreat to our place of stillness, peace and simplicity. And it is important that we do. At the same time, there is a need for balance and the need for us to bring that what we found in our stillness, peace and simplicity, back into the world. There is the beautiful Chinese term wu wei, effortless action, that exemplifies this. Wu wei implies that we are active in the world, but we are doing it out of an inner state of centeredness, balanced-ness and stillness. This can be achieved when we are not doing our own bidding but are acting in alignment with the cosmic. Jesus understood that when he said, "It is not me doing the works but the Father in me is doing the works".

By placing ourselves in alignment with divine will and intelligence, we are making ourselves available to cosmic intelligence that performs actions through us. Because there is no sense of agency (i.e., the belief that we ourselves are enacting or performing the acts), they cause little fatigue, effort and exhaustion. In fact, it is rewarding to do them. Idleness, the aversion against necessary and responsible action, is again caused by excess tamas in the mind, and yoga treats it like the previous obstacle above.

Idleness indicates not only an excess of tamas (mass particle, inertia) in the mind but also excess kapha in the body. Kapha in the body is reduced by Ujjayi pranayama, whereas Kapalabhati and Bhastrika pranayamas reduce tamas in the mind. The latter two techniques are used to purify and stoke inner fire (agni), which is the destroyer of tamas. Another technique to reduce tamas in the mind comprises external breath retentions (kumbhakas), which trigger the sympathetic nervous system. Additionally, the length of the inhalation can be increased, which promotes rajas (energy particle, frenzy) and reduces tamas.

Next on the list of obstacles is sense indulgence. Sense indulgence means to place too much emphasis on sensory pleasure and stimulation. We are not talking here about a healthy relationship with pleasure but the attempt to cover up a lack, an emptiness, a meaninglessness in our lives by drowning ourselves in pleasure. Up to a certain point, pleasure is necessary and healthy. But there are needs that sensory stimulus cannot fulfil. For example, human beings are wired to help and support each other and to further each other's development. There is no greater satisfaction than contributing to the growth and awakening of another. If we try to replace all of that with sensory stimulus, we become nihilistic and cynical, we lose our values.

CHAPTER 6

We all have this yearning in our lives for meaning and purpose. We should not try to replace it with pleasure seeking, but endeavour to find out what our life's purpose is and what the meaning of our life is. That means we need to use this unfulfilled yearning as fuel to power our vision practice. Sensory indulgence becomes an obstacle exactly then when we try to use it as replacement for meaning and purpose in our lives. Sensory indulgence is often caused by excess tamas in the mind and then is treated as above. The expression 'like a pig in mud', for example, indicates sense indulgence aggravated by tamas.

It can, however, also be caused by an aggravation of rajas (energy particle, frenzy). The phrase 'retail therapy', i.e., combating depression through shopping, indicates sense indulgence cause by rajas. Also, the demon king Ravana in the Ramayana shows us a great example of sense indulgence through aggravated rajas. Extending the exhalations combats sense indulgence brought about through rajas. Additionally, Chandra Bhedana pranayama can be practised, in which all inhalations are taken through the left nostril. This pranayama makes one docile and introverted. Breath retentions can also be employed, but whether they should be external or internal needs to be assessed on a case-by-case basis. It is also beneficial to add meditation.

Next in line of obstacles is false views. False views, in this context, means extreme views that do not manage to incorporate conflicting data points or data that does not fit our beliefs. Examples include materialist reductionism, social Darwinism, but also relativism and fundamentalism. An example of extreme views is also the belief that a vision should come automatically and without any effort. False views means that the mind falls into an extreme by not being able to embrace and consider the opposite of what it currently believes to be true. In yoga, we consider that to stem from a lack of brain hemisphere integration, which in itself is caused by an imbalance between lunar and solar prana. In this case, practise Nadi Shodhana pranayama to bring about balance and, in extreme cases, use either Chandra Bhedana or Surya Bhedana pranayamas to alleviate your particular imbalance.

Last in our list of obstacles are failure to attain a state and the inability to maintain it. Failure to attain a state could, for example, mean the failure to obtain a vision or insight into the nature of reality. We shouldn't expect that these things come automatically. Already, the indigenous people often undertook a monthlong walk-about or a vision quest, and these were usually preceded by lengthy preparation. On traditional spiritual paths, attainments were only expected after some time and effort had been put in. Failure to attain usually means that we do not value what has to be attained enough to put in the necessary time and energy. Especially in modern society, people often believe that the maximum effort they have to put in to obtain a vision is the price they have to pay for a psychedelic agent. Visions obtained through psychedelics often don't last long and usually don't lead to lasting change of a person's personality. This is because the change has not been brought about through our work and effort but simply by paying a few bucks at the entrance to peek in. 'Failure to attain' implies a lack of conquering solar attitude. Add Surya Bhedana and Ujjayi pranayamas. It is also helpful to increase inner fire (agni) through Kapalabhati and Bhastrika pranayamas.

Inability to maintain a state is closely related to this. An insight into the nature of reality is supported by the work, effort and energy that gave us the insight. If the insight was brought about by a psychedelic agent or the presence of a guru, then we may not be able to sustain the state in the absence of the stimulus. The question, then, is whether the state/insight is truly ours or if it is just borrowed. In yoga, both these obstacles are believed to be related to an inability to take the next evolutionary step. Yogis bring this about through Chakra-Kundalini meditation. 'Failure to sustain a state' also implies a lack of sustenance. Sustenance is a nurturing, anabolic, lunar quality. Once you have attained a state, use Chandra Bhedana pranayama to sustain it. The failure to sustain can also be caused by excess pitta and lack of kapha, in which case Shitali and Sitkari pranayamas are employed. Sustaining a state is also related to 'staying power'. Increasing breath retention (kumbhaka) length strengthens staying power. I have described all these methods, asana, pranayama, kriyas and meditation in great detail in a previously published series of textbooks.

FURTHER RESOLUTIONS (SANKALPAS) TO IMPLEMENT YOUR LIFE'S DIVINE PURPOSE

Here is another group of resolutions that will help us to integrate what we have learned so far. Again, it is not enough to read these resolutions once and then forget them. Write the headlines down on a list and contemplate them regularly, ideally daily, until they have become embedded in your subconscious.

I COME FROM A DEEP FEELING OF SERVICE AND WANTING TO HEAL OTHERS.

This sankalpa helps with expanding our sense-of-self. We now theoretically understand that our life is not just about us but about becoming a conduit for cosmic intelligence to express itself as the abundance of all life and its many life forms. To the extent to which our subconscious mind accepts this sankalpa, we become available to be such a conduit. The Divine feels invited whenever we come from service to community rather than just furthering our own satisfaction by means of consuming objects and experiences. Paradoxically, it is service to community that is ultimately the most satisfying that we can do. When we are lying on our deathbed, what truly matters is not all the silly things that we have knocked off our bucket list but the contributions that we have made to the lives of others.

Healing, we all need it. In our long journey through the evolution of life, we all have experienced hurt and injury, especially during the last few thousand years when humanity switched from more support-oriented matrilineal societies to male-dominated warrior cultures that resulted in increasing coercion, dominating, manipulating and stratification of society. Even at the time of writing this (2020), the transfer of wealth and power away from the global population into the hands of fewer and fewer individuals is accelerating every year. Inequality and domination have traumatized all of us in many ways and are continuing to do so. This sankalpa will help us bring the focus back to healing.

I DAILY PLEDGE MY ONENESS WITH THE DIVINE,
UPHOLD THAT I AM DIVINELY GUIDED AND THAT
EVERYTHING I DO IS FOR THE GOOD OF ALL
HUMANITY AND ALL LIFE.

It is easy to get side-tracked in modern society with a never-ending flood of often confusing and useless information bearing down on us at all times. It is therefore good to remind ourselves

CHAPTER 6

daily with this proclamation. However, it is not enough to simply think these words. We need to feel them from the bottom of our hearts, and that involves actually probing into where we are numb. Once we know what stops us from feeling these statements authentically, we can then let go of that.

We are all one with the Divine. As Krishna stated in the Gita, "I am the self in the heart of all beings". The pure consciousness within us is on the level of our individuality what the God transcendent is to the cosmos. In the Upanishads, this is affirmed by the dictum that Brahman (infinite consciousness) and atman (individual consciousness) are one. For the atman, the individual consciousness, the pure consciousness within us, this is absolutely clear. However, the atman does not process data, it does not think. It simply is present, is aware, is conscious. That means that on some level, the mere information that our consciousness is one with the supreme self (Brahman) does not help to elevate our surface-self, i.e., the egoic body-mind.

The thinker in us, on the other hand, is not aware but instead processes data. It is therefore important to make the mind remember that our essence, the consciousness, is one with the Divine. The mind can be intellectually trained to understand this, and we have hopefully taken steps towards that in this book. The mind, however, cannot by itself experience our unity with the Divine. This is because, for a deep unification with the Divine to occur, the mind has to temporarily suspend, shut down. At the end of this so-called samadhi, the mind will reboot and then wonders what has happened in its absence. Because the mind has not and cannot partake of the experience as such, it has the tendency to go on with business as usual. That can be very confusing to the novice-mystic. But it is to be expected. You have to carefully and regularly explain to the mind that in its absence, you have experienced unification with the Divine. I know that sounds funny, but that is technically exactly what has to happen. Mind and cosmic consciousness, by definition, cannot happen at the same time.

The next section of this sankalpa is then to remind yourself that you are divinely guided. The mind does better with this part of the statement than the first part. Let's recall that divine guidance, technically speaking, is an alignment between superconscious mind (the intellect of the Divine), your conscious mind and your subconscious mind. The mind can actually understand this information and also appreciate that it is the one to decipher and put into words the messages and visions that come down to us from the superconscious mind.

It is important that you don't just see your mind as an obstacle or enemy in your spiritual growth but as a friend and asset, albeit one that does have its limitations. You need to know and understand its limitations so that you can use the mind wherever it is helpful and go beyond it at times when it would impede your progress. The mind needs reminding that we are divinely guided and that we are actively looking out for its progress. The mind ultimately benefits from this as it does not have to supply meaning anymore in situations where it can't.

The third part of the present sankalpa is "Everything I do is for the good of all humanity and all life". This is, again, an important re-education process. For too long, we have been brainwashed by neoconservative and neoliberal mantras like "greed is good" and claims that all of our actions are selfish and egoic. But while we are right in taking care of our survival, the biosphere and life seen as a totality are largely bio-symbiotic. If all lifeforms would not have worked together to create more life, life on this planet would have collapsed long ago. Unfortunately, humanity has brainwashed itself into believing that to act selfishly is natural and normal. If you look at an organism, individual cells that have stopped contributing to the common good but go off to satisfy their own interests are called cancer cells. It would not be too harsh to say that, on some level, humanity is now acting akin to a cancer on its host organism, the biosphere of planet Earth, ultimately driving it towards destruction. The sooner we realize that this is unnatural (because the whole of life is aligned to bring about more life), the sooner can we again make a contribution to life on Earth in its totality.

I AM A VEHICLE FOR THE DIVINE.

A small single sentence consisting of few words but what an effect it has on our mental wellbeing. Most mental disorders are a result of disconnection or estrangement from the Divine, nature, ourselves and the community around us. This single statement will re-align you with an infinite power for good. There is no difference between the Divine, nature, ourselves and others. Nature is the crystallized body of the God immanent, and we and all others around us partake of the infinite consciousness, the God transcendent. There is nothing but the Divine. Every time when we can feel that we are nothing but its vehicle, we are aligning ourselves with our deep meaning and purpose in life.

Again, take some time to deeply feel the meaning of this statement in every fibre of your being. It may help to close your eyes and to visualize yourself as a conduit for the Divine and as being filled with Its love. Feel how this love touches everybody you meet throughout your day.

I KNOW THAT IT IS THE MIND OF THE DIVINE AND NOT MINE THAT IS MANIFESTING ITSELF AS MY HIGHEST POTENTIAL.

At times, we may know our vision, but we may struggle with how to implement it. This sentence is a reminder that it is not ours to answer this question. The Divine intended to become Itself as you before life on this planet started, in fact, before space/time started. Trust that It is an infinite power that will figure out how to manifest Itself as your life. Your mind does not need to know how. You only need to keep yourself open and available as a conduit and the intellect of the Divine will connect the missing dots.

How can it do that? Do you remember a time when you had a deep cut in your skin or maybe even a broken bone or were ill? Did you know how to heal? No, the body has an unbelievable self-healing capacity. It does all of that without you knowing how. You only need to give it enough rest and nurture it, and it will do the rest by itself.

Did you ever eat and know exactly how the body turns all the nutrients into tissue and function? No, never! Even today, we consider that in a simple piece of fruit there are 50,000 phytonutrients that we probably will never exactly analyse, because researching and identifying them is commercially not viable. We eat and then the body turns food into function without us knowing how. Similarly, the Divine expresses Itself as all life on Earth including us.

This resolution reminds us that the Divine is all-power, all-intelligence, all-beauty and all-love and that It is everywhere and at all times. It will find a way to express Itself as our life as long as we surrender us to It and let It do its seeming magic.

Chapter 7
RESULTS OF FINDING ONE'S LIFE'S DIVINE PURPOSE

This chapter deals with what we can expect when making progress and how we can recognize it. Let's firstly look into how the voice of the Divine would differ from the voice of the ego or the voice of the mind. Please remember that I do not use the terms mind and ego in the same condescending, moralistic undertone that they are often used with. They are important functional aspects of our psyche, just not necessarily the ones we want to consult when looking for spiritual guidance.

VOICE OF SILENCE

When we are asking the Divine for guidance, for a vision as to how to embody It, we may hear many voices. Of those, the voice of the Divine is the voice of silence. The term voice here is not necessarily used in an auditory sense. It is meant in the sense that aspects of your psyche have a way of making themselves felt, and that way depends on how you compute your sense-of-self. Whether you tend to compute more visually, auditorily or kinaesthetically (through feeling), the mind always communicates through discussion. It will discuss the pros and cons, it will tell you, for example, that you cannot do a because then b will happen. The ego, on the other side, usually communicates through fear. Fear-of-missing-out is, for example, a subset of the egoic thought.

When the Divine communicates, it will do so accompanied by silence, that is, there will be no conflicting comparing viewpoints but an uninterrupted broadcast of the vision not impaired or impeded by secondary noise. During the time of the broadcast or download, there is complete certainty. Insecurity will only restart once the mind starts commenting on the vision.

VOICE OF THE HEART

Amongst the many voices we may hear, the voice of the Divine can be said to be the voice of the heart. Heart here does not mean romance. The Sanskrit term for heart, hrt, actually means core, centre, consciousness. It is our innermost. In the Bible, it is called the secret chamber of the most high, and in the Chandogya Upanishad, it is described as a shrine in the chest that contains the entire vast universe. These descriptions are used because the heart, the consciousness, is the container that contains the world and all beings.

The metaphor *voice of the heart* implies the opposite of voice of the head. Most people, when referring to themselves, will automatically point to their chest. Indigenous people, when asked where in the body their sense-of-self is located, will always point to the heart. Only recently have modern people started referring to themselves as living in their heads. Interestingly, people who kill themselves with firearms will usually shoot themselves through the head (to kill the mind that tortures them) and not through the heart. If the voice that you listen to seems to come from the head, it is probably not the Divine. If it comes from your very centre, the core, or it seems to reach you in the centre, then it is likely to be the Divine.

There is some significance to the physiological dimension of following one's heart. When sitting in meditation and asking for divine guidance, this is more likely to succeed when the heart is carried in front of the head (when seen from the side), the head thereby following the heart. This is why yogis in deep meditation make efforts to pull up the heart and let it float in front of them as this leads to heart-brain entrainment. The heart has a magnetic field much stronger than that of the brain, and with the heart carried before the brain, the brain and mind are in service to the heart. This meditation position also helps with being completely present. If the head is carried behind the heart (as seen from the side) it is more difficult to be with one's mind in the future.

If, however, the heart collapses and the weight of the dropping chest pulls the head forward (therefore called forward head position), then the mind is likely to be in the future, and the brain controls and dominates the heart. In a forward hunched, slouching position, it is more difficult to obtain a vision. Notice that the alignment between superconscious, conscious and subconscious minds also has a physical component. I have profusely written about the physical aspect of meditation in my previous books on yogic postures.

ABSENCE OF INTERNAL DIALOGUE

In our head, there is often a conflict of competing opinions, and that can paralyse us. There is often an ongoing dialogue as to whether what we do is right, or whether another course of action should be adopted. We ask ourselves what are the pros and cons, whether something is endangering us, and whether it is too risky. We may wonder whether we are, in fact, living our own life or somebody else's. The mind and ego are constantly discussing why something should be done and why what we are currently doing cannot succeed. The sum total of these voices is here called internal dialogue.

When the Divine speaks, all of these voices fall silent, and there is certainty. After that, the voices may start again and confuse us. When we then start to enact the advice of the one voice, the other voices again fall silent. This is because by enacting on the one voice, we have brought ourselves in alignment with the Divine. Later, the voices may restart and tell us why we can't succeed with this newly adopted course of action. The art is to take the moments without internal dialogue, the moments of peace, seriously and enact on them. They are a sign of congruency, a sign of authenticity, a sign of alignment with the Divine.

BEING IN THE ZONE

There is no term that describes being in alignment with divine will better than the term *being-in-the-zone*. A friend of mine used to be an up-and-coming star in US college football. He was very physical and had no spiritual inclination. During one game, he suddenly felt himself fall into a trancelike state, during which time slowed down and something else took control of him, moving his body across the field. Somehow, he knew where the ball would appear a few moments later. His body was moved to that place automatically, and when he jumped and reached out, the ball appeared between his hands. He scored one goal after another and won the day for his team. After the game, although

CHAPTER 7

being offered contracts with major teams, he quit football because in his world and terminology, he could not explain what had happened to him. He went on a spiritual search across the world and became a serious spiritual practitioner.

The term being-in-the-zone is often used by athletes and musicians. It describes a state during which the shackles of ego, mind, and contracted sense-of-self fall away. Something greater than us takes hold of us and expresses itself through us. Everything that usually limits us is gone, and the skillset we were practising is often displayed to perfection.

Exactly the same applies when you follow your life's divine purpose. In whatever field you find yourself, there is no separation between the doer and the done, there is only the doing. And because this separation is gone, the doer becomes like a hollow conduit, like a bamboo flute, through which the doing is pouring forth.

There is a beautiful description of the in Robert M Pirsig's book *Zen and the Art of Motorcycle Maintenance*, where the main character, a retired professor of philosophy, takes his motorcycle on a tour through the US mid-west. At some point, he sustains damage to his exhaust and thinks to himself that he needs to find one of the old-style mechanics that get so absorbed in their welding that no thought of reward, no thought of finishing and going home, no internal dialogue whatsoever interferes with their work. Watching these old mechanics, you see the subject/object split disappear so that only the activity, in this case welding, remains. And because there is nothing to detract the awareness and attention of the one executing the skill, the skill itself expresses itself to perfection.

It is all of the other thoughts that deal with things not pertaining to this present moment that distract us so that the moment cannot be total and authentic. Anthropologists have described the same effect in traditional indigenous people. The anthropologists noted that indigenous people were completely present and absorbed in what to the modern observer seemed to be rather boring activities. But being-in-the-zone, there is no concept of wanting to be somewhere else, be somebody else or wanting to do something different, and the whole being is totally absorbed in the present task. Boredom is a result of not being present.

In many modern, still-existing, stone-age hunter-gatherer cultures, there is not even a concept of time. When Australian Aborigines were first thrown into the jails of the white colonialist, they often died after a short time. This is because they had not yet developed a concept of time, and therefore, there was no hope of a time in which they would again become free. They thought life was now being in jail and lost their desire to live. We can actually learn a lot from that. Our modern society has diverted most of our focus into the future so that it has become really difficult for us to totally experience the present moment.

Whether you are a sports person, a musician, a crafts person, etc., being in-the-zone and living your life's divine purpose means to be an expression of and being enacted upon by an infinite intelligence. For that to take place, the limited ego, for a time, has to disappear so that only the current activity and being in the present moment prevails.

SATISFACTION

Another result of living one's life's divine purpose is that of deep satisfaction. Because at times when you are acting in service of the Divine and all life, the subject/object split described above is gone and you are completely in the moment. The contracted sense-of-self that tells us we are flesh-encased survival-machines is gone, and there is a greater sense of purpose of acting in the service of all. I cannot think of any greater satisfaction than to feel that you are an expression of and being enacted on by a cosmic intelligence. There is a feeling of deep peace, acceptance, clarity, purpose, meaning and creativity.

QUALITIES OF FOLLOWING OUR LIFE'S DIVINE PURPOSE

The qualities that we feel when following our life's divine purpose are qualities in alignment with the fact that the Divine expresses Itself simultaneously through us and all other beings.

- Non-comparison. Because we are all unique and all unique expressions of that one cosmic intelligence, there is no point to compare ourselves with others. They are expressing a different facet, a different aspect of the Divine, so there is no point to compare our activities with theirs. Due to Its nature of unlimited potential, the Divine cannot, for example, limit Itself to musicians or, let's say, sports people or mechanics. Each one of these activities are expressions of divine creativity.
- Symbiosis rather than competitiveness. Because one intelligence expresses itself through all life as if through a super-organism, the basic quality of those in its service are defined by bio-symbiosis. Watch closely how deeply ingrained is our society's brainwash for us to be competitive. Recently, I saw a video of an older male supervising the sports activities of a few children.

He got them to run against each other and outperform each other on the track. They were too little to even understand competition and just wanted to have fun, but when they came closer to the finishing line, the trainer started screaming and making them artificially excited. He then celebrated the child going first through the finishing line, high-fiving her, but you could see that the children weren't even interested in it. They were more interested in having a good time together. A lot of the toxic activities and over-consumption of our society only exist because we think we have to compete and are being trained that way. Once the incentive for competition is gone, we will go back to what really matters, and that is supporting each other and other life forms rather than working against each other.

- Non-ambitiousness. Ambition is the desire for success. By deriving success measured through status, power and wealth and the ability to consume thereby bestowed, we are convincing ourselves that we are somebody. But how many successful people had all that and still fell for drug addiction, destructive behaviour, depression and suicide? The reason why we need to convince ourselves that we are somebody is because we have lost contact with that well-spring of divine love that comes with knowing that we are a beloved child of the Divine. By being in contact with our divine purpose, we can truly make a contribution to the life of others, and to the larger web of life. We then derive our value from our interconnectedness with all life, and no shallow ambition is needed to cover up our utter worthlessness and self-loathing.

- Life affirmativeness. As you might remember from the subheading *astrophysics* in the first chapter, cosmic intelligence has arranged the universe in a mysterious way so that no less than 140 different physical parameters align, making life possible. Not only that, but the universe is nothing but a giant incubator of life. It is fascinating to dive into the related physics such as the strong anthropic principle, John Wheeler's participatory universe, or Robert Lanza's biocentrism. For others more devotionally minded, it is possible to go directly to feeling that same phenomenon as divine love. Although the God transcendent as infinite consciousness seems complete in Itself, It also is infinite potential. Because of that, It expresses Itself in an infinite process as the sum total of computations and permutations that It can be. In philosophy, we call this the God immanent, and we have to thank Alfred North Whitehead that we now understand that the God immanent is a process (i.e., closer to a verb) rather than the God transcendent, which is a state (viz. more noun-like). Once we have arrived at the transcendent and the immanent, we realize that, like a father and mother, they reunite to form the divine child, life in its totality including us, you and me. In the Bible, we have beautiful descriptions of the love between the Father and the son, such as, "You are my beloved son in which I am well pleased". However, to limit the sonship to the man Jesus Christ is a theological error because Jesus said, "Ye all are gods ye all are children of the most high". The sonship collectively applies to all lifeforms including all humans and all non-human life. Natural and geological formations such as mountains, rivers, forests, and oceans are aspects of the divine mother, the God immanent, and have been down the ages identified by indigenous people as being in a parental and ancestor role to us. It is time for us modern people to understand this. For this very reason, the Lakota American Indians complete their rituals with the phrase, "to all my relations", affirming that, in this world, we are in a close familial relationship with all life and matter.

For our subject here, this means that living one's divine purpose cannot involve any forms of exploitation, domination, coercion and manipulation, neither of other people, nor other life forms, nor our ancestors in form of natural and geological formations. Our role must be one of being guardians of all life, which means to actively restore balance in the world and create more abundance of life on Earth.

- Giving-ness. When stepping into alignment with the Divine and living our life's divine purpose, we need to focus on giving and giving more. The more we give, the more we create a vacuum into which the abundance of the Divine pours itself. However, this is a magical outcome, and the focus should be on the process of giving and not on the outcome. In this, we then emulate the Divine, which cannot hold back. The belief that the Divine can withhold grace, or hear the prayers of one and ignore somebody else's, is a theological error. It came about because we extrapolated our own egoic state into the sky and created a god in our own image instead of realizing that we are made in the image and likeness of the Divine. The Divine has no ego from which to withhold abundance and grace. It is we who are cutting ourselves off. To be in

alignment with the Divine, we need to return to giving in abundance. The rest will take care of itself.
- Supportiveness. All life miraculously works together, and life forms support each other, showing that life is directed by one common intelligence. The greatest satisfaction we can experience is to make contributions to the lives of others. Like nothing else, this gives us self-respect and self-esteem, and nothing is so crippling to the psyche than feeling unworthy of contributing or not knowing how. To live our life's divine purpose is about learning how we can make such a contribution, and the reward will take care of itself. That's why Jesus says, "Seek ye first the kingdom of God and everything else will be added on".
- Nurture. Most of us will have experienced how much it gives to us to nurture another being, whether this be a child, an aging parent, a pet or somebody we pass skills on to. That's the way we are wired and that is good. What has changed, though, is that today we limit this nurturing to an ever-decreasing inner family circle. Living your life's divine purpose means to step up to nurture life in as many forms as possible because that's how the Divine is expressing Itself.
- Healing. Another quality that you can use to check whether you are acting in alignment with the Divine is that your activities are healing to those around you rather than causing further trauma.
- Love. The fundamental quality of the Divine is unconditional love. The Divine cannot perceive anything contrary to its own nature. It can reason and perceive only from the already established premise of divinity,

perfection and unconditional love. Because of that, the Divine can see us only in our original divine perfection, a fact that is beautifully expressed in Jesus's parable of the prodigal son. Because of that, if we do want to act in alignment with the Divine and embody our life's divine purpose, we need to see every being with the same eyes as the Divine. That means we need to see every being as an embodiment of divine love. This does not mean that we cannot correct others, stop them from doing destructive things or let them victimize us. It means, however, that all these actions, if they are necessary, will come from a position of compassion against the backdrop of seeing the essential divinity in all life and nature.

Epilogue
HUMANITY'S COLLECTIVE DIVINE PURPOSE

There is a deep connection between self-love, love for others and, ultimately, love for all existence. The more you love yourself, the more you can love others. To love oneself does not mean that because you love yourself, you need to prove it by spoiling and pampering yourself. The opposite is the case. We need to spoil, pamper and treat ourselves because, deep down, we lack self-esteem, self-respect and self-love. We are then trying to buy what is lacking by means of consumption, which makes us briefly forget our shortcomings and deep emptiness. True self-love, however, means to enter into a state of deep communion with the Divine. That is so because the Divine is our deep self. From the deep self, you can access an infinite reservoir of love for all beings. Then we abide in authentic being, and giving from this essence will fulfil both us and others.

Do not accept self-limiting thoughts because you are limitless and infinite. You are so because God has created you this way, and you are not powerful enough to change it. God did not create the multiverse by rolling up Her sleeves but simply by contemplating 'multiverse' into the divine creative force (prakrti, shakti, shekinah). Since God has created us in Her image, we have been given this same ability, which is to create reality through contemplation and to co-create together with the Divine.

If you think of yourself in terms of guilt, fault, shame or negative karma that you have to live through, then so will it be. If, on the other hand, you want to co-create with the Divine, then think of yourself as an infinite, eternal, stainless and sacred child of It. Your purpose is to be a canal, a conduit of and for divine love, creativity and intelligence. Practice this contemplation daily. Slowly, images and avenues will develop how this will express itself through you. Trust in this process because the power that will express itself through you is omnipotent, omniscient and omnipresent. You don't have to worry at all how exactly this expression will happen. The Divine will do that.

Although we need to employ science, politics, technology, social and economic reform, no amount of it can save us from the destruction of the biosphere brought on by our own confusion. What will save us is realizing that there is one cosmic intelligence that expresses itself as humans, animals, plants, microbes, rivers, mountains, forests and oceans. What we call human rights has to be extended to all of these entities. This amounts to no less than a spiritual revolution. After having made this realization, we need to then place ourselves into the service of this intelligence by serving the entirety of the biosphere. This means that in all situations, our actions must be life-affirmative, i.e., creating more life, especially non-human life. In devotional language, this means to lead a life of divine love.

Bibliography

Abram, D., *Becoming Animal*, Vintage Books, 2011.

Abram, D., *The Spell Of The Sensuous*, Vintage Books, 1997.

Aurobindo, S,. *Synthesis of Yoga*, Lotus Press, Twin Lakes, 2010.

Aurobindo, S., *The Integral Yoga*, Lotus Press, 2000.

Chapple, C., (transl.), *The Yoga Sutras of Patanjali*, Sri Satguru Publications, 1990.

Crick, F., *Life Itself: Its Origin and Nature*, Touchstone, Simon & Schuster, 1982.

Derrida, J., *Of Grammatology*, John Hopkins University Press, 2016.

Deussen, P., (transl.), *Sixty Upanishads of the Veda*, Motilal Banarsidas Publishers, 1980.

Diamond, J., *The World Until Yesterday*, Viking, 2012.

Eisenstein, C., *The Ascent of Humanity*, North Atlantic Books, 2007.

Eisenstein, C., *The More Beautiful World Our Hearts Know is Possible*, North Atlantic Books, 2013.

Eisler, R., *The Chalice & The Blade*, HarperCollins 1987.

Erdoes, R., *Lame Deer Seeker Of Visions*, Simon & Schuster, 1994.

Flannery, T., *Here On Earth*, The Text Publishing Company, 2010.

Frankl, V., *Man's Search For Meaning*, Beacon Press, 1959.

Gambhirananda, S., (transl.), *Brahma Sutra Bhasya of Sri Sankaracarya*, Advaita Ashrama, 1996.

Gambhiranda, S., (transl.), *Chandogya Upanishad*, Advaita Ashrama, 1983.

Gardner, J., *Biocosm*, New Age International Publisher, 2006.

Gardner, J., *The Intelligent Universe*, Career Press, 2007.

Gober, M., *An End to Upside Down Thinking*, Waterside Productions, 2018.

Goswami, A., *The Self-Aware Universe*, Jeremy P. Tarcher/ Putnam, 1995.

Holmes, E., *The Science of Mind*, Jeremy P. Tarcher/ Putnam, 1998.

Jensen, D., *A Language Older Than Words*, Chelsea Green Publishing, 2004.

Jung, C.G., *Collected Works of C.G. Jung*, Princeton University Press, 1981.

Lanza, R., *Beyond Biocentrism*, BenBella Books, 2016.

Lanza, R., *Biocentrism*, BenBella Books, 2009.

Maslow, A., *A Theory of Human Motivation*, Martino Fine Books, 2013.

Mohan, A.G., (transl.), *Yoga Yajnavalkya*, Svastha Yoga, 2013.

Muktibodhananda, S., *Swara Yoga*, Yoga Publications Trust, 1984.

Müller, M., (ed.), *Sacred Books of the East,* 50vols, Motilal Banarsidas Publishers, 1965.

Narby, J., *Intelligence in Nature,* Jeremy P. Tarcher/ Putnam, 2006.

Narby, J., *The Cosmic Serpent,* Jeremy P. Tarcher/ Putnam, 2019.

Nerburn, K., *Neither Wolf Nor Dog,* New World Library, 1994.

Nerburn, K., *The Wolf at Twilight,* New World Library, 2009.

Nikhilanda, S., *The Gospel of Ramakrishna,* Advaita Ashrama, 1984.

Pirsig, R.M., *Zen and the Art of Motorcycle Maintenance,* Bantam, 1984.

Plotkin, B., *Soulcraft,* New World Library, 2003.

Prechtel, M., *Secrets of the Talking Jaguar,* Jeremy P. Tarcher/ Putnam, 1999.

Prechtel, M., *The Disobedience of the Daughter of the Sun,* North Atlantic Books, 2001.

Prechtel, M., *The Smell of Rain on Dust,* North Atlantic Books, 2015.

Radakrishnan, S., (transl.), *The Principal Upanisads,* HarperCollins 1994.

Sapolsky, R., *Behave,* Penguin Random House UK, 2017.

Shepard, P., *Coming Home to the Pleistocene,* Island Press, 2004.

Some, M.P., *Of Water and The Spirit,* Penguin Books, 1994.

Subramaniam, K., (transl.), *Shrimad Bhagavatam*, Bharatiya Vidya Bhavan, 1988.

Tapasyananda, S., (transl.), *Srimad Bhagavad Gita*, Sri Ramakrishna Math.

The Holy Bible, New King James Version, Thomas Nelson Publishers, 1982.

Troward, T., *The Essential Thomas Troward*, Create Space Independ Publishing Platform, 2014.

Van Der Kolk, B., *The Body Keeps The Score*, Penguin Books, 2004.

Venkatesananda, S., (transl.), *The Supreme Yoga*, Divine Life Society, 1976.

Walker, R., *Lakota Belief and Ritual*, Bison Books, 1991.

Wheeler, J.A., *At Home in the Universe*, Amer Institute of Physics, 1994.

Whitehead, A.N., *Process and Reality*, Free Press, 1979.

Whitehead, A.N., *Religion In The Making*, Fordham University Press, 1996.

Index

Absence of internal dialogue, 275
Acceptance/ Receptivity, 256
Alignment of all three minds, 183
Archaea, 36 - 37, 50
Asking the question, 118
Astrophysics, 46ff
Being in the zone, 276
Bhagavad Gita, 86ff
Bible, 92ff
Bio parameters, 34
Bio-symbiosis, 50
Brain development, 52
Chakras, higher, 246
Conflicts, 237
Conscious Mind, 163ff
Contemplating the vision, 121 - 122
Daily cleansing regime of the subconscious mind, 187
Editing the description of the vision, 122
Embodiment of the vision, 127
Evolutionary Biology, 49
Evolving vision, 125
Forgiveness, 248
Frankl, Victor, 108
God as live, 31ff
God immanent, 25ff
God transcendent, 20ff
Gratitude, 253

Gunas, Gross State, 161 - 163
Gunas, Manifest State, 153 - 157
Gunas, Subtle State, 157 - 161
Gunas, Un-manifest State, 150 - 152
Hearing the message, 120
Homeostasis, 34, 36 202
Jung, Carl, 107
Letting go, how to
Listening for the answer, 119
Listening, 6, 100, 119, 129
Maslow, Abraham, 109ff
Materialistic reductionism, 54
Monte Carlo generator, 41
Multicellular life, 50
Obstacles, 258
Occam's Razor, 43
Panchakoshamodel (teaching of the five layers), 131ff
Particle state, 44
Practice of finding your life's divine purpose, 115ff
Practice, Place of, 115
Practice, Time of, 116
Principles of consecration, 194ff
Quantum physics, 42ff
Relationships, 237
Resolutions suitable for reconditioning the subconscious mind, 178
Science, philosophy of, 31, 56, 64, 144
Self-actualization, 109ff
Shariras/ three bodies, 149ff
Speciesism, 33, 144
Spiritual by-passing, 210

INDEX

Sri Aurobindo, 56
Stating your intent, 117
Subconscious mind, 166ff
Superconscious mind, 180
Surrender, 257
Taking notes, 121
Voice of silence, 273
Voice of the heart, 274
Wave function, 44
Wu-wei, 129, 263
Yoga Sutra, 64ff

Author Information

Gregor started his yogic practices in the late 1970s. In the mid-80s he commenced yearly travels to India, where he learned from various yogic and tantric masters, traditional Indian *sadhus* and ascetics. He lived many years as a recluse, studying Sanskrit and yogic scripture and practicing yogic techniques.

Gregor's textbook series consisting of *Ashtanga Yoga: Practice and Philosophy, Ashtanga Yoga: The Intermediate Series, Pranayama: The Breath of Yoga, Yoga Meditation: Through Mantra, Chakras and Kundalini to Spiritual Freedom,* and *Samadhi The Great Freedom* have sold over 85,000 copies worldwide and so far have been translated into eight languages. His blog articles can be found at **www.chintamaniyoga.com**.

Today Gregor integrates all aspects of yoga into his teaching in the spirit of Patanjali and T. Krishnamacharya. His zany sense of humour, manifold personal experiences, vast and in-depth knowledge of scripture, Indian philosophies, and yogic techniques combine to make Gregor's teachings easily applicable, relevant, and accessible to his students.

Contact Gregor via:
www.chintamaniyoga.com
www.8limbs.com and
https://www.facebook.com/gregor.maehle.

Printed in Great Britain
by Amazon